Chicken Soup
for the Soul.

My Kind (of)
America

Chicken Soup for the Soul: My Kind (of) America
101 Stories about the True Spirit of Our Country
Amy Newmark

Published by Chicken Soup for the Soul, LLC www.chickensoup.com
Copyright ©2017 by Chicken Soup for the Soul, LLC. All Rights Reserved.

The publisher gratefully acknowledges the many publishers and individuals who
granted Chicken Soup for the Soul permission to reprint the cited material.

Front cover photo courtesy of iStockphoto.com/PeopleImages (©PeopleImages)
Interior artwork courtesy of iStockphoto.com/mattjeacock (©mattjeacock)
Photo of Amy Newmark courtesy of Mary Fisher

Cover and Interior by Daniel Zaccari

Distributed to the booktrade by Simon & Schuster. SAN: 200-2442

Publisher's Cataloging-In-Publication Data
(Prepared by The Donohue Group, Inc.)

Names: Newmark, Amy, compiler.
Title: Chicken soup for the soul : my kind (of) America : 101 stories
    about the true spirit of our country / [compiled by] Amy Newmark.
Other Titles: My kind (of) America : 101 stories about the true spirit of
    our country | My kind America
Description: [Cos Cob, Connecticut] : Chicken Soup for the Soul, LLC,
    [2017]
Identifiers: LCCN 2017946572 | ISBN 978-1-61159-973-2 (print) | ISBN
    978-1-61159-273-3 (ebook)
Subjects: LCSH: United States--Literary collections. | United States--
    Anecdotes. | Americans--Attitudes--Literary collections. | Americans--
    Attitudes--Anecdotes. | Kindness--United States--Literary collections.
    | Kindness--United States--Anecdotes. | LCGFT: Anecdotes.
Classification: LCC E169.1 .C453 2017 (print) | LCC E169.1 (ebook) | DDC
    973/.02--dc23

PRINTED IN THE UNITED STATES OF AMERICA
on acid∞free paper

25 24 23 22 21 20 19 18 17   01 02 03 04 05 06 07 08 09 10 11

My Kind (of) America

101 Stories about the
True Spirit of Our Country

Amy Newmark

Chicken Soup for the Soul, LLC
Cos Cob, CT

Changing your life one story at a time®
www.chickensoup.com

Table of Contents

❶

~Our Common Ground~

❷

~Speaking Up for What's Right~

3
~3,000 Miles of Kindness~

4
~Honoring Those Who Defend Us~

5
~Community of Caring~

❻
~A Vibrant Melting Pot~

❼
~Where Kindness Counts~

⑧
~Making Things Happen~

⑨
~Our Dynamic New Citizens~

⑩
~Role Models~

Chapter 1

My Kind (of) America

Our Common Ground

Faith to Faith

*Remember there's no such thing as a small act
of kindness. Every act creates a ripple
with no logical end.*
~Scott Adams

The devastation started with a small malfunction in the plug conducting electricity to the kitchen refrigerator. Within minutes, the entire kitchen was engulfed in flames, destroying its stoves, ovens, and a storage closet filled with serving trays and table decorations used for bar mitzvahs and weddings.

The conflagration roared into the Social Hall, setting the walls aflame and leaping toward the rafters. The seventy-five-year-old certificate of the founding of the synagogue burned. The framed photos of all the temple presidents were consumed. The cabinet that contained the sound and recording equipment squawked, popped and died.

By the time the fire department arrived, minutes after it received the alarm, flames leaped toward the sanctuary, blistering its walls.

The last two rows of pews were burned, and the next four were scorched and blistered. The fire shattered the etched-glass entrance doors, obliterated the prayer books in their storage racks, and destroyed the classic chandeliers.

I had been the synagogue's rabbi for two decades before I retired, so I was receiving calls from worried congregants. "How widespread is the fire?" "Was anyone hurt?" "Are the Torah scrolls safe?" "Are we having services next Friday night?"

"I don't know," I said. "I'm on my way to the temple to find out. I'll call you back as soon as I can." I jotted down their names and phone numbers and rushed off.

By the time I arrived, the firefighters had knocked down the fire. The kitchen was in ruins. The closets that contained all our banquet tables and chairs were charred beyond repair. A few sections of the Social Hall walls and ceiling were smoldering, and the firemen continued to hose them down.

Thank God, no one was hurt. The fire occurred in the dark of night before any of our employees arrived to work. A few hours later, hundreds of children and their parents might have been caught in the conflagration.

I saw the current rabbi and the temple president talking to the fire chief.

"We thoroughly examined the school building for any damage or possible hot spots. There were none — not among the trees and bushes around the school, not on the roof, not in the library and not in any of the classrooms."

"So the fire was completely confined to the sanctuary building?" asked the rabbi.

"Yes. Unfortunately, the damage in this building was quite extensive."

"How extensive?" asked the president.

"The kitchen, assembly hall, board room, and storage closets were severely burned. I doubt that any equipment in those areas is still useable. The fire penetrated the ceiling and singed the rafters. My men had to open the roof to hose down all the smoldering sections they couldn't reach from inside," said the fire chief.

"Flames penetrated the folding door between the sanctuary and the assembly hall, and scorched the ceiling, walls, floor and pews about ten feet into the temple. Water and smoke damaged most of the rest. The chandeliers, pews, sound room and prayer books are probably damaged beyond repair."

"You'd be a better judge than I about damage to the Ark and the scrolls, but I do see some singe, water, and smoke damage."

"Do you think we can use the sanctuary for services?" asked the president.

"Or for weddings and funerals?" echoed the rabbi.

"I doubt it. I think you're going to have to remove all the pews, strip the walls and tear up the carpeting to discover all the damage — if only to figure your insurance claim and plan your remodeling."

"How long do you think that will take?"

"That all depends on your remodeling goals," answered the chief. "I'd make plans to use another facility for worship for at least twelve to eighteen months."

This was bad.

The president immediately divided the temple leadership into four task forces — one to assess in detail the damage to our facilities, another to press our claim with the insurance company, a third to draw up suggested plans for remodeling, and a fourth to secure a new facility wherein we might worship every weekend for the next year and a half.

Local synagogues invited our members to join them in their worship services, but they could not offer their facilities for our use. They had worship services already scheduled for the same Sabbaths and holidays.

A neighborhood Church of Jesus Christ of Latter-day Saints rescued us. The stake (the name of their administrative district) agreed to let us use their sanctuary for Jewish worship every Friday night and Saturday morning for eighteen months. They refused to accept any payment and assigned their own members to set up for and clean up after each worship service. They couldn't have been more kind or cooperative.

Fourteen months later, we began to plan our return to our newly remodeled facilities. A new chapel had been added to our sacred space. The temple offices had been refurbished. The temple entrance now included a pleasant lobby in which congregants could gather after services or before meetings. The sanctuary walls and ceiling had been completely remodeled with recessed lighting and windows to the exterior. The Holy Ark was pristine again, awaiting the arrival of its six Torah scrolls.

We moved hundreds of boxes back into the temple and began to load their contents into shiny new filing cabinets. Some cartons, covered with dust, included files dated decades earlier — board resolutions from the 1940s and 1950s, correspondence from previous rabbis, and the scripts of former temple musicals.

In one file, bent and stained over time, was a series of letters between the president of the Orange Stake of the Church of Jesus Christ of Latter-day Saints and our temple president. The stake was building its first facility then, and the stake president indicated how grateful he was for the Jews' willingness to house Mormon worship services and Bible study in the temple. The temple president refused to accept any fees and assigned the temple's staff to provide the stake's custodial needs. Amazingly, the very church that had been our temporary home had asked the temple decades ago for temporary housing. Jews had welcomed their Mormon neighbors to use their synagogue facilities and rejoiced with them when their own facility was dedicated.

Both Mormons and Jews marched the mile and a half from the church to the synagogue, carrying six Torah scrolls back to the Holy Ark in the newly refurbished temple sanctuary. Completely intermixed, members of both communities carried the sacred scrolls, walking a half block or so, and then handing a scroll to another person nearby. No one asked his neighbor's religious affiliation; no one questioned his neighbor's faith. We — temple and stake, Mormons and Jews — had discovered that a kind act is not a matter of belief. It is an expression of love from one human being to another.

~Frank Stern

Sunrise Pizza

Food is our common ground, a universal experience.
~James Beard

It was a midnight flight from John F. Kennedy International Airport to Minnesota, set to take off at exactly midnight on a Friday. After three "one-hour" delays, I was told the flight had been overbooked, and I was bumped to the 6:00 a.m. flight. Normally, I was not a complainer, but after twelve consecutive hours of traveling, and with stale granola as my only nourishment, no amount of free air points could ease my irritation.

I was directed to a small waiting room at a far corner of the airport. The phone signal was horrendous and there was no Wi-Fi. The tiny TV on the wall was streaming the same old depressing news.

I wasn't alone in those three hours of murky near-dawn. There were six of us: a quiet woman in a hijab, her small daughter who seemed unable to stay still, a heavyset man with stern eyebrows, a man in a startlingly pink suit, and a teenager whose music I could distinctly hear through her headphones.

If three hours seemed long on paper, it felt even longer surrounded by these strangers, who were just as disgruntled as I was. Thirty minutes had not passed, and I was ready to renounce my morning flight, book an overnight hotel, and take my chances with the airlines another day. I was done with hope.

A tiny voice suddenly fractured the stillness. "Mama, I'm hungry."

It was the little girl. Two half-eaten, unappetizing cereal bars lay abandoned next to her stuffed pony. The mother whispered something to her, placing a finger to her lips. The little girl was desperately trying to keep her voice quiet, but her words were distinct in the muted room. "But I have three dollars, Mama!"

"I got cash."

The gruff voice belonged to the old man with severe eyebrows — underneath which, I noticed, were soft eyes fixed on the girl. "How's pizza sound? My granddaughters can't go a day without it."

"Hey, I'm hungry, too." The man in the extremely pink suit smiled at the mother, who had begun to shake her head. "And I've got a few dollars lying around."

"I've been living on granola," I admitted, pulling out my own purse. "Count me in."

The teenager pulled off her headphones and said, "Extra cheese, please."

In fifteen minutes, two boxes of extra-cheese pizza arrived like the sunrise. I devoured my first slice in an embarrassingly short time and quickly reached for another.

The teenager mentioned how there was a serious lack of good, greasy pizza in Japan. "That's where I was this past week," she said, "to participate in a science competition." She told us of her keen interest in mental health, in the sicknesses that we have yet to understand. "Alzheimer's is the most interesting," she said. "There isn't a cure yet, but I know I'll find it."

The old man had his eyes downcast. "You'd better," he murmured. "My wife hasn't recognized me in years."

It was a solemn quiet until the little girl patted the man's arm. "Don't worry. When I grow up, I'll find a cure, too." Then she paused. "Or maybe I'll train horses."

She seemed perplexed when we all broke into giggles.

Slice by slice, speaking became much easier. We spoke of the ridiculous snow Minnesota had gotten. We discussed the increasing prominence of technology in our lives. We criticized the color choice of Princess Sparkle Pony's mane. "I hate pink," the little girl declared.

Her eyes widened a second later, shooting to the man in the neon suit. "No offense!"

The man just laughed. "I love pink!" His laughter slowly fell away. "Not sure if Ryan's parents do."

"Who's Ryan?" I asked.

The smile returned to his lips. "My fiancé," he said. "I'm meeting his parents this weekend, but… they're not too happy about me."

The old man reached forward to squeeze a pink shoulder pad. "If they love their son, they'll learn to be happy."

The smile didn't leave the young man's face after that.

The woman in the hijab told us that she was on her way to visit her husband. "I travel a lot," she said. "I get many air points! Especially today, since I offered to take the next flight."

The teenager gasped. "You offered?"

The woman said, "Maybe someone needed the seats more than we did."

"Are you a saint?" the teenager asked.

The woman laughed. "No, I am a doctor."

The teenager's eyes widened. "That is so cool. Wait — aren't you going to tell me that loud music is bad for my ears?"

The woman smiled. "I figured you already know."

"I do," she admitted. "Still, I like it. It helps me drown out the world."

"Why do you want that?" I asked.

The teenager glanced at the TV. I'd forgotten it was there. It was blasting clips of bloodied children waiting to be treated in a makeshift medical center. Then, it cut to armed men peering through smoke.

The teenager said quietly, "Why wouldn't you?"

"Because, despite everything, hope defeats fear." It was the mother speaking. Her voice was quiet, but her eyes held fire. "No matter what happens, you can't forget that."

The old man murmured, "Hope begets happiness."

The teenager shook her head. "It's more complicated than that. I mean, what is happiness? It's not easy to define."

"Yes, it is!" The little girl's voice turned our heads. "Happiness is when it's a snow day, and Mama lets me eat cereal in front of the TV."

We couldn't stop roaring at that. Still chuckling, the teenager said, "Maybe it's not so complicated, after all."

Somehow, without really realizing it, the hours disappeared — as did the strangers around me. The old man with the strict eyebrows became Jim, a grandfather anxious to reach his granddaughters. The quiet mother with the hijab was Mina, a gynecologist with the most vibrant four-year old I had ever met. The newly engaged Ming had a smile as bright as his suit. The sullen teenager was the incredibly brilliant Ruth, and I knew that it wouldn't be long before she was making headlines.

We were no longer strangers connected by only a delayed flight to Minnesota. We were inventors, healers, dreamers, and lovers, Americans who respected each other and embraced our differences.

Almost too soon, it was time to board. We folded our pizza boxes, gathered our belongings, and pulled out our tickets. We knew it was time to say goodbye.

The little girl turned to me. She said, "Wait a minute, miss! What do you do?"

I smiled at the girl. "I'm a writer," I said. "I write about the things that give me hope."

~Sabrina Forest

The Folded Flag

*Patriotism is the admission that people who share
a land, a place, and a history have a special
obligation to that place and to each other.*
~David Ehrenfeld

I had traveled to California to say farewell to my sister Rose, who died suddenly of a heart attack at the age of fifty-four. She had served in the Women's Army Corps during the Vietnam War and received a military funeral at Riverside National Cemetery in Riverside, California. I was presented with the commemorative American flag and the three brass casings from the volleys fired by the honor guard, and then I rushed off to the airport.

I was carrying the flag, which had been folded into the traditional tri-corner form with the blue field of stars visible from both sides. The three spent shell casings were carefully tucked inside.

Going through security, which was at an all-time high due to the recent September 11th attacks on our nation, was quite an ordeal. I was ushered to a highly visible, roped-off section, flanked by security officers. The casings, still containing gunpowder residue, had been detected.

I tearfully explained over and over that the casings were from the commemorative rounds fired at my sister's funeral. Still, they closed the security line, and passengers were redirected to another area as they strained their necks trying to see what was happening. After several phone calls and discussions, security finally let me through with the flag and casings intact.

I held the flag even tighter as I looked for my gate and began my walk through the airport, which turned out to be an unexpectedly emotional experience. People looked at the flag and then at me with compassion and respect. "I'm sorry for your loss," many said as they hurried past.

While on the automated walkway, I thought of my sister. I held back tears as I held the flag to my chest. Across the aisle, headed in the opposite direction, a dozen or so young men — perhaps a high-school sports team — looked at me and simultaneously gave the thumbs-up. My sadness mixed with pride as I realized this was their salute, their show of respect.

Arriving at the overcrowded gate, a gentleman respectfully stood up, took off his hat, and gestured to his seat. I thanked him and sat next to a young mother who was explaining to her child why I was carrying the flag.

"Someone died who had served our country," she explained.

As I boarded the plane, people ushered me ahead, patting my arm and expressing condolences. A young man offered to take my carry-on. He smiled, gave a half salute, and swung it into the overhead compartment. Thanking him, I sat in my seat and placed the flag in my lap. The exhaustion from the emotional roller coaster of losing my sister so suddenly, and the quick cross-country trip for her funeral, were finally catching up to me. I decided to try and relax, but just as I was on the verge of settling down, I heard my name over the plane's PA system. "This is the captain. Linda Feist, please come to the front of the plane."

Was I being called back to security due to the casings? Full of apprehension, I made my way up the aisle amid the stares and low murmurs of the other passengers. I was greeted by a flight attendant, who took my arm and politely pointed to a seat.

"The captain and the crew asked me to extend this courtesy to you," she said. It was a first-class seat! I thanked them and thought about how I would always remember this day... the day I buried my sister, the day of immeasurable kindness, the day I felt patriotism so profoundly.

During my connecting flight, a passenger looking for her seat stopped in the aisle when she saw me. She looked at the flag in my lap and said she had noticed me walking through the airport. "It was quite an impressive sight," she said, "to see the commemorative flag being carried, and so many knowing what it symbolizes."

Arriving home, I was anxious to share these extraordinary experiences with my husband and daughter. During dinner, I told them about the funeral, my flights, and the respect and kindness I received from total strangers. "I was in awe of how many people were genuinely affected by seeing the flag," I said. "I felt a universal reaction, whether it was from those who knew what it symbolized or not." My daughter, in her early twenties at the time, was quite moved.

"Mom, do you have a renewed sense of faith in our country by this show of patriotism?" she asked.

I thought carefully about her question. "I've always felt it, sensed it," I answered. "I was just one of the fortunate ones to experience it."

That day, on March 6, 2002, I felt my sister traveled with me. I proudly carried the flag in her honor. I realize now that the flag is a symbol for all those who went before and will continue after her. When we honor the flag, we honor them.

~Linda Ann Feist

Getting to Know the Sicilian

When you really know somebody, you can't hate them.
Or maybe it's just that you can't really know them
until you stop hating them.
~Orson Scott Card

I was never a big genealogy buff, but I did know that I had some Italian in me. I thought that was pretty cool until I discovered I'm not really Italian at all — I'm Sicilian... at least a little. The rest of me is German, Welsh, Cherokee Indian and, well, you get the picture.

My maternal great-great grandparents immigrated to the United States from Palermo, Sicily. This knowledge didn't stop me from proudly and erroneously proclaiming my Italian roots anytime I met someone with a remotely Italian-sounding surname. And that's exactly what I did when I met Alonzo Ricci.

I was in my early thirties and working a civil-service job at a local military hospital. Alonzo was the born-and-bred Italian husband of my co-worker, Sergeant Julie Ricci. Sergeant Julie met Alonzo while stationed in Italy. They fell in love and married, and he accompanied her to Texas. Alonzo looked every bit the stereotypical beefcake Italian guy I'd seen on my favorite television shows. Having lived in America for only a short while, he sounded the part, too. I'd never met a "real"

Italian before, but of course he had, and it didn't take long for Alonzo to call my bluff.

As the holidays approached, I sent an open invitation to my enlisted co-workers to spend Thanksgiving at my home. I was pleased to learn that Alonzo and Julie would be joining us. As my guests ate and mingled, I noticed my mother visiting with Alonzo across the room. Suddenly, the look on Alonzo's face changed, and he seemed perplexed. My mother had shared her maiden name with our new Italian friend. Our "secret" was out.

I learned that day that Alonzo hailed from a family of Italians who despised the Sicilian people. He seemed conflicted over the fact that he had just broken bread with "the Sicilian," as he began referring to me. I assured him it was fine — we were actually one hundred percent American. Besides, he had just celebrated the quintessential American holiday with us. How could he possibly dislike someone who had fed him turkey and mashed potatoes?

Julie felt the need to apologize repeatedly over the next week for her husband's sudden and apparent disdain for me. I assured her it wasn't necessary. I felt so bad for her embarrassment that I found myself inviting her to my family's annual Christmas caroling hayride. She seemed surprised.

"Alonzo, too?" she asked, incredulously.

I laughed, "Yes, of course, Alonzo, too."

I'd like to think it was my winning personality, along with my mashed potatoes and gravy, that convinced Alonzo to revisit the home of "the Sicilian." Whatever it was, there he was, sitting on a bed of hay and reluctantly singing along to the American Christmas carols I had grown up with. I offered him a cup of steaming hot chocolate, which he first refused. Sergeant Julie gave him a discreet but swift elbow to the ribs, and he begrudgingly accepted my peace offering.

Alonzo seemed to relax as we wound through the streets of our picturesque small town. He even joined in when our group periodically broke out into laughter. At the end of the evening, Sergeant Julie gave me a heartfelt hug. "That was so much fun! Thank you! We would have been alone for the holidays if not for your hospitality." She turned to her husband and looked at him expectantly. "Isn't that right, Alonzo?"

"Yes, thank you, Sicilian," he added stiffly. I could swear I detected just the faintest smile from him. I smiled back and nodded.

The following day, Alonzo showed up at work to have lunch with his wife. They were passing me on their way out of the clinic when Julie stopped. "Melissa, why don't you join us?" Alonzo looked just as surprised by his wife's invitation as I was. I tried to decline politely, but she was insistent.

We settled into our booth at a local diner. There were a few minutes of awkward silence as we pretended to study our menus. I finally couldn't take it anymore. "Why don't you like Sicilians?" I asked Alonzo point-blank. He looked startled and a little embarrassed as he fumbled with an answer. Nothing he said made any sense to me, and I told him so. He actually seemed to appreciate my candor.

We spent the next hour talking about our families and our experience growing up in our respective countries. He shared about his life in Italy. I told him what I love most about America is that when push comes to shove, we care about one another, regardless of where our ancestors started out. He listened, and I do believe he was surprised to learn we weren't as different as he had been conditioned to believe.

Alonzo extended his hand to me as he dropped off Julie and me at work. I gladly took it. "I enjoyed our conversation, Sicilian," he offered gruffly.

"Yeah, me, too, ya big Italian," I answered with a smile. Much to my relief, he laughed.

A few days later, Alonzo arrived back at the clinic. This time, it was he who extended the invitation to join him and his wife for lunch. The conversation seemed to flow much more naturally this time. I found Alonzo to be pretty charming when he wasn't consumed by hating my Sicilian heritage.

"Ciao, Melissa. I see you soon, no?" he asked as we parted ways. I nearly fainted. It had taken one Thanksgiving dinner, a hayride, and two lunches, but he had finally called me by my name.

That weekend, my family and I rang in the New Year with food, games, and the Riccis.

When the clock struck midnight, Alonzo called his family in Italy. "You're never going to believe where I am!" he practically yelled into the phone. "I'm celebrating at the home of a Sicilian!" There was a pause before he continued. "No, no, no... these are good ones!" he finished. And I could tell he really meant it.

As our guests gathered their things to leave, Alonzo took me by my shoulders and kissed each side of my cheek. "Ciao, my friend... my American friend," he said in his thick Italian accent.

Sergeant Julie hugged my neck. "Thanks, again. I can't believe you kept inviting us back, but I'm so glad you did."

I shrugged my shoulders. "It's what we do... we good Americans." I winked at Julie as she stifled a laugh.

I don't know much about my Sicilian ancestors' arrival in America, but I'm willing to bet there was at least one "good American" who showed them kindness and hospitality, who made them feel welcome in a country where they knew no one. More than one hundred years later, their great-great granddaughter continues to pay it forward.

~Melissa Wootan

America Carried Me

My iPhone screamed the news as I stood in front of the open closet door in my hotel room. "49 DEAD IN MASSACRE AT GAY BAR!" I tried to take a step back and sit on the bed, but the unexpected grief kept me frozen. I'd just finished the Lake Placid Half Marathon, and spent the last several hours slogging through the rain and cold, daydreaming about collapsing into bed. But now, even with 13.1 miles behind me, I couldn't sit down. I just stood there, reading through the horror.

The words bounced around in my head, scrambling my thoughts into an ugly fog of anger, fear, and sadness. I transformed back into that little girl in elementary school, when I was always under attack.

"If you don't wear a dress to school, I'm going to fail you," said my fifth-grade teacher.

"Let's play 'Kill the Queer'!" yelled the kids at recess.

"What are you, a dyke or something?" sneered a boy in the lunch line.

Even as a young child, I knew I was different. Teachers and peers alike made sure to remind me every day. I didn't even understand the words "tomboy," "homo," "queer," "faggot," or "dyke." I had no idea what they meant, but somehow I knew they were me. More importantly,

I knew that all those words were the worst thing anyone could ever be. Shame, fear, loneliness, and desperation all went hand in hand with whatever "gay" was. As a child, it meant being hated — that was all I knew for sure. Back then, my best hope in life was to be invisible, to shrink back into the depths of the closet in my childhood bedroom, blanketed by the shadows and the darkness, alone but safe.

I'll just kill myself if it's true... I remember thinking matter-of-factly at seven years old.

Seven years old.

In the 1970s and 1980s, when one of the queers "got themselves killed," there was laughter. There was snickering. There were jokes. Even worse, there was silence. That was the majority opinion. If I turned out to be gay, then all of those sneers from the playground at recess were right. I'd be a queer, a faggot, a homo — a sin so great that my death would be a joke. Better to just kill myself to spare my family the humiliation, spare them the unbearable shame.

"That queer had it coming. One less pervert to worry about!" my young ears overheard from the TV in the other room.

I was terrified to be gay. Gay was expendable. Gay was perverted. Gay was a dead, bloodied body being mocked and laughed at by the masses.

My heart started pounding, and sweat beaded on my forehead as I relived the dark past of gay history in America.

Then my son's high-pitched toddler voice cut through the silence and snapped my mind out of its tailspin.

"MOMMY, I NEED GO PEE!"

Finally, I stepped back and sat on the bed.

"Okay, buddy. Good job using your words. I'll help you."

I stood up and followed him into the bathroom, my knees cracking in protest. As my son peed all over my sneakers, my mind wandered. I began to assume that a quiet indifference would settle in the air, and the country would move on without skipping a beat. That's what almost always happened in the past when these tragedies occurred.

After I sopped up my son's pee from the bathroom floor, I nestled into the couch next to my wife, with him lying horizontally across our laps. I braced myself for the hate and turned on the TV.

I was blinded by the rainbows. Politicians, news outlets, TV channels, companies, entire cities — all mourning, shrouded in colors. My parents called in tears. My wife's father called, outraged. In my grief and horror, I was not alone, I was not shrinking into the shadows, not hated. I was loved and giving love. President Obama released a statement condemning the violence and embracing the gay community. This time, the hater was the outcast, and the country was behind us. My wife and I looked at each other, teary-eyed and amazed.

A sad, deranged man with a gun stole forty-nine lives and affected countless others. It was unimaginable and tragic. The darkness came calling, urging me to retreat in fear, to hide myself in the shadows. But the love and support from family, friends, and country pulled me back from the darkness that day. I felt the weight of my profound grief spread across millions of shoulders. Even though the country I know hasn't always been kind, after the Pulse nightclub massacre on June 12, 2016, America carried me.

~Julia Pfeiffer

Just Lucky

How often we fail to realize our good fortune in
living in a country where happiness is more
than a lack of tragedy.
~Paul Sweeney

Just my luck. Right in time for Thanksgiving, one of my favorite pearl earrings broke. I'd had the pearls for years, and they were deeply sentimental, not to mention they matched everything. Besides that, I felt good with them on. Most people buy earrings to go with their outfits, but in this case, I'd bought my Thanksgiving sweater to match my earrings — a wheat-colored pullover with pearls and rhinestones encrusting the crewneck collar.

One of the pearls popped off the post right in the middle of a yoga class, and by some miracle, I managed to wrestle myself out of extended side angle to retrieve it off my mat before it had a chance to roll across the studio's bamboo floors to be lost forever. I groaned inwardly. Now I'd have to get it fixed if I wanted to wear it to the formal holiday dinner we were sharing at a dear friend's house. As if I didn't have enough stuff to do already. I mean, the day before I'd gone to three different grocery stores trying to find cardamom, plus I had three pies to make on top of two different kinds of sweet potatoes. I had to pick up my brother at the airport, and my kindergartner had some sort of school project due that involved feathers and poster board. Did I mention that I also work two jobs?

A friend had recommended an excellent jewelry repair spot in the mall closest to my house. I needed to go there anyway because my six-year-old had outgrown her dress shoes, so I thought I'd pop in, pick up some new shoes, and hopefully get the earring fixed.

The mall was predictably packed, and it was definitely beginning to look a lot like Christmas. Garlands were hung, and the stores were jammed with merchandise that promised to be the perfect gift. "Silver Bells" piped in from invisible speakers, and I couldn't help but notice the signs in every shop window, blaring in all caps about upcoming doorbusters for Black Friday. They annoyed me almost as much as trying to find a parking spot in the crowded lot just minutes before.

Located in the back of a card store was the jewelry repair counter. A young Muslim woman stood behind a glass case filled with gold chains and various charms. Crosses, crescents, Stars of David, and even little silver American flags all sparkled together in velvet trays. She wore a beautifully patterned green hijab and a loose tunic with long sleeves. She smiled warmly as I showed her my broken earring and explained the situation.

"I would have to send these out, and it would be a week to get them back. Then you couldn't wear them for Thanksgiving, so let me tell you what. Please go to my competitor instead — he's a friend of mine. He will fix them for you right now, and for less," she said.

Then she told me how to locate his kiosk in the center of the mall across from a store that sold luxury bath products.

What I found shocked me. The kiosk sold Judaica. I'd passed it a hundred times and never paid much attention, but this time the jewelry, wind chimes, wall hangings, and what my mom would have called "tchotchkes," caught my eye. Selling the Chais, Hamsas, and Star of David bracelets was a young, religious Jewish man. I knew he was observant because he wore a head covering. He spoke with a thick Israeli accent, which I recognized because my dad is also from Israel. In ten minutes, my earring was fixed, ready to go, and I was only out six dollars.

That afternoon, I gained a lot more than my favorite earrings repaired. I got a new perspective, a spark of hope. After a vicious election, headlines furious with scandals every day, and a twenty-four-hour news cycle with its endless loop of worldwide hate, brutality, and unthinkable violence, I realized that the anger and fear had gotten to me, made me cynical, and stolen my normally unshakable optimism. I understand that a broken pearl stud is but a minuscule inconvenience in the grand scheme of things, but I'd needed it to bring me to this experience and to see that what we read in our news feeds and see splattered across our screens isn't all that exists. There is friendship, honesty, and integrity, too. A lot of it.

It was Thanksgiving, and I was really grateful for something I normally took for granted — the United States of America. A Muslim woman sending me to her friendly competitor, a Jewish Israeli, so that I could wear my favorite earrings to a holiday dedicated to gratitude may not seem like a big deal, but to me it represented everything that I love about America. Suddenly, my pride in my country returned.

The news is filled with terror and vitriol. These things exist and shouldn't be downplayed lest we become complacent, but real life in America is also, just as importantly, filled with real human beings getting along, being decent, kind, and honorable, and we must recognize and celebrate this, too. The freedom we love in the USA lets people from all over the world work, own businesses, observe their differing faiths as neighbors and, best of all, be friends. As I left the mall that afternoon, right before Thanksgiving, I thought, *It's just luck that this is where I get to live.*

~Victoria Fedden

Working at the Muslim Community Center

I do believe in religious tolerance and finding the
commonality between all of us. I think that's
how we're all going to come together.
~Dennis Quaid

"A lright, everybody, how are we doing?" I shouted, trying to heighten the energy in the room. I glanced around, recognizing my normal participants: an Egyptian woman, the women who worked in the office upstairs, a Peruvian, other Americans practicing Islam, and my aunt and mother.

My class looked toward me with big smiles. Some of them had already removed their headscarves because in this women-only space they could be comfortable. I pressed Play on the stereo and started the warm-up, noticing my participants already relaxing, even though some of them were a little shy about shaking and grooving to the Latin rhythms of the Zumba routines.

At first, my friends and relatives didn't really understand why I was doing it.

"If you're not Muslim, why are you going to work at the Muslim community center?" they asked, confused.

I hadn't really thought of it like that. I was just finishing my first year of college studying Arabic language and culture. A summer internship at the Muslim community center seemed like the perfect place to put my theoretical skills to practical use. The center helped new immigrants settle into the Indianapolis area, it helped the refugees with legal matters, and it had a space for Muslims to join together to celebrate holidays or hear a lecture about religion or history. These were all things I was curious to learn more about. Plus, once the center learned I taught Zumba, they quickly arranged for twice-weekly classes for women — not just Muslim women, but any women who wished to join. I was only one of two non-Muslims working there, but I was accepted just the same.

That summer, I met refugees from Eritrea, Ethiopia, Burma, and Iraq I participated in an intercultural, interreligious community night where I made spring rolls with a Vietnamese-American co-worker and ate too much baklava. I went to a lecture about the Syrian civil war, which had then just erupted. The Zumba classes weren't only chances to get fit and have fun; they provided a space where my participants forged unlikely friendships.

People are busy in their daily lives. They normally go from home to work to home again, scrambling to make dinner, helping their kids with homework, and taking care of the house at the same time. It's not surprising that many people never branch out of their immediate social circles, which usually include people similar to them.

But at this special Zumba class, to which I had invited everyone from different areas of my life to join, there was a range of people as diverse as the city itself.

One of my most loyal participants was my supportive aunt, who lived nearby. She, like all of us, has a big heart. She always remembers birthdays and gets excited about all of my achievements.

What I hadn't realized when I started to invite her to the Muslim community center Zumba classes was that she never really had an opportunity to spend time with people different from her. I watched her in the class, dutifully following my instructions, and leaving with a big smile and drenched shirt.

She came to almost every class, but I didn't think it was a big deal — she always supports me. Then, the summer ended, and so did my internship and Zumba classes. I went back to school. But a few months later, when I got together with my aunt, she confessed something to me.

"You know, Allie, I was kind of scared of Muslim people before the class," she said, lovingly. "But then I got to know them at Zumba and realized they are normal just like everyone else."

When I heard her say that, I felt a wave of gratitude and achievement. I was so grateful for the Muslim community center for providing a space — not just for Muslims, but for people like my aunt and me. Because of their openness, there was the opportunity for an encounter that might not have happened. My aunt could have continued to be hesitant to trust a woman in a headscarf or afraid of a man with a long beard. But it was because of this shared space that maybe we did something to better our country.

And that's what makes America so wonderful. It is a willingness of different people — on all sides of the spectrum — to share and create together. We are inherently tolerant. We just need a chance to express it.

~Allison Yates

The Kindness of Strangers

I have always depended on the kindness of strangers.
~Tennessee Williams

My husband and I are avid rock-art fans. We are fascinated by the art of the Native Americans who chiseled, pecked or incised on rocks to produce images that depict the spirituality, daily life, travels, and other facets of their culture. I got hooked on this form of artistic expression the first time my husband took me west not long after we were married, and it has been a mutual passion of ours for many years.

Recently, we were in Mesa Verde National Park in south Colorado and wanted to see what petroglyphs (the name given to this art form) were found in that park. After much frustration, we found that only one site within the park was open to visitors, and that was on a two-and-a-half-mile trail, aptly named Petroglyph Point Trail, near the museum of the park. Now, two and a half miles didn't sound like a very long hike. We are both in our seventies and fairly fit, and we can pretty easily do two and a half miles if the hike is not too strenuous. I suppose I must have really wanted to do this hike because I was only halfway listening when the ranger said that the hike was pretty strenuous, and it was steep and rocky over most of the first mile and a quarter. After all, I had my hiking boots. Surely, I could do this!

Another thing she said was that *if* we could negotiate the stairs, we would find that the last mile and a quarter or so would be on level ground and extremely easy. I realize now I minimized that "if."

On the appointed morning, we got up fresh and rested, ready to go on our petroglyph hike. First, we would have a good protein-filled breakfast. We waited for a café near the trail to open at 9:00 a.m. This was our first mistake. Turns out that café did not serve breakfast. We rushed four miles back to a place that *did* serve breakfast, but we had already lost a few good morning hours waiting for the other place to open. It would be nearly ten before we could get on the trail. In June, every minute of early-morning coolness counts.

Sure enough, when we did get started, it was beginning to get warm. We headed out for our big adventure. The first quarter-mile of the trail was not too bad although it was pretty much downhill all the way. Then it became treacherous. The trail twisted and turned between huge boulders. I grabbed onto trees, rocks, and anything I could to find a handhold to steady me. Gordon, my husband, was watching my every step as well as his own.

The sheer drop-off below us was awe-inspiring. One misstep and we could be plummeting over the edge. Nevertheless, younger hikers were passing us by with nary a worry.

Sometimes Gordon walked ahead of me, and sometimes he thought it best to follow me. He was always close by, and I did appreciate him. He held my hand often when he thought I might need the extra support, and it was definitely needed. I was embarrassed that I needed help. A couple of years earlier, I was in better shape, but now I had serious back problems and three joint replacements.

The park had placed a couple of rangers at strategic places on the trail to check on hikers and make sure everyone was okay. That was reassuring. They were both encouraging, making us feel that we could indeed make it to the end.

A little before we got to the petroglyph panel, we met up with a man who looked vaguely familiar. After speaking with him briefly, we realized we had encountered him the day before on the Southern Ute Indian Reservation at a fry-bread stand. This man, his wife and her sister, who were Hopi Indians, were also having bread. As we visited with him, he said that he would see us at the petroglyphs, and we thought no more about it.

The man passed and we continued on the trail to the stairs we had been told about. But we found our Hopi friends there waiting for us! They wanted to help us up those challenging stairs! It turned out that I would never have made it up those stairs without their help.

After we got to the top of the mesa, they continued to watch out for us. If we lagged behind on the trail, we would find them waiting for us to make sure we were all right. They acted as our guardian angels the rest of the way back to the museum. It was hot, and we were out of water. I think we would have survived, but I was in bad shape, and they realized it. After the hike, one of the women rushed to her car and brought back a container of Gatorade for me.

It was such an eye-opening experience to know that people wanted to help us. They demonstrated their brotherhood and faith to us by simply befriending us.

~Carol Nash Smith

Provisions

More things are wrought by prayer
than this world dreams of.
~Alfred, Lord Tennyson

I was in Charleston, South Carolina, on the night of the infamous attack at Mother Emanuel A.M.E. Church in June 2015. My husband and I had just arrived at our hotel when the story came on the news: Bible study becomes a bloodbath as an unknown white gunman mows down African American worshipers who had welcomed him into their circle. It seemed impossible that such a horrific event could occur here, in Charleston, a place routinely lauded as one of the friendliest cities in America. We stayed up long into the night watching the reports, trying to make sense of the madness.

The following morning, I had to go out for groceries. Everyone in the store was shuffling around in a fog, still in shock. We ambled about like robots, mechanically going through the motions of filling carts and lining up to pay for purchases.

I had picked up a few basics and was standing at the register when a young black man walked up to my cashier — who was also African American — and gave her a gentle hug. He stood back and took a folded newspaper from under his arm, opening it to reveal the glaring headline: "Church Attack Kills Nine."

"One of the victims is my neighbor's cousin," the man said solemnly. "And Pastor Pinckney is gone, too." He shook his head and put down the paper. Then the two resumed their silent embrace.

I glanced at the woman behind me. We were both white, and I think we instinctively felt some shame and guilt at our racial commonality — however incidental — with the gunman. I wanted to say something, but couldn't think of anything that wouldn't come off as insensitive, or worse, patronizing. The lady behind me also seemed to be struggling with the awkwardness and angst of the situation.

But before either of us could muster a comment, the cashier stepped away from the distraught man and walked over to where we stood.

"We need to pray," she said, looking from her friend to the two of us in line. "Let's join hands and ask Jesus for a blessing."

Without another word, we all reached out our hands and formed a circle — four strangers of various races, ages, faiths, and economic statuses. (I'm not even sure, really, because we knew literally nothing about one another.) And we prayed there, in the checkout line of a Charleston grocery store, for the victims, for their families, and for the police, who had to tell mothers and fathers and children and friends that their loved ones were gone and then risk their own safety apprehending the murderer. We also prayed for Charleston, the "Holy City," and for cities everywhere that suffered such heinous events — that this might be the last.

"And Lord, we ask your grace be upon the killer, too," she said at the end. "And on his family. This is a terrible thing he's done; please turn his heart back to you, and give his family some measure of peace. Amen."

That evening, candlelight vigils were held along Calhoun Street, and the gates of Mother Emanuel A.M.E. Church were adorned with white satin bows. By Friday, the suspect had been arrested (I will not use his name; he does not deserve to be memorialized within these pages), and he appeared in court for a bond hearing. Family members of his victims came, too — not to demand blood, but to forgive him and encourage him to repent. "May God have mercy on you," said a woman who survived the massacre but lost her son to the very gunman she was now blessing. Another explained she would respond to his violence with compassion, so "hate won't win."

In the days that followed, South Carolina's Governor Nikki Haley removed the Confederate flag (a symbol the killer used as his personal emblem) from the State Capitol. An outpouring of love and support swept over Charleston from around the country. President Obama came to the Holy City and led a chorus of "Amazing Grace" that resonated throughout the nation. Hate didn't win.

The villain who committed these vile atrocities sits behind bars for the rest of his life. The victims' families will never be the same, but have crafted beautiful mosaics from the broken pieces fate handed them that June evening, confident in the knowledge they will see their loved ones again. Mother Emanuel Church is stronger than ever, focusing not on past brutality but on everlasting glory. And the heart of the Holy City, once cruelly broken, continues to beat.

I will never forget that summer morning, the smell of salty sea air and bread baking in the grocer's ovens, the feel of a stranger's hand in mine as we said our improvised prayer, the affirmation that good always overcomes evil.

That is the real Charleston. That is the real America. That is who we are.

~Miriam Van Scott

My Kind (of) America

Speaking Up for What's Right

10

The Other Bus Story

It ought to be possible, in short, for every American
to enjoy the privileges of being American without
regard to his race or his color.
~President John F. Kennedy

I n the early 1950s, in a small South Carolina town, a little girl refused to sit at the back of the bus. Her mother gave her the evil eye and insisted she move. But the little girl continued her protest as she sat in a front seat beside a white woman, leaving barely enough room for air between them. The white woman looked back at the little girl's mother and said, "Oh, it's okay. She can sit here beside me so she can have a better view." The bus doors closed, and they all proceeded to their destinations without incident.

This story has not been recorded in any history books or newspapers because I am finally writing it down for the first time. My mother was that little girl, and the white lady is an unnamed character in a story that has helped to shape my image of life in this country. I remember my mother telling this account to my sister and me on more than one occasion, and it has stuck with me all these years. That incident on a bus in segregated South Carolina is the picture of America that I am determined to keep in my heart. While numerous outrageous lines were drawn throughout the southern United States at that time, every person on the bus that day, black and white, made a conscious choice to maintain peace.

Hearing this story as a child was significant to me in a few ways.

First, it demonstrated that, regardless of how dire the circumstances, there is hope. At the very core of American life, there has always been hope. Despite the obvious turmoil that plagued the country during that time, there was hope that great things were still possible. On that day, my mother hoped that her determination would result in a better seat, and she prevailed. It was a small victory for a little girl, but an enormous victory for humanity that would reach the next generation.

Second, I learned that "we the people" are just trying to make it — just trying to live a good life and make it home without incident. I do not know if that white lady was just tired, a secret freedom fighter, or a mother who had a little girl waiting at home for her. But I feel certain that she, like most Americans, believed in "life, liberty and the pursuit of happiness" for all people. It can be hard to cancel out the chaos that surrounds us, but that lady was able to focus on doing the right thing.

And, third, this story taught me the importance of storytelling. How many other little girls and boys of color were brave like my mother? How many small victories have been won in some quiet corner of this nation? The only way to begin to answer these questions is through storytelling, so that we can help paint a more complete picture of this place we call home. I have shared this story with a few people over the years, and they always seem happier after having heard it. I have often wondered if that lady shared this story with her children. I like to believe she did, and that they, too, were inspired and encouraged to share the story as I am doing now.

No, my mother's name is not famous, nor is the name of the white lady. And, no, my mother's actions did not lead to the desegregation of South Carolina buses. But that one incident has survived history because it helped shape the heart of a post-segregation African American woman: me. My mother's decision to share this story helped me focus on the common thread of humanity that is sewn into all Americans. I am constantly grateful that my parents chose to tell positive stories like this one. Their memory sharing helped me form a more complete vision of the world around me — one that acknowledges the trials, but is not embittered by them. I definitely have my tough moments when I am sure that hell in a hand basket is just around the corner. But remembering the incident that took place on a bus in the 1950s helps me know that moments like that have happened all throughout our history and continue to happen today.

~Cynthia M. Gary

11

Keeper of the Principles

God has given us many faiths but only one world
in which to co-exist. May your work help all of
us cherish our commonalities and feel
enlarged by our differences.
~Lord Jonathan Sacks

I first attended interfaith groups as a high school student in the 1960s in Bethlehem, Pennsylvania. I was raised in a Jewish family with an awareness of racism, anti-Semitism and oppression of many kinds in our country and in the world. My ancestors had suffered from pogroms in Russia, prompting them to immigrate to this country. Because of them, I was lucky enough to grow up in America. As a young person, I thought a lot about becoming a civil rights lawyer so I could help people who had been discriminated against, although I abandoned that plan when I discovered how many years of school that would require!

I studied Comparative Religions in college, and participated in many spiritual, peace and civil rights events over the years. Yet more than thirty years after my first interfaith experiences in high school, despite decades seeking greater understanding of the struggles of other people, after 9/11 I realized I didn't know any Muslims.

I knew that Muslims were going to suffer discrimination and persecution from the anger that was to come. So while some called for war, I went looking for peace groups to work with.

The one I liked best was JAM and All (short for Jews and Muslims and All), founded by a South Florida imam and a Jewish businessman shortly after 9/11. I loved this group's positive emphasis on creating and working for peace, rather than fighting against war and injustice, and I've been an active member since 2002.

Through JAM, I've met wonderful people of many faiths, and had numerous enlightening experiences through our community events featuring spirited dialogue, shared prayers and educational panels. And some of the most meaningful connections I've made have been with Muslims.

One thing about JAM events: There's always food! And breaking bread together really seems to help people connect and overcome differences. Spicy chickpea salad and potato samosas with tamarind sauce have become favorites of mine! And I've fallen in love with the gorgeous colorful fabrics worn by my Muslim friends who wear the traditional, multi-layered clothing items known as hijabs, abayas and jilbabs.

I've learned how wholeheartedly Muslims practice charity, compassion and generosity. I've seen it through their devoted and consistent support of our local community events and charities, as well as personal acts of generosity and support toward myself and others.

I've been able to support them, too, by playing music for hospital visits with sick members, writing letters in support of imams who were unjustly removed from planes, and in many other ways. I've also learned how much Islam and Judaism have in common. I've learned that Islam is a religion of peace and teaches that: "If you save one person, it is as if you have saved the world. If you harm one person, it is as if you have harmed the world." We have this same teaching in Judaism. There are many other common values and teachings as well.

In our JAM group, I became known as Keeper of the Principles because I typeset a nice copy of the twenty principles we created to guide our dialogue groups and events. I make sure there are copies to give newcomers at every JAM gathering. Some of our JAM Principles include:

- Respect our differences
- Non-judgment
- Keeping each other safe
- Listen and hear

Over the years, we've developed traditions in JAM. One of our favorites is sharing "JAM Stories," examples of wonderful things happening as a result of some kind of interfaith interaction.

One of our most memorable JAM stories happened in October 2005 after Hurricane Wilma, one of the most devastating hurricanes we've had in Florida. Electricity and water were out in many places for weeks, and in some cases for months, leaving many without food, water and other crucial resources.

In the Holiday Springs condominium in Margate, many elderly Jewish residents were trapped in their upper-floor apartments with no elevators, electricity, or water. This building was next door to Masjid Jamaat Al'Mu-mineen, known as the Margate Masjid, a mosque that many of these Jewish folks had adamantly opposed when it was being built.

Nevertheless, when members of the Margate Masjid discovered their neighbors were trapped in their apartments, they immediately organized food and water deliveries, walking up all those stairs to deliver this vital nourishment to their neighbors, people they didn't even know. The Margate Masjid had a generator so they were able to make hot coffee to go with the countless sandwiches they put together. These deliveries continued daily for weeks until electricity was restored to the building.

I heard about this while it was happening from JAM friends who belong to the Margate Masjid, and later from some of the condo residents themselves, who attended a JAM meeting at the mosque some months later. The hearts of these elderly Jewish people were transformed by this generous act of charity by their Muslim neighbors, and they spoke warmly of those who had helped them. The fact that they were now willing to attend an interfaith meeting held at a mosque spoke even louder than their words.

Later, when the Margate Masjid needed to expand and build a larger facility in a different area, some in the new area opposed the new building project. These same Jewish neighbors who had once opposed the building of the mosque next door now spoke to the County Board on behalf of the mosque, along with many of us in the community, supporting them in building their new and much-needed facility. And the new mosque was built.

This is just one of many transformations I've experienced, observed and participated in through our JAM and All interfaith group. I had the opportunity to speak on an interfaith panel at an Islamic Society of North America convention. I've been warmly welcomed (and fed!) at many iftars, the breaking of the daily fast during Ramadan. I've attended many inspiring services at churches, temples and mosques to support JAM brothers and sisters who were leading or speaking at the services. I've attended countless JAM events and board meetings, and proposed and managed our JAM Listserv for group communications and community notices.

Now if I hear someone slandering or repeating a negative stereotype about Muslims, I always say: "If you knew the Muslims I know, you would feel differently. Let me introduce you to my friends!" I have Muslim friends who feel more like members of my family than some members of my family.

Though it's not a big group, it feels to me like this JAM group, which comes together in love, caring and mutual respect, is practicing the principles of America in a deep, authentic way. And that makes this group one of the most beautiful examples of the kind of America that I am proud to live in.

~Laura Sue Wilansky

12

Pats on the Back

The best protection any woman can have… is courage.
~Elizabeth Cady Stanton

"We're with a group of strong, beautiful women. We're fine." These were the words that my travel companion and dear friend Cassondra uttered to her concerned mother by telephone as we made our way into Washington, D.C., by metro train for the Women's March on Washington early on the morning of January 21, 2017.

I've had to replay Cassondra's words many times in my head in the days since. I've needed the reminder that those simple words provided. I've needed the strength, the affirmation, the love. Because, let me tell you, the days following that beautiful Saturday have not been easy.

I live in a very small, old-fashioned town in the mountains of North Carolina. Many of the locals have never been anywhere else. Their minds haven't stretched far enough to take in all that is out there in this big world. I've become used to it. I've become accustomed to the responses I receive any time I go against the flow (which is pretty often). This is nothing new. I knew there might be negativity associated with participating in the march. I was prepared for it. It's pretty much the status quo for me as someone who is not from the area.

But what I wasn't prepared for?

What took me by surprise?

The response from some of my friends, and one response in particular: "No one was there to 'fight' anything. You just walked around getting pats on your back from people who already agreed with you."

Coming from a day filled with love and acceptance, I felt shell-shocked to hear those words. And from one of my closest friends even.

Were we just looking for "pats on the back?"

After some thought, however, I realized that she had it backwards. It was the other way around. We were there to *give* those pats on the back.

To the woman I overheard trying desperately to hear on her cell phone as the crowd thickened and the decibel level rose because she was calling to make sure her son made it to soccer practice — this pat is for you.

To the man who married a strong woman and showed up to show his support and love for her and all women like her by wearing his "I married a strong woman" T-shirt — this pat is for you, sir.

To the woman carrying the sign that said, "I'm the lesbian daughter of a Muslim immigrant" — this pat is for you, you strong, beautiful, brave woman. And here's another one for your mom.

To the many women in the crowd who carried their babies on their person for hours at a time so they could be part of an historical event to have their voices heard — this pat is definitely for you. What a story you'll have to tell them. Kudos to you, mommas.

To the little Latino girl on her daddy's shoulders beaming as she watched six-year-old Sophie Cruz, daughter of Mexican immigrants, give arguably the most rousing speech of the march. I remember the smile that covered your little face as young Sophie told you, "I am here to tell the children, do not be afraid." Oh yes, little one, you get a big pat on the back. And you would have gotten the biggest hug you've ever gotten from a redheaded stranger if I could have reached you, you sweet little thing.

To the teenager holding the rainbow sign showing the USA and the words, "No hate, no fear, everyone is welcome here" — a pat on the back for you, little warrior woman. I know full well how tough it is for a teenager who is "different." How brave you were to walk through the streets of that big city and show the other kids of the world that you were on their side.

To the woman wearing the race bib on her shirt that said "Sarah bear" — being a runner myself, I had to ask about it. When you told me you were wearing that bib in honor of your young daughter who had just passed away, I couldn't stop my tears. You definitely get a pat on the back. A big one. You possess a strength that I couldn't possibly know. You are my hero.

I could list a million more "pats on the back," but I'll finish with a final one.

To the woman who stood by my side through it all. The woman I watched feed a homeless man; defend a woman who was being verbally attacked by a stranger on the street; force a parting of the crowd to help a woman break through to find her son. The woman who continually asked people's stories. Who felt people's pain. Who engaged everyone in conversation. Who shed tears on countless occasions simply because she was standing where she was and doing what she felt in her heart to be right. The woman who never wanted to be in front of the camera because she was too busy behind it — documenting the happiness, strength and, sometimes, the pain. The woman who lost her job while we were on this trip because of a landslide in our small town, yet who set that worry and grief aside long enough to focus on the matter at hand, and do her part in preserving a piece of history. I laughed with her; I cried with her; I raged with her.

We became sisters.

So, to my travel companion and dear friend, Cassondra — an extra special pat on the back for you, lady.

This is what this trip was about. This is what this weekend was about. This is what that day was about. This was what that march was about.

This is what America is about.

Sisterhood.

Togetherness.

Connection.

Strength.

Love.

Determination.

We are going to be there for one another. We just are. Not just Cassondra and me, but every woman and man who stood there side by side in collective love. That day was just the start of something big and beautiful.

We are not through yet.

This movement won't be stopped. Maybe you don't understand that right now, but one day you will.

One day, you will.

~Melissa Edmondson

The Top of the Stairs

*The tears of the red, yellow, black, brown
and white man are all the same.*
~Martin H. Fischer

In August 1957, in Central Texas, a well-dressed young woman perspired as she climbed the steps to the public library's children's room.

"Can you help me?" she asked. "I was graduated from college in May, and this is my first job as teacher, second grade. I've made a list of books that I'll need. The school where I'll teach does not have them."

"Well," I said. "I was graduated in May, too, and I'm working here while my husband completes two required courses for his bachelor's degree, plus a couple more courses toward his master's. I DO know books. I've read all my life, and helping you will be fun."

Together, the teacher and I searched for books. Teachers were allowed to check out twenty books on their library cards. We laughed and figured out which books would fit into her teaching, and which would be just plain fun for her kids.

She thanked me for helping her carry the books downstairs. We were both sweating. She eyed her underarm stains. "I just bought this suit," she said. "I usually make my own dresses, but I wanted to splurge to get ready to teach. I could not try on this suit in the store. That's their policy. Do you think it fits?"

After the woman left, I went back upstairs and had begun shelving books when the children's librarian confronted me.

"Why did you help that girl?" she asked.

"She's a teacher. She needs books."

"THOSE people don't come in here," said the frowning woman. "We send a bookmobile to the part of town where THEY live, and they can check out books once a week. Teachers can send me their lists, and I decide what is right for their grades. You were choosing books from shelves all over the place. We probably won't get back the books she took."

"She had a library card," I said.

"She can use the bookmobile. Don't forget, and wipe those books she didn't take. She sweated on them. And don't let her come up here again, or any of THOSE children. They don't belong here."

Because I needed my $190-a-month pay, I stayed quiet, cleaned, and straightened bookshelves. But the more I thought about the eager teacher, the more I boiled. The children's librarian had already limited all children to books at their grade level only. I'd grown up thinking of my hometown public library as my special place, where I could choose any book I wanted. But this was not my hometown.

Finally, I asked for a private word with the head librarian. I told her that I intended to work with any teacher and any child in the *public* library. The head librarian had known me since childhood back in my hometown, and I knew of civil-rights battles she'd fought throughout the state. She was also an excellent librarian.

"I'll take care of this," she said.

And she did. Before the city council, she reviewed the intention of a public library, and she presented a resolution that called for the library to be open to all. Her resolution passed unanimously and was published in the local newspaper.

I'd like to say I stayed and became part of that quiet revolution, but my husband was graduated. We moved away to his first job. Besides, I was pregnant, and a baby bump was beginning to show. The children's librarian said, "No child should see you in that condition."

"At least," I thought, "she's a bigot on several levels. Surely, she and her ways will go away soon."

I have worked in other states, as librarian at a grade school, and with many children and teachers. I know of several students of color who lived in that 1957 community and became scientists, writers, performers, and teachers. I hope they sometimes think of their second-grade teacher, who climbed some steep stairs to help them. I was proud to meet her at the top of the stairs.

~Shirley P. Gumert

Bridging a Gap

Every man is rich in excuses to safeguard his
prejudices, his instincts, and his opinions.
~Egyptian Proverb

When I heard the news, I cried. On a Monday evening in late November 2001, the week following Thanksgiving, three gun-wielding teens shot and killed two men at a neighborhood grocery store in the eastern part of Tuscaloosa, Alabama. One of the victims was Hassan Serag, the grocery store's owner. The other victim was Mosaad Abdelkerem, one of the co-owners of Hooligan's Mediterranean Restaurant downtown.

Both men were Muslims, and both were from Egypt. They were friends.

Abdelkerem had taken a prepared meal from his restaurant for his friend to break the day's Ramadan fast. He knew Serag was at the store alone and wouldn't have an opportunity to eat otherwise.

Along with shock and profound sadness, shame overwhelmed me. I had never bothered to find out the names of the people at Hooligan's who reliably served me whenever I walked in the door.

For two and a half years, I had been eating lunch two or three times a week at Hooligan's. It had the best mint tea in town, fast service and was just a block from my office at *The Tuscaloosa News*.

Hooligan's was one of the most popular downtown restaurants in this thriving university metropolis. The staff consistently and politely accommodated the onslaught of customers who lined up all the way to the sidewalk on some days. No one was overly talkative, but then everyone was usually busy, including the two co-owners who often managed the order window.

How could I frequent this place of business for so long and never take the time to get to know the people I saw more than some of my own family members?

Just a couple of months before, Hooligan's had sent all of its employees to donate blood following the terrorist attacks on September 11th. They all wore T-shirts with "United We Stand" imprinted on the back to show their solidarity.

They were an inspiration to the entire community despite the suspicion and fear hovering in the background toward all Muslims during that period. They wanted everyone to know they condemned the attacks, and were as appalled and shocked as everyone else.

Many in the community, including me, initially assumed the shooting was a hate crime. There had been a number of death threats in the past few months. Tensions ran particularly high in the Muslim community.

Even after police said the shooting deaths were the results of a botched robbery by the teenage thugs, apprehension and trepidation remained.

When Hooligan's reopened two days after the shooting, I went there to find out more about the man whose name I hadn't known. I also wanted to introduce myself to all the employees and the other owner, and to apologize for my indifference. The other owner wasn't there; he was in Birmingham, Alabama, making arrangements to have the victims returned to their families in Egypt.

But I introduced myself to the employees, who also knew me by sight but not name. I asked them to tell me about Abdelkerem.

A seventeen-year-old server said the six or seven months she'd been working at Hooligan's was the longest period she'd worked anywhere. And a lot of it had to do with Abdelkerem's generosity of spirit. He listened to, counseled and encouraged her.

"He was just the sweetest man. We're all like a big family here," she said with tears in her eyes. "I can't believe he's not here. I keep thinking he'll be here any minute, just running late."

Co-worker Khaled Ismail, who had been at Hooligan's for about five months, was close friends with both of the victims and still in a state of shock over their deaths.

"I just talked to Mosaad five minutes before he was killed," Ismail said. "He was laughing, just calling to check on things here at the restaurant."

He said Abdelkerem had returned three weeks earlier from his wedding in Egypt and was working to bring his wife to Tuscaloosa. Serag had just recently become engaged.

Ismail said both men were deeply loved by their families in Egypt, as well as their Islamic community here. Their deaths hit everyone hard.

"I'm happy for them because they're going to heaven," he said. "But I feel very sorry for us who don't have them around."

I went back to my office and composed a column expressing my sorrow and regret. It included a more personal account of the men based on the comments I received that day at Hooligan's.

On Thursday, my column ran on the front page of *The Tuscaloosa News*. Many of our readers expressed empathy and thanked me for publicly acknowledging my shortcomings.

Several in the Muslim community also let me know how much they appreciated the tribute. The president of the Islamic Society even invited me to speak at the memorial service on Sunday. I was honored to be included and given the opportunity to express my condolences and apologies.

Also speaking that day were Tuscaloosa's assistant police chief, the mayor, the district attorney and several other religious leaders in the community. Everyone expressed their concern for the terrible tragedy and their appreciation of the victims' contributions to the community.

"I am so ashamed that I never took the time to let Mr. Abdelkerem know how much of a difference he made in my life, how much I enjoyed doing business with him, how much he brightened my day every time I walked into Hooligan's and was greeted by him," I told the people in the mosque that day. "I didn't have the conversations with him that I wish I had. His death has made me realize how unconscious I've been, and I don't like what I've seen."

I recalled how excited and proud I had been when I moved back to Tuscaloosa in 1998 after being gone for nearly twenty-five years. I happily discovered my hometown had become an international community, a culturally richer place.

The deaths of the two young men jeopardized what we as a community were achieving.

"There have been unconscionable threats against some of you and rumors that some of you may want to leave here. I hope that's not true," I said, directing my comments to the Muslims. "You strengthen the tapestry of our lives. You make our lives better, more interesting, larger. You open a refreshing window to the world. The cultural and religious diversity I see in front of me today is awesome — it's beautiful. I don't want to lose that. And that's what scares me about the deaths of these men. We're all grieving because of it."

That day, the members of the Islamic Society heard from all of us who spoke that Tuscaloosa grieved with them and shared their pain. They were part of our community, and we were better for it.

~Jane Self

Making Choices

Before God, we are all equally wise and equally foolish.
~Albert Einstein

I skipped all the way home from school. I was so excited. Thursday evening was our school's annual roller-skating party. The rink would be filled with children from our Catholic elementary school, and many teachers had also promised to attend. I couldn't wait to have fun with my friends.

Our teacher had made an important announcement just before dismissal. "As you know, some of our classmates live quite far away. They won't be able to attend the party unless arrangements are made for them to spend the night with a friend. If any of you would like to host Robert, Nathan or Shauna, please bring a note from your parents tomorrow."

As the bell rang, I rushed over to Shauna's desk. "You can stay with me!" I assured her.

Shauna was one of my best friends in the third grade. Her face lit up as she did a quick twirl. "That would be so much fun!" she answered. "I hope your mom says it's okay."

I laughed and assured her, "She will. I have lots of sleepovers at my house." We chattered all the way out the door, parting at the line of yellow school buses. I would be walking home, while Shauna boarded the bus that was headed to the inner city.

It was the 1960s, and in an effort to achieve racial balance, black children were bussed in from the city to attend suburban schools.

Desegregation was a term that meant little to me at the age of eight. The only thing I noticed was that the bus carrying the black children often arrived late, and I was jealous that they got to miss a bit of school. I had no concept of the hardships involved in their long daily commute.

Arriving at home, I plopped my lunchbox on the counter and quietly reached for the cookie jar on the counter. As I lifted the lid, the scent of cinnamon made me lick my lips. My older sisters loved to bake. My mother walked into the kitchen. "Mom, can a friend spend the night on Thursday?" My mother put a finger to her lips, her way of reminding me not to talk with food in my mouth. I swallowed fast, and then continued. "It's the night of the skating party."

Mom let out her usual sigh when I asked for a sleepover. "You never sleep when friends are over," she protested, "and you have school on Friday." I clasped my hands as if in prayer. "Please, Mom, I promise we will sleep," I begged. "Shauna is so nice. You will like her." She looked at me for a long time, as if in deep thought. She opened her mouth to answer, then starting wiping the kitchen counters vigorously. I snatched another cookie and stepped back outside to play. As the screen door shut, I heard my mother's answer: "Ask your father."

At the dinner table, I swiveled my chair from side to side as I played with my peas. I waited for my father to finish talking to my brother, and then quickly asked about Shauna. "Dad, can my friend spend the night on Thursday?"

He glanced at me, then at my mother, who was stirring the gravy. "I guess so," he muttered. I held my breath as I savored the joy that was filling my body. I was smiling so big it was hard to chew my food. I instantly started planning, mentally choosing which pajamas I'd wear.

"I have to bring a note to school saying that it's okay for her to stay here," I informed my mother. That's when my father dropped his fork. He turned to me. He seemed angry as he asked, "Is she black?"

I looked up into his face, feeling both frightened and confused. "Yes, she is," I answered quietly.

His fury was now apparent as he snapped, "Then she's not staying here!" He went back to his roast.

I was so stunned that I could hardly move. I bit my lower lip as hot tears filled my eyes. *What had I done that had made him so angry? Why did it matter that Shauna was black? Why didn't he like my friend?*

As I crawled into bed that night, the scene replayed in my mind. I kept twisting the facts about, trying to make sense of it all. But after what seemed like hours of thought, I came to the conclusion that this simply was not logical in any way. I had always trusted my father and would have followed him down any path. But even at eight years old, I knew that he was leading me astray this time. I had never heard the word racism, but I knew in my heart that it was wrong to judge others based on differences. At that moment, I felt a profound sadness. I loved my parents. But I was ashamed of them.

Thankfully, Shauna was able to spend the night with another classmate and attend the skating party. As we skated together, hand in hand, I told her how sorry I was. "It's okay," she said with a smile. But it wasn't okay, then or now. As years passed, I had to close my eyes and ears to the prejudice my parents displayed. I vowed to come to my own conclusions about people, based not on their race or religion, but rather their effect on my heart and soul. And I'm pleased to say that my diverse array of friends has my heart humming and my soul singing.

~Marianne Fosnow

16

Sleeping on the Street

*I was standing there, waiting for someone to
do something, till I realised the person
I was waiting for was myself.*
~Markus Zusak, Underdog

As crazy as it may sound, many Americans will willingly sleep on the street. We'll trade in our feather-down pillows, duvet comforters, and Sleep Number beds, and pull up a corner of concrete for the latest iPhone, concert tickets, and Black Friday specials. A few hours on the sidewalk is well worth it when the prize is right.

Many Americans will also willingly step up for others when a need arises, regardless of what country they are from. We'll pull out our credit cards, organize fundraisers, or simply lift up a prayer for people in Syria, Haiti, or Africa. On April 29, 2006, I did both of these as I joined more than 80,000 Americans and others from around the world as we lay our pillows on the street for a Ugandan boy named Jacob.

When I first heard Jacob's story, I was a junior studying education at Union College in Lincoln, Nebraska. Jacob's face was one of many children known as "night commuters," who fled their homes nightly and walked several miles to sleep in cities' empty bus stations — all to avoid being enlisted as child soldiers by the Lord's Resistance Army in northern Uganda. Images of rows and rows of children sleeping restlessly were imprinted in my mind. I was so wrapped up in my studies and social life that I had been oblivious to what was happening around the world, particularly in Africa. Yet when I was introduced to the *Invisible Children* documentary that highlighted Jacob's story, I knew I wanted to help in some way.

Naturally, being a college student, I was broke most of the time, so pulling out my credit card wasn't an option. However, I heard that one night I could join thousands to raise awareness and show my solidarity with Jacob and others like him by sleeping outside in our own Global Night Commute.

As my friends and I made T-shirts for this occasion, I thought about what it would be like to constantly lay my head down in a different place every night and sleep the restless sleep of worry… worrying whether my family was okay… worrying whether I would be able to escape and survive the following night… worrying whether I would someday be forced to carry a gun and kill or be killed.

The Global Night Commute occurred on a beautiful Saturday in early spring. Because most of us still stayed in the dorms, we had obtained special permission from our college to sleep away for this occasion. After prayer, we set out and walked the four miles from our school to our state capitol building. We would sleep across the street from it. We joined young children with their parents, high schoolers with their headphones, middle-aged adults with their careers, retirees with their experience, and fellow college students with a purpose. We were all there to write letters and engage in meaningful dialogue with one another as well as with local news networks. We were all vastly different, yet we were all willingly united in our goal: to protect innocent lives like Jacob's from being destroyed by violence.

Later, upon watching footage from across the country of that night, I was in awe to see so many who had walked the miles and gone the distance for the children in Uganda. There were people of all ages, races, and demographics. I saw footage of high schoolers dressed in their prom dresses and tuxes walking the miles for Jacob. The Invisible Children organization had even flown Jacob in for this occasion; I smiled when I saw his face on the screen, for it was filled with hope. The slogan, "One American Sleeping on the Streets for One Ugandan," was adopted by all of us who participated that night.

Needless to say, when I finally laid my head down on the ground that night, I didn't sleep… I couldn't sleep. The sounds of downtown Lincoln, Nebraska, certainly contributed to this insomnia, but it was more than that. The sounds of America at its finest kept me awake. At that moment, thousands of others across the country were taking a stand by lying down on the streets of cities such as Oklahoma City, Los Angeles, New York City, and Washington, D.C.

The next morning after a group photo in front of the capitol building, my friends and I made the trek back to campus. Even though I was tired, my mind was cognizant of many things that early Sunday morning. As the sun stretched its rays between budding trees, and early-morning traffic began pouring down the streets, I thought about Jacob and others like him. I thought about being able to go back to my dorm and go straight to bed while the children of Uganda would still have to sleep on the street that night. I thought about the impact our one-time night commute may have had, and I frowned. *What if it didn't change anything?*

But then, I thought about the fact that it did change something: *It changed me.* I wasn't the same person I had been... and I'm pretty sure others were not either. We may have only exchanged our cotton comforters for one night, but that one night on the street allowed us to see the kind of America we should be, one where we do pay attention to the hardships faced by others.

~Elizabeth Harsany

17

Being Black in a White World

It is never too late to give up your prejudices.
~Henry David Thoreau

A s a white kid growing up on the lower west side of Detroit, Michigan, in the 1940s, I never experienced any prejudice or discrimination. Most of the people in the community were white and Jewish.

Although I didn't experience religious or racial bigotry at this early age, I certainly did hear about it from my father. He was the only survivor from his family during the Holocaust. The Nazis exterminated his parents, seven siblings, and all his aunts, uncles, and cousins because they were Jews. At some point as a teenager, I told my father that I thought it was wrong to hate the new German babies being born.

His reaction was, "Today, a nice German baby, tomorrow a Nazi."

He felt that hating Jews was ingrained in the German culture. I understood why he felt the way he did. Even so, I could never bring myself to feel the same way.

The first time I experienced racial discrimination, not for myself but for a co-worker, was in 1964 while I was working at Litton Industries, an aerospace company, in Canoga Park, California. There I met George Green, a twenty-eight-year-old, single, black male who was an electronics technician like me. One day, he told me how far he lived from work. At first, I thought maybe he had no choice but to live where he did.

But when I pressed him about living closer, he told me he had tried to rent an apartment closer to work.

"What do you mean you 'tried'?" I asked. "I've seen all kinds of vacancy signs close to work."

"Benny," he said, in surprise, "are you that naïve? I just accept it. I know this is the way it is. Maybe you haven't noticed, but I'm as black as the ace of spades. I can't prove it, but I know that's the reason."

My initial reaction was disbelief. "George, this isn't Alabama or Mississippi."

I told him he was overreacting and being overly sensitive. I explained to him that the State of California had recently passed a new law, which prohibited discrimination in housing because of race, color, religion, or national origin. It was called the Unruh Civil Rights Act, named after the Speaker of the California State Assembly, Jesse Unruh.

I then told him I had an idea. "George, this is what we are going to do. At lunchtime, we are going to take a ride down Ventura Boulevard. The first sign we see that says 'For Rent,' I will go and see if they have already rented the apartment. If not, I will leave, and you will go and try to rent the same apartment."

"Whatever you say, Benny."

The following day, we drove in my Volkswagen to an apartment complex on Ventura Boulevard, not far from where we worked, that had a vacancy sign on the front lawn. I went first while George sat and waited in the car. I was dressed casually. The manager showed me the bachelor's apartment and said that it was available. She said all that was required was the first and last month's rent. I thanked her and left.

I walked back to the car where George was waiting nervously. I told him exactly what I asked for, a bachelor's apartment, and how much the monthly rent would be. We waited for a few minutes while watching to make sure that no one else entered the building. George, who was wearing a sports jacket, white shirt and tie, certainly looked presentable enough. I sat in the car and watched George knock on the manager's door. Within a couple of minutes, I saw George walking back to the car.

He got in and just stared out the window.

"What happened?" I asked.

"I told you what would happen," he replied. "She said, plain and simple, there were no vacancies."

I couldn't believe it. I sat there for a while and decided to go back and check it out again. The manager easily recognized me and asked if I had decided to rent the apartment. I told her I had changed my mind and wanted to rent the one-bedroom apartment. Once again, she showed me the apartment and said it was available. I thanked her and left.

George and I repeated our efforts three more times at different apartment complexes. When they didn't have exactly what we asked for, we asked if we could leave our names and phone numbers. They always took my name and phone number, but they never took George's name and phone number. I had seen and heard enough to convince me that there was something drastically wrong. At this point, I told George he had to get in touch with the Fair Housing Commission and register a complaint. Within two weeks, George heard from the FHC and was told to try again.

I was so happy for George.

But instead of being happy, George was now full of anxiety.

"Benny, now I'm not sure if I want to follow through."

"Why not?"

"I don't know if I want to live around people who hate me."

"I understand, but now it's your choice. Just remember this. Once people get to know each other, this whole racial thing will go away. It's all about the fear of the unknown."

The following day, George courageously found an apartment on Ventura Boulevard about three blocks from work.

A few months later in March 1965, George and I were discussing race once again. I casually mentioned that we didn't have any areas in Los Angeles that were all black.

"Have you ever heard of Watts?" George asked.

"What's Watts?"

"It's an entire community in Los Angeles that is all Negro."

"You have to be kidding, George. How would I not know that?"

"That's because you live in a bubble."

When I got home that evening, I told my wife that on Sunday the two of us and our two small children were going to take a leisurely ride to Watts.

As we drove through the neighborhood of Watts, around 101st Street and Central Avenue, it became obvious that everyone we saw outside was black.

Then I heard my wife say, "ROLL UP THE WINDOWS!"

"WHAT?" I screamed. "Why would I want to do that?"

"I'm scared," she declared.

"Why are you scared?"

"I've never met a Negro before."

"Well, you are about to meet one. I've invited George Green from work over for dinner."

I felt that, together, George and I had made some small progress toward breaking the barriers of prejudice and discrimination in our country.

Our country may not be perfect, but it does get better all the time.

~Benny Wasserman

18

There's No Place Like Ommmmm

Music can change the world because
it can change people.
~Bono

The day before a Women's March, I received an e-mail from a friend warning me to be prepared because it could get ugly. She cautioned there might be people protesting the march, and she gave me a list of strategies to avoid getting swept up in the violence, including staying out of the center of any frenzy, and writing my name and an emergency contact phone number in black marker on my arm in case I got caught in a police raid.

She said that her sister had recently been holding hands in prayer with a group of activists in a peaceful protest and was shot in the eye with a rubber bullet. With this dark cloud hovering overhead, my friends and I gathered on the eve of the Women's March in a ceremony that included prayer, meditation, and soul-to-soul sharing, plus gobs of chocolate (because chocolate, well, no need to explain).

We all expressed how scared, nervous, and unsure we felt about the march the next morning. We questioned if putting our lives at risk was worth it. None of us felt particularly strong, but we all felt it was important to show up anyway. Come hell or high water, nothing would stop us from marching.

Until then, I'd not been the type to be politically active. Okay, that's not entirely true. I attended several Marianne Williamson for Congress rallies, and I have always taken a very strong stance in the Pepsi/Coke debate.

I've also suffered from a severe case of the "Disease to Please," which is why I've not been more vocal about my political feelings. I've cared *way* too much about not offending anyone and wanting everyone to think I'm the nicest person on the planet. But, thankfully, that is no longer the case. It's safe to say that the beast has been awakened... and it's okay if people unfriend me on Facebook, which happened as soon as I attended the women's march, by the way.

It does hurt my feelings when people unfriend or unfollow me on Facebook (especially when it's my own godmother), but I'm learning to come to peace with it. The beauty of gathering with women is that, in addition to celebrating each other's highlights (career, relationship, or hair), we can express our pain, angst, and drama without having any clue what the solution might be. It's in the simple act of sharing, caring, and listening that the healing alchemy takes place... and that night, it did.

By the time we arrived on the metro in downtown Santa Monica, we were buoyant, our tanks were full, and we were ready to take on the day, come what may, even if that meant, God forbid, getting shot in the eye with a rubber bullet.

We were among thousands of mostly women, and some brave men and children, smooshed together like sardines into the train compartments.

Even though we were packed to the gills, the metro was automatically programmed to stop at all its normal twenty-five stops along the route to downtown. Every time we'd stop, we'd see a bustling mob of hopeful people waiting to get on. Upon seeing how crammed in we were, despite their disappointment, they'd take a breath and resign themselves to wait for the next train, while encouraging us as we pulled off to the next stop.

Luckily, we were a jovial bunch that made light of the fact that we were all up in each other's business. I joked and said, "We're definitely getting our daily hug quotient today. At least, we're all good sports about this."

I spoke too soon.

At the next stop, a huge, irate man barged his way into our compartment like a punk rocker in a slam pit, and started yelling: "MAKE ROOM, YOU SELFISH IDIOTS! THERE'S ENOUGH ROOM. DON'T BE SO SELFISH!"

In seconds flat, our happy Girl Scout camp became helter-skelter, fraught with screaming, yelling, and pushing. The louder that people shouted at the man, the more adrenalized he became, and this lit match was quickly becoming an out-of-control forest fire.

On a dime, I realized there was no fighting fire with fire. This ugly scene would only continue to escalate, so I did the only thing in my power I could think of to do in that moment...

I OMMMMMED... loudly!

Because my friends and I were on the same wavelength from our ceremony the night before, they instantly jumped on my Om bandwagon and together our OMMMMM escalated. This incited the rest of our compartment to join in, and we suddenly became a single voice of the loudest OMMMMM I'd ever heard.

I've ommmmed a lot in my day, but I've never ommmmmed like that... with such intensity... at such a volume   with such a purpose: to snuff out fear with love. This was no light and fluffy Om; it was an Om on a mission.

After about eight rounds of Ommming, as if we all shared one mind, we gently lowered our volume and noticed that the man had stopped ranting.

Absolute silence settled in upon our compartment. We felt a cautious optimism that we'd successfully snuffed out the rage with our Om, but we didn't know for sure the fire was all the way out until we got off the train in downtown Los Angeles. We all took a deep sigh of relief and were grateful our Om put out the fire.

I reflected on the Singing Revolution in Estonia in 1988, when spontaneous mass singing demonstrations led to the restoration of the independence of Estonia, Latvia, and Lithuania. The people of Estonia literally joined hands and hearts and, with a unified voice, sang their way out of the bonds of the Soviet Union.

Then Martin Luther King, Jr. and Gandhi came to mind. They taught that "non-violence" is not merely the absence of violence, but a force unto itself — a soul force — stronger than hate and fear. It is a force that, if engaged in, will have the final word.

I felt elated because for the first time in my life, I truly felt the power of "non-violence," not just the intellectual understanding of it… and I suddenly became incredibly thankful for the irate man.

I pray for him because I know he must be incredibly troubled to carry around that level of incendiary rage. But for my girlfriends and me, he was a strange angel who taught us how powerful we can be in the face of hate.

Luckily for us, the incident with the man was the only troubling event during the day. In fact, the march itself was incredibly peaceful and good-spirited. My sister Shannon nailed it when she said, "Being at the Women's March was like being on the winning team at a sporting event."

We felt like we had won because we all had an opportunity to have our voices heard, and to be shoulder to shoulder with hundreds of thousands of people (and millions worldwide) who realized how powerful we can be when we join our voices (literally and symbolically) to ensure that peace, freedom, and liberty have a voice (or at least a loud OM!).

Dorothy said it best when she realized the great, terrifying, and powerful Oz was just a little man with a big God-complex. In the end, she realized that all she needed to do to get back to her place of power was to tap her heels three times and say, "There's no place like Ommmmm!"

~Kelly Sullivan Walden

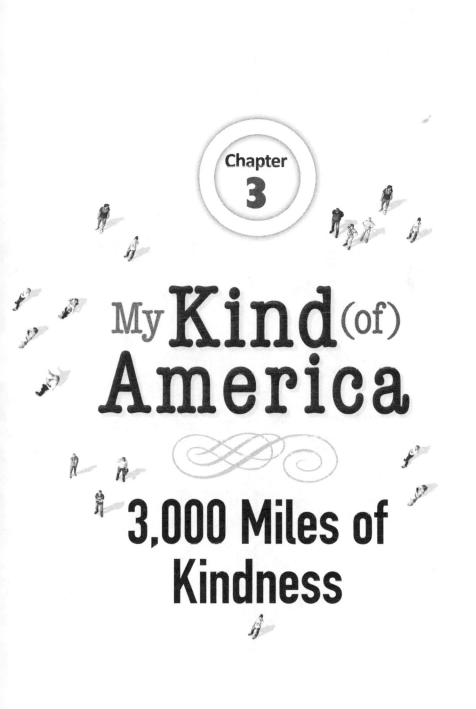

My Kind (of)
America

3,000 Miles of
Kindness

19

Audrey and Annie

*My mom once told me that when I see tragic disasters
and accidents to look for the good. People are
always helping each other out. There's still
some good left in this world.*
~Marisa Stein

udrey: Paul left for the airport before the sun came up. I held our baby in one arm, and we waved to Daddy as the cab pulled away. Relishing the last day of my maternity leave, we were off to the YMCA and then to visit Grandma.

Annie: September 11, 2001, was a home-office workday for me. I had been traveling a lot with my job at American Airlines and was happy to have the day to catch up on paperwork.

I turned on the TV as I organized my desk. A news flash reported that a plane from Boston had hit the World Trade Center. I was paralyzed with shock and fear as billows of smoke poured from the north tower.

Audrey: With my son happily in childcare, I was oblivious for one marvelous hour to anything but the form of my backstroke. By 8:45 a.m., we were back in the car, headed toward the highway.

Ten minutes later, my phone rang. Paul's boss wanted to know if Paul had made his flight to Los Angeles. He told me what had happened to the Twin Towers. "People miss flights all the time," he assured me.

But Paul hadn't missed his flight. He had called me from his seat aboard the plane. I'm sure I stopped breathing. I turned on the radio and pulled into the breakdown lane.

Annie: My fear that it was an American Airlines plane was confirmed when I checked my computer. The morning BOS/LAX flight was blacked out. I knew what that meant. It was time for me to pack and be ready for my call to duty as a CARE (Customer Assistance Relief Effort) team member.

Audrey: I don't know how long it took me to get home.

Still incredulous, I checked the flight itinerary Paul had taped to the fridge.

I was a widow.

I walked outside into the pristine air. Wally, our mailman, waved. He was the first person I told. Wally must have told everyone on the block because my house was full of people within thirty minutes.

Annie: The call came, and I was told to drive to the Marriott at Boston's Logan International Airport. The turnpike was eerily empty. Even the tollbooths were unmanned. The whole world must have been glued to their TVs.

Upon arriving at the hotel, I learned that the last name of the family I would be assisting was Friedman, the same as mine. The woman's first name was Audrey. Her husband had been on the first plane to crash into the towers. The fact that our surnames and religious culture were identical made me feel a kindred spirit to this family.

I called Audrey. She took the call, but clearly was in no frame of mind to talk to some stranger from the airline.

Audrey: A woman from American Airlines called. Her name was Annie. She assured me they would do everything they could to help. Did we need money? Childcare? Food? I was numb. No, thank you. None of those things was what we needed.

Annie: Being able to help and comfort people during a crisis has always helped me as much as I'd hoped it helped them. But this time I was scared. I could hear how fragile Audrey was by our fragmented phone conversation.

After extensive briefing about this crisis, I was finally allowed to visit Audrey at her house. I was very nervous and didn't know how I would be received.

The house was full of company, but I focused on Audrey, the baby, and Hercules, the little Yorkie that never left her side. I knew I was where I was meant to be.

Audrey: Although everyone who came to my house during the days and weeks after 9/11 wanted nothing more than to comfort me, I felt exhausted and "on display." When Annie introduced herself, I felt an immediate connection. I wasn't sure why she was there, but I wanted her to stay.

Annie: I called and visited frequently. This was a challenging time for me because I hurt so badly for Audrey while still trying to understand what was happening in the world around us. I struggled to keep it together. Alone in my hotel room, I often broke down in tears.

Audrey: It was a terrible time. I was inconsolable, and my family and friends struggled to know how to comfort me.

Annie came as unexpectedly as the events that jettisoned her into my life. Maybe I saw her as particularly strong and steady because that's what I needed her to be. Annie was totally "in" but objective; open hearted but sturdy; pragmatic but able to absorb my rants and mood swings.

She lingered into the evening after everyone else had gone home. This gentle stranger, with a name that reminded me of a well-loved rag doll, showed me the joy in my baby's eyes when all I saw was pain.

With Annie, I could crumble.

Annie: Some nights, we talked for hours on her flowered couch. Some nights, we just sat in silence. A hand on her knee or a hug brought us closer than words. To this day, I picture the baby in his swinging chair and Hercules staring up at me from the floor, protecting his humans.

Audrey: How long was Annie in town? Weeks? Months? It never occurred to me that she would go away someday.

I don't remember the day she told me she would be leaving. But somehow, my pre-9/11, polite self invited her for a thank-you dinner.

Annie: Nothing could have shocked or endeared me more than when Audrey invited me to dinner. Her kindness seemed surreal in light of what she was going through. I felt like I had known her for years.

Audrey: It felt so good, so normal, to have Annie sitting at my dining room table. It was the first time I had cooked a proper meal in weeks. For the first time, I asked Annie about her life. Did she have kids? (Yes.) Was this her first time responding to an air emergency? (No.) Where did she live? (Upstate New York.) I had assumed that Annie's role as a CARE member was part of her job. It wasn't until this dinner that I learned it was strictly volunteer.

Annie: In the early years after the tragedy, I hesitated to contact Audrey because I didn't want to be a reminder of that terrible time in her life. When I brought this up, she assured me that would never be the case.

Some years, we speak often; sometimes, only on 9/11. But I think of Audrey and her son frequently. The silver lining of that horrific experience is that I got to know and love her.

Audrey: Annie played a huge role in my recovery from 9/11 and will always be part of the loving circle that got me through those wretched first months.

Annie is in my thoughts more often than she knows. Far from triggering bad memories, she reminds me that healing sometimes enters unannounced; gently offering support and friendship, and never really saying goodbye.

~Audrey Ades and Annie Friedman

20

South Dakota Hospitality

I've been helped by acts of kindness from strangers.
That's why we're here, after all, to help others.
~Carol Burnett

After my initial visit to South Dakota, when I'd decided to move to the western part of the state, I planned a return trip. I'd only spent time in Spearfish and Rapid City, both of which I thoroughly enjoyed. But were there other areas worth considering?

I decided on a swing through the southwestern part of the state and started making plans for the last two weeks of July. I was surprised that motel reservations were hard to come by in some places, and a few prices were surprisingly high compared to my previous spring visit. South Dakota sure was popular as a tourist destination in the summertime!

And so I left the sweltering, humid heat of a New York City summer. As soon as I exited Rapid City Regional Airport, the magnificent views of the distant mountains soothed my soul. Amazingly, I also found my body reacted beneficially to the dry weather. Yup, this was definitely the place for me. As a matter of fact, in case I decided to stay for a longer span of time this visit, I intentionally left my New York City return date open.

Scratch one off my bucket list — I finally got to see Mount Rushmore! Scratch another off the list — the monumental mountain carving of Chief

Crazy Horse. And then I embarked upon a carefree, lovely, meandering, circular drive farther south that took me through a number of South Dakota's famed westernmost Black Hills sites and towns.

I'd stayed a couple days longer than expected, and as time progressed I suddenly found it difficult to extend my motel reservations. And then, my last night before departure, I simply couldn't find a room anywhere. I'd never run into anything like this before. I've been fortunate, for work, to travel the world, and I'd always been able to secure a reservation somewhere — even in the most remote places. But there didn't appear to be a single available room in the entire western half of the state! What the heck? I called motels, hotels, inns, B&Bs — nothing! I had a very early morning flight — and here I was trying to book accommodations over an hour away.

What in the world was going on?

After being turned down on the phone yet again by a B&B owner over a good hour's distance from the airport, I finally asked, "Is there a convention or something in town tomorrow? All rooms everywhere seem to be taken."

His matter-of-fact answer: "Honey, it's Rally." As if I should have just realized it.

Pregnant pause...

Me: "It's what?"

Him. "The Rally. It's Rally time. Don't tell me ya never heard of it. What rock you been hidin' under all ya life? Beginning August is always Rally time. You're not gonna find a room within four hours of Sturgis this time of year."

Me: "Sturgis? That's near Spearfish, isn't it?"

Him, losing patience: "Yeah, that's near Spearfish. Sturgis is Rally headquarters."

Me, totally stupefied: "What's this Rally?"

Him, dumbfounded: "Lady, where are you from? You don't know about the Sturgis Rally?"

Me: "Haven't a clue. What are people rallying for? Is something political going on?"

There was an audible groan over the phone. "It's not a political rally, lady. It's a motorcycle rally — the largest in the world! A couple hundred thousand of 'em."

Well, that would certainly explain why I couldn't find a room... Now I would probably have to sleep in my car at the airport the night before my flight. I explained I was planning to move to the state and asked if by any chance he knew anyone at all who had a room available... and it was his turn to pause.

"Look," he said, "you have to understand you're not goin' to find a room anywhere. These dates are booked up a year ahead, from Rally to Rally. And, by the way, that's why prices are higher — this is prime time.

"But since you're gonna be a neighbor, so to speak," he continued, "I can offer you some South Dakota hospitality. Won't be fancy because I'm completely full, running my tail off."

"Anything, please. I'll take anything at this point."

"Okay. My son is bunking with a friend over in Sturgis. You're welcome to use his room. I have no idea what condition he left it in. I'm not even goin' to charge ya for it — I don't have time to clean it up. But at least you'll have a bed — ya won't have to sleep in your car. The airport is crazy now with everyone arriving and all the motorcycles being flown in.

"Whenever you get here, just drive up to the main house and go inside — the door's unlocked. My son's bedroom is up on the second floor. It's the first door on the right. The bathroom's down the hall — take a towel from the linen closet. And whatever ya do, be careful driving here. There'll be motorcycles swarming all over the place."

And so I spent the eve of my first world-famous Sturgis Motorcycle Rally in the empty dormered bedroom of an eight-year-old boy, rumpled Superman sheets and all. With playthings scattered all over the floor protected by superhero figures lined up along a windowsill. With a blue-and-yellow wallpapered wall depicting our solar system, and Little League trophies on a couple of shelves. With an orange plastic basketball hoop dangling from the ceiling.

Sometime during the night, I was awakened by the bedroom

door being nudged open. A huge, furry dog bounded onto the bed to snuggle…

When I left at 5:00 a.m. to make my early flight, the house was silent. I hadn't seen a soul since I arrived the night before. The bikers had been out partying then and were fast asleep now. I put fifty dollars as a thank-you on a kitchen counter with a note — in case my move wasn't yet finalized, I asked for reservations for the following year.

Well, now, I really did have to see just what this huge Rally was all about…

…and thank my anonymous benefactor, his son, and their big, furry dog — in person — for all their very kind hospitality.

~Marsha Warren Mittman

A Side of Kindness, Please

Help one person at a time, and always
start with the person nearest you.
~Mother Teresa

It was Christmas Eve and we decided to have breakfast at Cracker Barrel. We got there early, shortly after eight. It was busy, but to our delight there was no wait.

As we looked at our menus, the conversation between the server and two Hispanic men at the table next to us caught our attention.

"We just want to pay," one of the men said. "Check, please?"

"There is no check. It's all taken care of."

"We don't understand."

"You don't owe anything."

"But we ate. We must pay."

"Not today. Merry Christmas!"

Apparently, someone had paid their bill. The waiter was having trouble getting the men to understand that, though. He walked away to help another table, leaving them looking uncomfortably at each other.

They spoke in hushed tones in Spanish. They looked around at the other tables. Most of the ones directly around them, like ours, looked back, smiling.

They didn't smile back. They looked nervous. I wondered what they were thinking. Did they think it was a joke or a setup of some kind?

They had a right to be suspicious. It was a tense time in the world. Donald Trump had just been elected president. Hispanics and Muslims were the target of a lot of derision and hatred.

After several minutes, they got up to leave. They walked out slowly, cautiously. Were they hoping their kind benefactors would reveal themselves so they could thank them? Or were they expecting to get stopped and accused of dining and ditching?

I wiped tears from my eyes, which was the moment our server came to take our order.

"I'm sorry," I apologized. "I just witnessed a random act of kindness that melted my heart."

"I know. That was one of my tables that did it."

"Really? What a very cool thing to witness. Especially on Christmas Eve."

A short time after we placed our order and were waiting for our food to come, I noticed a man get up and walk in our direction. He'd been seated at a table with a large group of people next to where the Hispanic men had been sitting. He approached an older couple behind us. They were gathering their things to leave.

"Excuse me. Were you the ones who paid for those men?" he asked them.

The man had a thick Southern drawl, wore a trucker hat, and fit my stereotyped view of someone who was not in favor of immigration. The older couple was white and in their seventies.

I'm ashamed to admit it, but I judged them both. I doubted an older white couple would've noticed the Hispanic men and bothered to pay for their meal. But if they did, I feared this guy in the hat was going to say something nasty about it.

"Yes," the husband said humbly.

The redneck removed his hat and reached out to shake the man's hand.

"That was a mighty nice gesture, sir," he said. "Can I give you a little something toward it?"

"Oh, no, son. That's nice, but not necessary," the husband said.

"Save it for another time," the wife said. "If you ever see a chance and feel so compelled to do something, do it then."

The man nodded, replaced his cap and went back to his table.

"That was really awesome of you two," I said as they approached our table.

The wife smiled at me and put a hand on my shoulder.

"There's been a lot of ugliness in the world lately, hasn't there? Some people have seen it more than others. We saw a chance to let someone know not everyone is against them."

She gave my shoulder a little parting squeeze, and then she and her husband left.

Our food came, and a short time afterward a mom and dad and their two small children were seated at the table the Hispanic men had vacated. The family was also Hispanic.

I saw the man in the hat looking at them. I wondered if he was thinking the same thing I was. I knew he was when he stopped the server and motioned toward the family. The server looked, nodded and walked away.

I was pretty sure he'd just arranged to pay for the family's meal. I grabbed my napkin because the tears had started flowing again.

"Why are you crying now?" my husband asked.

"It's a Christmas miracle. Or maybe just the Christmas spirit made visible. I'm not sure which. Maybe both. Whatever it is, what a great breakfast this turned out to be."

Both my tummy and soul were nicely filled up.

~Courtney Lynn Mroch

22

A Gift at the Bank

To be impulsive is to be fully alive.
~Marty Rubin

On my weekly run to the bank, I had just made some deposits and withdrawn funds. As I moved down the counter to organize my paperwork, the woman behind me stepped up to the teller. I could see that she slid over a withdrawal slip. Then I heard the teller refuse her request for cash, saying her account was overdrawn.

The woman let out an anguished cry, and several customers turned to see where it came from. I looked more closely. She was a small, dark-haired woman, dressed in respectable old clothes. Involuntarily, her hand went to her mouth, and her voice broke. She wailed with a thick accent, "What am I going to do?"

The words reverberated through me, triggering a discomfiting memory. Before my current, well-paying work, in the not-too-distant past I had asked myself the same question. *How would I meet the coming month's rent? How would I have enough for food? How soon would the electricity be cut off?*

Without thinking, I did something I never did before or since. I reached almost automatically into the cash envelope I'd just received, took a step closer to her, and held out a hundred-dollar bill. She stared at me, unbelieving. Then she looked suspicious. "Qué?"

I smiled and extended the bill closer to her. "Please," I said.

She looked at me, her eyes tearing.

Other people in line stared and murmured. A couple shook their heads, unbelieving. I heard murmurs of "Wow!" and "Wonderful!" One man said loudly, "Hey, as long as you're giving it out…" A few giggled.

Their comments didn't interfere with my focus on the woman. My hand still held out the bill. "Please," I said, "take it."

She started to say something — perhaps a refusal at such a miracle — but my insistence changed her mind. She took the money.

Her face glowed as if she'd seen a saint. Crying, she hugged me and exclaimed, "Madre de Dios, bless you!" As she turned and left, still crying, she kept glancing back at me.

Some of the other people continued staring at me. I kept my eyes down, wanting to cherish the moment.

I can't report that this act — which surprised me as much as it did the woman — had any direct or immediate consequences for me, like those we read about. I didn't receive a check for quadruple that amount in the next day's mail, a surprise gift of an expensive piece of jewelry, or a registered letter of an inheritance from a third cousin.

But what I gained was much more important.

I carry the image of the woman's face and hear her blessing. We never even exchanged names, but the memory continues to warm me.

I never missed the money, but I felt certain it met the woman's immediate urgent need.

My spontaneity, as I reflect now, must have come from a profound empathy, feeling another's complete dismay in a situation that instantly called up similar ones of my own. Now, every time I am tempted to get sucked into that money-worry vortex, I remember this experience. The woman in the bank didn't know it, but she gave me a precious lesson: Just as she was provided for, so, if ever needed, will I be.

My lingering memory of this incident has taught me more: Whatever we are impelled to give — whether it is money, a smile, a hand, a suggestion, or a few minutes of undivided attention — we should. Yes, the receiver gains what is needed. But, as givers, we gain incalculably from our spontaneous acts of kindness from the heart.

~Noelle Sterne

23

Sheltered Beneath the Open Sky

Wherever there is a human being, there
is an opportunity for a kindness.
~Lucius Annaeus Seneca

The first time I got on my scooter, I didn't have the faintest idea how to drive it. I revved the gas, shot up my inclined driveway and instantly toppled into a hedge. My neighbors helped me out of the shrubbery. It was that same sort of youthful, spontaneous whimsy (reckless lack of preparation) that landed me as the fifth man (well, woman) in a tiny, three-man tent during a rain shower (relentless deluge) in the wilderness of Washington State.

A few days after my practice ride on my gutless mini-motorcycle, I began to drive my scooter to my part-time teaching job because buying a car was not in my budget. Summer vacation was weeks away, and I'd been dreaming of travel, but the costs were daunting. Then I had an epiphany. *Why not just take my scooter on a camping trip?* Sure, it topped out at 35 miles per hour, but still I resolved to explore the Pacific Northwest on my puttering steed.

I borrowed a small tent and a tarp, bought a sleeping bag at the thrift store, and took fifty bucks out of the cash machine for gas and campsite fees. I rigged a clever milk-crate contraption to the back of the scooter and shoved in my supplies: the camping gear, a rain poncho, my rattan purse (hey, it was all the rage) and a plastic bag filled with a traveler's perfect food — peanut-butter-and-jelly sandwiches.

My destination? Hurricane Ridge at Olympic National Park. As the light came up over Puget Sound, I lined up for the ferry behind a row of cars, but the port employee waved me out of the area. He guided me toward a spot by the foot passengers and bicyclists. Thus demoted, I began my travels as second-class citizen of the road.

On the peninsula, cars honked and trucks whizzed by my ear as I drove on the road's shoulder at half the posted speed limit. At this rate, I thought, I'd be lucky to make it to the campground by midday. At least it was a pleasant day. I'd been enjoying the drive... until distant thunder interrupted my thoughts. The air cooled off rapidly as the dark clouds rolled my way. I pulled over and fastened a tarp over my belongings, grateful that I'd thought to pack rain gear. In minutes, the downpour was upon me. I slowed to a nervous crawl along the edge of the slippery asphalt.

Beside me on the road, enormous trucks flew past, hauling pine trunks on their flatbeds. Cars honked as they passed me, but I could not speed up. One car drove behind me, honking repeatedly. Finally, the driver pulled over and rolled down her window. My helmet and the sound of the pounding rain muffled her shouted question. "Did you lose some stuff on the road?"

With a sick feeling, I turned behind me. All of my belongings were gone. Only the plastic crate dangled from the bungee cord. "How far back?" I asked.

"Maybe five miles ago? Or ten? I kept honking, but you didn't hear me."

Deflated, I turned back and rode through the rain. After almost half an hour of retracing my steps, it occurred to me that my stuff had either been picked up or had blown over the hillside. Whatever the case, I had nothing. No purse, no tent and no sleeping bag — nothing but the clothes on my back. My thin, drugstore poncho had sprung a leak. I barely had a quarter tank of gas left.

What could I do but limp onward? Just when my gas gauge read empty, a small filling station appeared on the horizon. I told the attendant, "I've lost my wallet, but if you give me your address…" He shook his head in wonder at my drenched appearance and wordlessly filled the tank. "Where can I send…?"

"Don't worry about it," he said, already walking back to the station. "Be careful driving. You're not too far from the park entrance."

By the time I rolled into the national park, the rain had died out, but darkness was creeping in. "Do you have a reservation?" the ranger asked.

Reservations! Why hadn't I thought to reserve a campsite? I shook my head pathetically, fighting back tears of exhaustion and frustration. The park ranger looked at my soggy state and told me gravely that all the campsites were full. "But feel free to take a look around," he offered kindly.

I drove the campsite loop hoping to happen upon an open campsite, but every site was taken. The grounds were quiet. The damp weather had made cooking on a campfire impossible, and folks had probably headed to the nearby town for supper. I washed up in the cold water of the bathroom sink and considered that I might spend the night sleeping on the linoleum floor. Then, I sat in a stall feeling sorry for myself and allowed myself a brief cry, wondering how my brave adventure had gone so wrong. I kicked myself for my lack of preparations.

I heard the bathroom door open. "Are you okay in there?" I didn't answer at first, embarrassed. When I heard her brushing her teeth, I came out. When she saw my puffy face and waterlogged clothes, her blond eyebrows arched in surprise.

Quickly, she collected herself. "Hey," she said as if we were old friends getting together for tea. "What's wrong?"

I told her everything. It poured out of me like the afternoon rain shower.

Her name was Joanne, and she took me back to her campsite where her husband Arlo was busy dressing their toddler in pajamas while simultaneously cradling a baby in a sling. They spoke together in low tones, and then he waved me over. "Look, we have space. Why don't you come in with us?" I peeked at their crowded, three-man tent and politely declined, even though I desperately wanted to climb inside.

"We insist," Joanne said. She loaned me a dry sweatshirt, and I wolfed down the leftover hotdogs and crackers they offered me. I was so sleepy that I curled up against the tent wall and fell asleep quickly.

I woke shivering in the middle of the night. The rain had started up again in earnest, and the nylon walls of the tent were wet. Joanne insisted that I squeeze onto the inflated mattress next to her. She unzipped her sleeping bag, and we shared it as a blanket. It was tight quarters, but we were cozy, especially for near strangers!

Come morning, we all unkinked our bodies. As I stretched, my hand landed on the back of my jeans. Something flat and solid was in my back pocket. My credit card! When I took money out of the cash machine, I must have put it back there.

"Can I take you all out for breakfast?" I suggested.

"That's okay," Arlo said. The wood was already crackling in the fire pit, and he was making eggs and coffee. "I prefer to eat outdoors beneath the open sky."

I couldn't have agreed more. I looked up at the wide blue sky, dotted with puffball clouds. It was turning out to be a fine day.

~Ilana Long

Small Fortune at the Car Wash

*Riches do not consist in the possession of
treasures, but in the use made of them.*
~Napoleon Bonaparte

"**Y**ou kids get the hell out of the house! It's a beautiful summer day, and I won't let you waste it watching TV."

We obeyed, but we knew our exile was not imposed out of concern for our health. Our mother wanted to spare us from listening to her and our father fight. And so we wandered off in opposite directions down the street in front of our house. My sister went to her best friend Carla's house, where they'd probably play out in the back yard with their Barbie dolls, and I rode my bike down to my pal Frankie's house. I felt a little morose, mainly because my folks weren't getting along, but also because there wasn't much for kids to do in the summer in our little town, especially kids with empty pockets.

Our family was not extremely poor when I was a kid, but before I got my first paper route at twelve years of age, money seemed hard to come by. My parents worked hard and didn't give it away. In the summertime, Frankie and I would wander the alleys and streets, imagining out loud what kind of candy we'd buy or what movie we'd go to if we only had fifty cents or a dollar. We weren't lazy, but we didn't live in a big town, and there were only so many lawns to mow or yards to rake.

We tried to be resourceful. Sometimes, we'd ride our bikes around, checking the coin slots in every telephone booth and vending machine, hoping to capture a stray nickel or dime that someone in a hurry might have left. One afternoon we hit the jackpot when we rode through the stalls at the carwash and found a neat stack of quarters — two whole dollars! — tucked into a corner of the control box.

It was a small fortune to two ten-year-olds in 1976. Eight quarters would buy four comic books and a handful of candy bars, or two tickets to a matinee. I remember how finding that pile of change lifted my spirits and made me feel that even if things between my folks didn't work out, some power or force in the universe was looking out for me.

We were young enough still to believe in magic, at least a little bit, and our imaginations were fertile enough to concoct a dozen narratives behind our discovery.

"Maybe the guy was washing fingerprints from his car because he robbed a bank," I suggested.

"Yeah," Frankie agreed, "and he left his quarters there because the cops drove by, and he got spooked." Or maybe someone had had a heart attack and an ambulance had taken him away before he could wash the car. Maybe an absent-minded professor like the guy in the Disney movie pulled in to wash his car, but then remembered he was supposed to go to the store for his wife. We explored various scenarios as we pedaled to the corner store.

Once there, we probably idled away most of the afternoon wandering the narrow aisles and debating the best way to make use of our wealth. In the end, we bought two huge sacks of sunflower seeds and a couple glass bottles of Coca-Cola, and rode off to a spot in the woods we liked. I remember lounging away the afternoon feeling like we were the luckiest kids in the known universe.

I'm sure it's mostly nostalgia driving my memories now, but I have never forgotten the thrill I felt at finding that stack of quarters.

In all of our scenarios, we never considered the possibility that whoever had left that stack of quarters there had done so on purpose, but over the years I've come to realize that's almost certainly what happened. A random person felt some inexplicable impulse to leave the leftover change on the machine, never imagining that a small kindness intended for the next person in search of a clean car would instead create a whole afternoon of bliss for two ten-year-olds.

When I came home that evening for dinner, my mom and dad had made their peace, and we all enjoyed a pleasant meal together. I still had one shiny quarter left in my pocket, which I gave to my sister. I went to bed that night feeling like John D. Rockefeller.

To this day, I never reach for my change in a soda machine, and I leave a few extra quarters behind at the car wash. You never know who might be down on their luck and find a smile waiting for them.

~Alf Pettersen

The Guest Room

*The everyday kindness of the back roads more than
makes up for the acts of greed in the headlines.*
~Charles Kuralt, On the Road With Charles Kuralt

A s a single woman in my thirties, I bought a three-bedroom house. Now that I share it with my partner, he laments that we heat so many unused rooms in winter, and in summer we dehumidify them. It's wasteful, he says, and we don't have the money.

He's right. We sketch drawings for our future — a tiny house with a loft bedroom, just big enough for two.

"We need an outbuilding for guests," I insist, and he nods, distracted. It's an old conversation by now, my need for a guest room, and although he doesn't fully understand, he knows it's important to me.

Years before, I hadn't been in any position to buy a house. A couple of weeks after finishing college, my friend Jennifer and I moved into my Ford Escort station wagon. We'd become friends in our American Studies classes, reading about westward expansion, Jeremiah Johnson, John Muir, and Gifford Pinchot. When the professor passed out a blank map of the United States in our last semester, we realized how much of our country remained blank to us, unmapped in our own minds.

Armed with about $2,000 each in graduation money, camping gear, and two audio collections of Charles Kuralt's essays, we set off to see as much of America as we could before our money ran out. It was five years, forty-nine states, and dozens of seasonal jobs before I returned in any settled way to New England, to graduate school, and to the safety nets of my family and my education.

Although we carried pepper spray, a lead club, and personal alarms to guard against stranger danger, we never needed them. While Jennifer and I, and then I alone, crossed back roads and highways from east to west, north to south, we relied on the kindness of strangers.

In Madison County, Iowa, we searched for a free campground we'd read about in our AAA guide. We stopped to ask directions at the local pharmacy, one of the disappearing icons of the American Main Street. The pharmacy counter and divider still sported the original stained-glass panel, and instead of the half-dozen pharmacy techs we'd have seen at any of the larger chains, a single elderly pharmacist gave us directions to the campground. He added a small, hand-drawn map to his house. "I'm not sure if the campground is still in use. If it turns out you need a place to stay, follow these directions home. The door is open. My wife should be there. Just tell her I sent you, and she'll take care of you."

We didn't take him up on his offer, and I think we must have found that campground, but I don't remember it. Like Charles Kuralt, who wrote about his regret over a Boundary Waters trip not taken, I regret not walking through that pharmacist's open door. Had we stayed in his farmhouse, had we eaten at his wife's table, I'm certain we'd remember that night.

But there are others I do remember.

In Breckenridge, Colorado, Jennifer and I walked into a high-end hotel and asked for a discounted room. The young men behind the desk said they couldn't alter room rates, but they could let us use the pool. After we swam and showered, one of the men behind the desk, Chris George, offered us shelter in his shared apartment. He had queen bunk beds, and Jennifer and I slept on the top while he and his friend slept below. The following morning, Chris woke us with blueberry pancakes before heading out to ski. "Just lock the door behind you," he said.

In Jackson Hole, Wyoming, Jennifer and I spent twelve minutes on an aerial tram with a retired couple, Ray and Marge Smith. Ray had been a history professor in Fresno, California, and he was curious about our travels. When we disembarked at the top of the mountain, Ray gave us his business card and said, "Look us up if you're in the neighborhood."

We hadn't planned to use their phone number, but months afterward Jennifer came down with the flu in Death Valley. She couldn't bear another night in the tent or stretched out across our bags in the back seat, so she called the Smiths. A few hours later, we were in their living room, Jennifer's head bent over a eucalyptus steam bath and I on a tour of the family photographs. We spent the night, and Marge made us scrambled eggs and bacon the next morning. Two decades later, the Smiths still write to us at Christmas. Although they were the ones who opened their home to strangers when we needed respite, they always write, "Your visit was the best thing that ever happened to us!"

Near the Canada/Alaska border, I met Dustin Renner at a truck stop. He invited me to visit his family, who'd built a homestead in the woods outside of Palmer. He took me to dinner at the local diner, then hiking by the light of the midnight sun. He taught me to identify the carrion smell of bear and wolverine, his father read to me from the Bible, and he and his siblings taught me how to shoot a rifle. Two days later, Dustin drove the winding roads in front of me, leading me back to the highway.

In another small town in Alaska, before the last of the frost had melted, I met a woman on the street who asked where I was from and where I was going. She invited me to do laundry at her house while she fed me a peanut-butter-and-jelly sandwich. She said people had always been kind to her when she traveled, and she wanted to pass that along.

Over and over again, people opened their doors, schedules, tables, and wallets to show us this country we call home. I hardly remember Mount Rushmore, but I'll not forget the names of those who fed and sheltered me along the way, the taste of Marge's scrambled eggs, the way the light played off the stained glass of the pharmacy in the afternoon sun, and the sweet relief of clean clothes when I least expected such kindness. Traveling, vulnerable, I saw the best in people. Now I want to be the best for someone else. I need a guest room.

Last fall, my partner and I were on the road in South Dakota. He's Finnish, an immigrant, and we're twenty-seven states into my piecemeal attempts to show him this country. A friend of ours phoned, and we learned she was between graduate school and employment, moving as unobtrusively as she could between her mom's in New York, her dad's in Connecticut, and her sister's in Massachusetts while she interviewed for jobs. She didn't have money for an apartment and didn't want to sign a lease before she knew where she'd be hired. I told her where she could find our keys.

"Help yourself to the garden tomatoes," I told her. "We'll be back in three weeks, but please plan to stay as long as you like. We have plenty of room."

~Sayzie Koldys

Soldier's Homecoming

There's nothing half so pleasant as coming home again.
~Margaret Elizabeth Sangster

I was sitting in an airport one day. We'd had rain for three straight days, and it was coming down hard. Some of the flights had been delayed, which is why I was still sitting there waiting to board my flight. As I sat there, I saw a group of soldiers come in. Apparently, they had just disembarked, and they were immediately surrounded by family and friends who had come to welcome them home. At least, this was the case for all but one soldier.

He was one of the last to walk in, and as his buddies hugged and kissed their loved ones, he walked away slowly. Taking a seat not far from me, he sat staring out the window. His face had a tired, sad look on it, and that look went straight to my heart.

I couldn't bear to see him sit there all by himself, so I picked up my carry-on bag and walked over.

"All right if I sit here?" I asked, giving him a smile.

As soon as I spoke, the soldier got to his feet and removed his hat. "Yes, ma'am."

After I had taken my seat, he sat back down. For a while, neither of us said anything, but I could see his reflection in the window. He kept glancing over at me, so I decided to try talking to him. It was no use in having both of us sitting there in silence.

"Just off deployment then?" I asked.

"Yes, ma'am. I've been gone for about fifteen months."

"I'm glad you got back safe and sound."

"Thank you. It's good to finally get home."

The laughter of the other soldiers drew his attention for a moment. He smiled as he looked over at them, but still seemed sad.

"Do you have family in town?" I asked as he turned back to me.

He didn't answer right off. In fact, I began to feel very uncomfortable and wondered if I shouldn't have asked such a personal question.

"No, ma'am. They live about 200 miles from here. My dad has been ill for months, and they couldn't make the trip."

"Are you going to be able to get home?"

"Yes, I'll head out in a couple of days."

Even though I knew he had a home to go to, I still felt sad that no one was at the airport to welcome him. I doubted that he had any friends in the city besides his fellow soldiers, and they'd be busy with their families.

"Excuse me, I need to check on my flight," I said. I rose quickly and went to the ticket counter.

I gave my flight information and found out that it would leave within twenty minutes. Glancing back, I saw the soldier still sitting there, and my mind was made up. I requested a ticket on a flight that would leave in a couple of hours. Thankfully, this arrangement was not a problem, and my business could wait.

Walking back to my seat, I said, "Looks like my flight won't leave for a couple of hours. Would you join me for lunch?"

The soldier looked surprised and seemed to seriously consider refusing my offer. I wasn't about to let that happen.

"I do appreciate it, ma'am, but there's no need to go to all this trouble."

"This is no trouble at all. There's a nice restaurant not far from here. You have been serving our country, and now you are home. In the absence of your family, I would like to give you a welcome home lunch. It's the least I can do."

He seemed very touched by the gesture and offered no further objection.

The next two hours were very enjoyable. We exchanged stories, and he told me a little about his time overseas. I really regretted having to catch a plane. He saw me back to the airport and thanked me for everything.

"This is a nicer homecoming than I expected to have when we first touched down. God bless you, ma'am."

I gave him a hug and told him that I'd keep him in my prayers. My plane left a short while later, and I thought about that soldier through the whole flight. My goodwill gesture surely didn't change the course of history, but it did change the homecoming for one soldier.

~Carla Erin Wiggins

Sam and the Visitor

*Gratitude is a currency that we can mint for ourselves,
and spend without fear of bankruptcy.*
~Fred De Witt Van Amburgh

Aunt Marian, my mother's sister, asked Mom and me to stop by; she had something for us. When we arrived, she led the way to her kitchen, where she handed Mom and me each a cellophane bag tied with a twist-tie. The bag was crammed to the top with fresh, gorgeous pecan halves. We took turns thanking her for this delicious gift, one we would have welcomed any time, but particularly now. It was the Christmas baking season, and I knew that Mom and I would use those plump pecans in at least one of our Christmas cookie recipes.

Curious about the generous quantity in each bag, I asked, "Where did the pecans come from?"

I'd known from childhood that Aunt Marian had married Sam after his first wife passed away from a heart ailment, and that he had a young son and daughter who needed a loving mother, while he needed a loving wife.

I'd also known that Sam's Italian immigrant parents reared their family in St. Louis. Sam moved his first wife and young family to our small Illinois town, and right away set himself up in the food business.

Sam had made a very comfortable living for his first wife, and then his second wife. He and Marian grew their family to four with the addition of their two sons.

I knew that Sam's work centered on connecting with vegetable, fruit, nut, and poultry farmers to buy truckloads of their foods and arrange for delivery to our community. Of major importance before sealing any deal was to have pre-sold the shipments to area grocery-store owners. Essentially, Sam acted as the middleman between the farm producer and the grocery store. Throughout his working life, he had always worked out of a basement office in their comfortable home.

Sam's business success later inspired two of his three sons and my two brothers to follow him into the world of food.

What I hadn't known before was the story my aunt was about to tell us about the pecans Mom and I held in our hands. The story warmed my heart, then and now.

It was a wintry December night in the mid-1950s. Marian and Sam had finished their evening meal not long before the front doorbell rang. Sam had been awaiting the arrival of a shipment of Georgia pecans for a good part of that day.

He walked to the door and opened it to a black man, who stood shivering in his lightweight jacket.

"Mr. Sam," the man began, "I got your load of pecans here."

"It's too late now to deliver them to the store," Sam told him. "We'll deliver them first thing tomorrow morning."

"Know where I can go find me a room for the night?" the man asked. He looked worn out from his long haul to central Illinois from Georgia.

Sam scratched his balding head. "Hmmm, that's going to be a problem. No place in town will rent to you," he replied.

"I'll just sleep in my truck then," the man said, about to head for his half-ton truck parked on the street in front of Sam's house.

"Hey, just a minute! It's too cold for you to sleep in your truck. Come inside," he said, and opened the door wide so the man could step into the warm home.

They stood in the small vestibule as Sam called out, "Marian! Set a place at the table. Let's feed this man. He's hungry!"

The man took a step back. "No, no, that's all right, Mr. Sam. I'll get me somethin' to eat somewhere."

"Nonsense. No, you won't. We have plenty of good food right here. And when you've eaten, we have a nice place for you to sleep."

Marian set a place at their dining table and called the man to come and eat the hearty meal she had laid out for him.

While the man ate, Marian scuttled downstairs to make up the day bed with fresh linens in the living area opposite Sam's office, and to place fresh towels in the bathroom for their visitor.

Later, Sam showed the man where he would sleep. "Make yourself comfortable and get a good night's sleep. Marian put fresh towels in the bathroom for you," he told the weary visitor. "We'll leave around 7:00 in the morning to deliver the pecans."

The next day, the men left for the downtown grocery store, Sam in his car, his houseguest-driver in his truck.

When the man returned to Georgia, he told his boss, the plantation owner, what had happened.

The following December, and every December for decades to come, the boss sent twenty-five pounds of shelled Georgia pecans to Marian and Sam as a thank-you for kindly looking after a cold and tired man who had no hope of finding food or a bed in a town that, at the time, was prejudiced against men and women of color.

Sam was no stranger to discrimination. A local country club had blackballed his application for membership because of his Italian heritage. Sam's eldest son, an Eagle Scout, made it his mission to end that lopsided practice, and the next time Sam applied for membership, he and his family were admitted to the club. That standout act of discrimination stung Sam's heart, but it didn't stop him from joining his church choir or the barbershop singing group he so loved. Nor did his Italian heritage keep him from volunteering with the local Boy Scout Council. Throughout the years, he helped the Scouts make their special events a success. He encountered no discrimination in his church or the other groups.

Without fanfare, Sam helped raise up others who felt the sword of prejudice. Obviously, the plantation owner didn't believe in prejudice, either. No one will ever know how many others showing kindness to his employees were thanked with gifts of Georgia pecans. Clearly,

Marian and Sam had turned a color-blind eye to the man standing on their doorstep. They only saw a fellow human being in need, and they wanted to help him.

When Aunt Marian's storytelling ended, Mom and I stood quietly for a time, pecan bags still in hand. I looked down at my bag, replaying the scene my aunt had just unfolded to us. Uncle Sam was gone by that time, yet the pecans kept coming, despite Marian writing to the plantation owner about the sad news.

Those yearly gifts from a grateful Georgia businessman were a reminder of the night Marian and Sam had welcomed a tired and hungry visitor into their home.

~Natalie M. Rotunda

28

Serving Dinner to Friends

If a natural disaster strikes your community,
reach out to your friends, neighbors, and
complete strangers. Lend a helping hand.
~Marsha Blackburn

I thought I'd feel pretty good after my first night of volunteering with the local flood-relief efforts. I was wrong.

My family had been spared during the storm and the flooding that followed in the wake of Hurricane Irene. I decided to help those who weren't. I was in awe when I walked into the church hall that had been turned into a volunteer command center. Meals were being readied for hundreds of flood victims; helpers scurried with boxes filled with donated items; several small groups waited in lines for their afternoon jobs, while those already assigned were leaving with tools and buckets filled with cleaning products.

And soon I'd be a part of this altruistic endeavor — a mere foot soldier serving in this great volunteer army, ready to do battle in an area that only two days earlier had been submerged beneath several feet of murky floodwaters. I was ready — or so I thought.

My team was given a simple task: remove the drywall and insulation from a home that had been inundated during a flash flood. As we neared our jobsite, what we saw was disturbing: At house after house and on street after street, the contents of entire homes were piled curbside in heaps, awaiting disposal. I felt like an intruder trespassing into the private lives of these people. But we had a job to do, and so we went to work. We labored for hours and when it became late, we wished the family well, and left for our clean, dry homes.

I felt an overwhelming sadness when I realized that whatever we might've accomplished, it did little to address the totality of needs facing this young family or countless other families suffering similar circumstances. I began to realize that what I'd witnessed far exceeded my comprehension of the sheer magnitude of the devastation.

Later that night, I thought about the family whose flood-damaged home I'd worked in. When I put myself in their place, I realized that I would have been grateful for the help. We were not really intruders.

I had been depressed, but now I began to feel slightly better. Tomorrow, we'd try again — another assignment, another location, and another opportunity to make a small difference in the life of another family.

The waters receded, and families slowly began returning, determined to rebuild their damaged homes and shattered lives. At the same time, I became part of a distribution team that went into the devastated areas delivering hot meals. In the days that followed, we got to know many of the victims, people who'd lost everything and somehow remained thankful for the opportunity to start over. We also met formerly flooded residents who surprisingly declined our free meals and asked that they be delivered to the homes of their needier neighbors instead.

I was humbled.

Our deliveries eventually became opportunities for us to have conversations with those we were serving. The simple thank-yous we'd received in the beginning soon morphed into longer, more heartfelt expressions of gratitude. More often than not, they came with hugs and, sometimes, tears. Something else was happening, too, that I'd yet to understand. My wife, Karen, who also volunteered, said she felt it as well. One afternoon, she told me what it was.

After bringing meals to yet another home, Karen mentioned how she'd gotten to know many of the families on our delivery route. She knew their problems and learned their stories. She said that she was no longer just bringing hot meals to victims; she was now serving dinner to friends.

And, of course, she was.

Since the hurricane, I've come to realize that as much as I'd like to lend assistance to everyone in need and to feed everyone who may be hungry, I can't. Mother Teresa once said, "If you can't feed one hundred people, feed one." I get it now. Following Irene, my little team served more than one thousand meals to those in need — no, wait, we served more than one thousand dinners to *friends*.

Finally, I'm starting to feel good.

~Stephen Rusiniak

29

Paying It Forward

The right shoe can make everything different.
~Jimmy Choo

"Hey, you think you could give some money?" A young man was tapping the arm of the woman in line in front of me as she opened her wallet to pay for her purchase.

It was obvious by the look on her face that she didn't know the kid, who appeared to be about seventeen. She shook her head. "Sorry."

The kid shifted his weight from one foot to the other. "Really?"

"Sorry," she said again as she tucked her credit card into her wallet and walked away.

Before I could set my bag of cat food on the counter, the kid took a step forward and made eye contact. My elevated stress and deteriorating patience were doing overtime. *Oh, come on,* I thought to myself. *I don't have time for this. I have to be back to work in twenty minutes. I can't believe he's going to ask me for money.*

He was holding a pair of Nikes. "So, can you help me out? I'm like…" He paused and looked at the price tag, then counted on his fingers. "A couple dollars short."

"I don't think so," I said.

He sighed. "Seriously? Why not?"

I wanted to tell him that it wasn't nice to ask for handouts, and that he should learn to manage his money. But I replied instead, "Because I have my own things to pay for. Sorry, but I'm not giving you money."

He broke eye contact and looked down at his feet.

"These are my cousin's shoes," he said. I glanced at what he was wearing—a pair of dirty, tattered work boots. Unlaced. "He's been letting me wear them to work all week. They don't fit very good. And it's kinda gross wearing someone else's shoes."

I motioned to the man in line behind me to go ahead.

The kid looked up at me. "Are you sure you can't help me out? I thought I had enough. These are real good shoes, and they're on sale for $58. It's the only pair they have left in my size."

I felt my heart shift into mom-mode. "Why are you wearing those, anyway? What happened to your own shoes?"

"They're back home. I guess I forgot them."

"So just go home and get them." I assumed his house was across town.

"Well, I can't. They're in Nebraska."

"Nebraska? How do you forget to put shoes on your feet when traveling from one state to another?" I heard my voice shoot up an octave, as if I were scolding my own son.

He looked down again. "Well, my cousin came to get me, and I grabbed all my stuff and threw it in his car. We were in a hurry, and I guess my shoes weren't in there. I know it was dumb."

From outside, a car horn beeped. "I gotta get to work. My cousin's out there waiting for me." He looked at the cashier and asked, "Can you hang onto these? I can come back tomorrow and get them. If I have the money."

She shook her head. "I can't. It's a clearance item. And we can't hold clearance merchandise."

He turned and looked toward the back of the store. By now, three people had refused to help him out. I watched his face as he contemplated the journey to the shoe department, then back past the registers. Empty-handed.

Standing there in the checkout line, my mind flashed back to when I was a single mom, in constant financial worry and struggling to provide for my family. Fifteen years ago, the owner of a local shoe store stopped by my workplace and handed me a gift certificate. Aside from the business logo and my own name, it was blank. The giver's name and dollar amount weren't filled in. The storeowner explained that "a friend" wanted me to take my daughter shopping and let her pick out any pair of shoes she wanted. I stood with the certificate in hand and asked, "Why?"

"Maybe someone just wants to do something nice for you," she said with a smile.

That weekend, my eight-year-old daughter got to pick out a pair of shoes without her mother telling her we couldn't afford them. Even after all these years, I don't know who paid for those shoes, but my heart swells with gratitude every time I think of it.

Now, here I was listening to this kid's excuses as to why his shoes were 400 miles away. I didn't know why he left home in a hurry. Maybe his cousin had rescued him from a bad situation. Maybe that's why he left his shoes behind, because he had to leave fast. Right now, it didn't matter. A voice in my heart spoke up and told me it was my turn to pay it forward.

I nudged his arm. "Put the shoes on the counter."

"For real?"

He sat the shoes on the counter and pulled a crumpled wad of cash from his jeans pocket. The cashier scanned the tag as he handed over the money. She looked at me. "There's an $11.86 difference."

I took a $20 bill from my wallet and laid it in the kid's hand. The cashier counted back $8.14, and he turned to me with the change. "Here, I can pay you back the rest next week when I get paid."

"You keep it," I said. "Spend it on something useful."

His eyes were wide and sincere. "Why? I didn't need the whole $20."

"It's your lucky day. Somebody wants to do something nice for you."

He folded the money neatly and slipped it in his pocket. "Friday is my sister's birthday."

"Well then, buy something for your sister." He lunged toward me with open arms and a chorus of thank-yous, but before he could hit me with a hug, he turned his attention to another round of beeps from the car waiting outside.

He kicked off the old boots as he shuffled toward the door. "I'm never wearing these again." He slipped on the sneakers and waved a final thank-you as he ran outside.

I was now the only person left in line. My five-pound bag of cat food seemed so insignificant. The clerk scanned the bag of Purina and said, "That was really nice of you. I think you totally made his day."

"You know," I smiled, "every kid deserves to wear new shoes." I realized that the kid who was $11.86 shy of a new pair of sneakers had no idea who I was and likely never would. And I was okay with that.

~Ann Morrow

My Kind (of) America

Honoring Those Who Defend Us

Random Acts of Breakfast

Always be a little kinder than necessary.
~J. M. Barrie

My husband Dan and I were just finishing breakfast at a bustling diner when a young soldier, his wife and their two school-aged children were seated at the table next to us. As soon as they all sat down, the woman dipped into her purse and opened a small blue wallet.

"Eighteen," she said softly to her husband after carefully counting out the bills inside. "And about another two in quarters and dimes."

He nodded silently and then began going over the menu, reading off food selections to the children.

"They have bacon and eggs," he told the little ones. "Blueberry muffins, French toast, cinnamon rolls, silver-dollar pancakes..."

"What are those?" asked the girl, who appeared to be about seven years old.

"They're mini-pancakes," her mother responded. "Just like regular ones only smaller."

"That's what I want!" the tyke declared excitedly.

"Me, too!" her little brother chimed in.

When the waitress came, the kids ordered the silver-dollar pancakes while their parents requested scrambled eggs and sausage, his with a side of hash browns.

"We can add fresh strawberries and whipped cream to the pancakes for only $1.99 extra per order," the server offered.

Both children squealed in excitement.

"Ooh! Can we get strawberries, puh-leeeeeeeze?"

Mother and father exchanged an uneasy look.

"Sure," the man spoke up. "They'll both have the strawberries, but I'm rethinking my order… Can you just bring me some coffee for now?"

"Same for me," Mom said. "We'll take another look at the menu, but can you go ahead and get their food going?"

"Of course," the waitress smiled. "I'll put that order in and be back in a few minutes to check on you two."

When the server walked away, the couple looked at the menus again, weighing their options. The soldier suggested they split something, but his wife said she would just get toast or a muffin so he could enjoy a real meal, reminding him he had a full day ahead. Though they spoke in hushed tones, we couldn't help but overhear them in the crowded space. As the two were conducting their deliberations, our waitress brought us our check and indicated we should pay at the front counter.

Dan and I got up and began making our way to the cashier to settle the bill. On the way, he stopped me and whispered, "We should help those two get a decent breakfast. It's the least we can do for a family that's serving the country."

"I know, but how can we do that without embarrassing them?" I asked. "What if we offer them money and they refuse? That might make things worse."

Dan thought for a moment, and then came up with an idea. At the register, he handed the cashier our check and asked if she could also add in a $25 restaurant gift card.

"After we leave, can you have someone take it over to that family?" he asked, discreetly pointing out their table.

"Sure," the cashier responded. "Whose birthday is it? I have a clown card if it's one of the kids, or one with candles and a cake if it's for Mom or Dad."

Dan looked at her blankly, a bit confused that she had immediately assumed this was a birthday gift.

"Um, no one's, I don't think," he responded, trying to figure out how to explain the purchase and delivery request.

"Oh, I just figured one of them was having a birthday today," the cashier continued, "because you're the third person in the last few minutes who bought a gift card to send to that same table."

~Miriam Van Scott

31

Faith, Hope, Life

None of us knows what might happen even the next
minute, yet still we go forward. Because we trust.
Because we have faith.
~Paulo Coelho

I stood on the cliff overlooking Omaha Beach in Normandy, France. My hands rested on the handles of a wheelchair. The old soldier I was assisting slowly stood and pointed to where he came ashore in the second wave on D-Day, June 6, 1944. Tears formed in the corners of his eyes as he recalled wading past wounded comrades he could not help, as his job was to hit the beach and fight for a stronghold to liberate Europe. Medical corpsmen would attend to the wounded.

He remembered the machine-gun fire, the sounds of heavy artillery, the smell of diesel fuel from friendly tanks that sat disabled on the beach from enemy fire, and the utter fear that nearly overwhelmed his nineteen-year-old body. He was one of the lucky ones that day. He lived and continued to fight across Europe — through France, Belgium, and to the gates of the German concentration camp, Dachau. As he sat back down, he wiped his eyes and said he would do it all again for his great nation and its flag — the Stars and Stripes.

I was on a ten-day trip with eleven World War II veterans visiting Paris, Normandy, Belgium, Luxembourg, and Germany. As a twenty-one-year veteran of the U.S. Air Force, this was a bucket-list trip for me. Eight of the men fought in Europe, while three fought in the

Pacific. The youngest was eighty-nine, and the oldest, ninety-four. They were on this Forever Young Senior Veterans Trip of Honor to heal from the emotional scars they had carried for more than seventy years. Their faces may have shown many years of life, but their minds were sharp — remembering minute details about their time spent fighting for freedom against tyrannical powers. They shared freely, talking of hardships, successes, fears, and regrets, of duty, honor and country.

They asked for nothing special, continuing the humble nature they and their brethren of The Greatest Generation have demonstrated since returning from the war. They were proud patriots who felt the only heroes were their fellow soldiers who are buried in cemeteries like the two American ones we visited in Normandy and Luxembourg. They didn't get to go home.

One member of our group was approached by a beautiful, young lady as we were visiting a battlefield. She knelt down in front of his wheelchair and asked about his service as a Navy Seabee during the war. After a few minutes, she told him that she was a Seabee and had just returned from Afghanistan. They talked of her service, she gave him a hearty hug, and then she left with tears in her eyes. I looked at the old vet and said, "How about that!"

He smiled and said, "Well, I know now I left the Seabees way too early; we didn't have any that looked like that." We laughed, and then he said, "She gave me hope that her generation still holds the values that we fought for — she inspired me." And that is what our hard-fought freedom does: inspires the youngest and even the greatest Americans to have faith and believe in the goodness of our country.

Well into our tour, we walked through the Ardennes forests of Belgium, where the frontline of American troops faced the force of the German Army at the Battle of The Bulge. I looked over my shoulder and saw Bob, a ninety-year-old Marine veteran who fought in the Pacific Campaign and later elected to continue his service in Korea and Vietnam in the Air Force.

Bob stood looking at a double foxhole dug between trees by soldiers who fought in this iconic battle. He slowly came to full military attention with a straight back and head held high. His right hand slowly rose into a military salute. He held the position for nearly two minutes. As his arm slowly returned to his side, I saw his shoulders sag, and he nearly collapsed. I hurried to his side and put my arm around his back to support him. I whispered that I was there and knew this time must be very difficult. After a few minutes, Bob breathed deeply and said through tears, "I lost many friends over here. Now that I have traveled where they fought and honored their memory, maybe I can start to heal."

My time with these veterans was coming to an end, and I started to reflect on my own life. As a young boy, I remember attending movies where we all stood with our hands on our hearts as the National Anthem played and the American flag waved on the big screen. Newsreels from World War II would be shown as the lead-in for the main feature. These newsreels taught us about the gallantry of our Greatest Generation and inspired me to join the military, too.

When they came home, these heroes would not talk about their service or the war. They melded right back into society, building careers and raising families. They wished to forget and move forward, though many could not.

Early in my own career, I had a commander who had spent nearly six years in captivity at the Hanoi Hilton, the infamous Vietnamese prisoner-of-war camp. I asked him how he survived those years of torture, isolation, starvation and humiliation. He hesitated for a few seconds, then looked very intently at me and explained. He survived because he had faith: faith in his God, faith in his country and faith in his fellow POWs. He said, "When you have faith, there is hope; and if you have hope, you have life." His words of faith, hope, and life were the exact mantra I heard from the World War II veterans as they spoke of their lives.

I now have a different perspective when I look at the American flag. I don't just see the Stars and Stripes. I see a cold and ragged army crossing the Delaware River under the leadership of General Washington; I see brother fighting brother at Gettysburg; the gassed trenches of World War I; the beaches, hedgerows, bombing, and concentration camps of World War II; the cold mountains of Korea; the rice paddies of Vietnam; and the deserts of the Middle East. I see the men and women of this great nation who sign up to give it all — including their very lives — to defend the freedoms that bind our nation. I also see a nation that is first to offer assistance to friend or foe when disaster strikes. I know our flag has some tattered edges, but through faith, hope, and love, we can live and continue to honor a flag that, as Lee Greenwood sang, "stands for freedom, and they can't take that away."

~K. Michael Ware

32

Make America Grateful Again

*Make it a habit to tell people thank you. To express
your appreciation, sincerely and without the
expectation of anything in return.*
~Ralph Marston

The way I see it, America is already great! What we need is to make America GRATEFUL again. For the past fifteen months, that has been my mission. I am finding that all it takes to inspire gratitude is a little time, love, and appreciation for those who fought for, bled for, and defended our way of life in this country and in our communities.

I have a bachelor's degree in Communications. I'm also a hopeless romantic who sees great promise and purpose in having a pen in hand. Thus, a simple idea was sparked: spreading love one thank-you note at a time.

In an age consumed with digital technology, text messaging, and social media, it is my hope to replace the negativity in our country with gratitude and love — and good, old-fashioned, handwritten thank-you notes. I like to think of them as love notes, thanking our nation's heroes, those who have served and sacrificed for something bigger than themselves. These everyday heroes are walking among us, some of them in uniform and some of them in plain clothing, and some of them dating as far back as World War II and the Korean War.

When I handed out my first thank-you card, I had no idea the weight behind it. It was just a simple handwritten note thanking one of our nation's heroes for his service and sacrifice to our country. I walked up to him in a Home Depot in the doorknob aisle. He was a small, elderly gentleman whose shoulders were hunched, but who stood ten feet tall underneath his Korean War veteran cap. I introduced myself and handed him the thank-you note. He opened it slowly with bent fingers and read it aloud. His aged blue eyes began to water, and his shoulders began to shake uncontrollably. He asked for a hug, and so I held him in my arms as he wept, this frail stranger who, when he served in the Air Force as a young man, was the backbone of our country. "Thank you," he whispered. "No one has ever thanked me in such a beautiful way."

This Korean War veteran then spent thirty minutes talking to me about his life and his service. I was moved in that moment — changed forever.

And then there was a young Army veteran who served in Iraq. I met him in the parking lot of a grocery store late one Sunday afternoon. The desert sun was setting when I left a thank-you note beneath the windshield wiper of his truck. I knew he was a veteran by his veteran license plate. As I turned to walk away, I heard a man say in an angry tone, "What did she leave on my truck?" I hadn't realized the veteran himself was standing there, so I quickly retreated to my car on the other side of the parking lot to avoid an awkward situation.

As I got to my car and began loading my groceries into the trunk, I looked up and saw the veteran jogging toward me, thank-you note in hand. My heart stopped. I thought, *This is either going to be really good or really uncomfortable.* By the time he reached me, I could see he had tears in his blue eyes. His arms were outstretched, and as he swallowed me up in a big bear hug, he said, "Thank you so much! You don't know what this note means to me."

He and I have been friends ever since.

There have been countless stories like these, veterans and first responders who have opened up to me about their service. Many have admitted to suffering from PTSD. Some have lost friends in wartime, and some have lost limbs. Some have received honorable medals, and some have fallen on hard times and homelessness. Some are doing hard time. And almost all — Marines, sailors, combat soldiers, police officers, and firefighters alike — have been brought to tears.

Vietnam veterans, in particular, seem especially moved by these thank-you notes, having not received a warm welcome home from war. It never ceases to amaze me that these men and women are so easily disarmed by such a simple but genuine gesture. One young Marine Corps veteran who served in the Middle East said it best. "Human kindness can bridge our gaps," he said. "This act of kindness puts an angry veteran's cold heart back in its place."

With the help of my mother and the community at large, we have written and delivered more than 3,000 thank-you notes across the country, and we don't plan on stopping anytime soon. This mission has opened up a conversation, not just with our nation's heroes, but with their families, friends and social networks.

Many of these men and women who have courageously and self-lessly served and sacrificed have seen and done the unfathomable. Nine times out of ten, they will tell you it was their job. However, the truth is that serving our country and our community is, and will forever be, more than just a job. It is a gift.

And I was brought up to believe that when someone gives you a gift, particularly something as precious as peace of mind and freedom, whatever the cost, it is good manners to pen a thank-you note in return. It's the right thing to do. Like the blood, sweat, and tears these heroes have spilled for our sake, the ink spilled to handwrite a thank-you note will leave a long-lasting impression.

~Natalie J. Reilly

Saluting the Flag

*The American flag represents all of us
and all the values we hold sacred.*
~Adrian Cronauer

O
n national holidays, my dad carried a metal pole to the middle of our front yard. He sunk it into the ground and attached a flag. I can still hear the crank of the pulley as the flag rose, splaying stars and stripes in a suburban neighborhood, where big flapping flags were rare.

I watched as Dad saluted our flag. He was fiercely loyal to America and, because of that, I was, too.

"This is the best country in the world," he'd often say. "We're so lucky to live here." He was referring to his grandparents, who'd arrived penniless from the Jewish ghetto of Vilnius, Lithuania. They had been second-class citizens there with no chance of economic or social advancement. Yet here in America their children graduated from high school and moved into the middle class.

During World War II, my father served in France and Germany. A year before Pearl Harbor, he was drafted as a private, later rising to the rank of Major. He was willing to die to defeat fascism and make the world safe for democracy. His service to our country was deeply ingrained into his identity.

Although his patriotism was palpable, he never spoke about his war experiences, the gory side of bravery, or how many people he saw die. Instead, Dad reminisced about his men and the bland, powdered food the Army provided them. They sometimes traded coffee grounds with French farmers, who gave them fresh eggs and homemade bread. These meals were the highlight of those dark days.

Dad spent countless months in trenches, through rain and freezing temperatures. He came home from the war with a back injury, which dogged him for the rest of his life, causing excruciating pain and days lost from work.

At the end of the war, the Army offered him a military career, but he felt better suited to civilian life. He was a furniture salesman, and I remember him giving me pieces of discontinued upholstery fabric that I turned into dolls' clothes.

When I was twenty-five, my father died suddenly. The day after his funeral, a box was delivered to my parents' house. Inside was a flag crisply folded into a triangle.

"It's from the Army," my mother said. "For his military service."

"I'm impressed they sent it so quickly," I said.

She sat in a chair and wept for half an hour, cradling the flag. She displayed that cloth triangle on a shelf in our living room, where everyone could see its white stars shining against a blue background. She never moved it from that honored spot.

When I'd visit, I was disturbed that dust had seeped into the creases. I tried removing it with a feather duster.

"Don't touch the flag," Mom said. She was afraid I'd loosen the folds.

Because I lived in a New York City apartment, I had no front lawn, no way to erect a flag. But twelve years after Dad's death, my husband David and I bought a charming cottage near a lake in Massachusetts.

"Do you think we could hang a flag from the front porch on Memorial Day?" I asked. "It's something my dad always did on American holidays. It would mean a lot to me."

"Let's hang a flag all year," David said. "We're Americans every day, aren't we?"

We went to Kmart and bought a flag. I was a little surprised that they sold only nylon flags, not like the thick cotton ones of my childhood.

"There's no such thing as a bad American flag," David said. "Besides, nylon is durable and will hold up well since we're planning to hang our flag every day."

Whenever I see our flag hanging off our porch, I think of my father. Sometimes, I'm emotional because I miss him. But most of the time, I think about how proud I am to be his daughter, to be an American, and to carry on his patriotic tradition.

Five years ago, David and I visited Normandy with another couple. We were incredibly moved to see those big wide beaches, so sunny and quiet, belying the thousands of young men who perished there in the dawn hours of June 6, 1944.

But nothing prepared me for the scope of the American cemetery. Row upon row of pristine white crosses, with the occasional Star of David, marked where 9,387 heroes were buried. Those young men sacrificed their lives to keep our country safe. I felt heartbroken for their families whose sons, husbands, or brothers were buried so far from home.

We were traveling with a French guide named Jacques, who'd intentionally brought us to the American cemetery just before 5:00 p.m. He knew that my father had fought in France and that our friend Arnold had been a Captain during the Vietnam War. Dozens of people swirled around us in the shadows of two gigantic flags.

Unbeknownst to us, Jacques ran off and spoke to some officials about our military connections. He returned, walking quickly. "They'll lower those two flags any minute," he said. "Two groups of people have the privilege of participating in a ceremony. The four of you have been chosen!"

Before I knew it, we heard the whine of Taps playing as the flags crept downward. Arnold saluted. The atmosphere was somber, as if World War II had ended yesterday, instead of sixty-seven years earlier.

We held the flag in silence, first folding it in half and then into a triangle at the tip. We moved the flag back and forth in that shape until it became a triangle as thick as a pillow. Covered by stars, it was just like the one that had been delivered to my mother forty years ago.

My eyes welled with tears, wishing my dad were here to see this.

I was humbled to honor him and his service to our country with something he loved dearly — the American flag.

~Linda Morel

The Christmas Tree

*Christmas is not as much about opening
our presents as opening our hearts.*
~Janice Maeditere

It was late November, and I had been out of the military for less than a year. The holidays were quickly approaching, and money was tight. My wife and I had uprooted our life in the military to move back to my hometown in a quiet suburb of Chicago. We had not yet gotten fully into the civilian swing of things, but we wanted to make sure it was a festive holiday for our seven-year-old son.

When we looked at Christmas trees in our local Target, I sat on hold with my credit card company, determining whether we had enough spending power to buy a tree. My wife pointed at a tree that she and my son had selected. I was forced to shake my head sadly. Like the champ she is, my wife smiled and walked back to our son to begin swaying him toward a less expensive tree.

While watching them shop, I saw an older woman begin to walk toward them. I walked in their direction, too, wondering what possible reason this woman could have for approaching my wife. She walked up calmly to my wife and said something, and then my wife gave her a hug. I was now more confused than ever. After being freed from my wife's embrace, the woman walked away without a word.

My wife explained that the woman had heard us talking. She asked if I was a veteran. When my wife said yes, the lady had handed

Honoring Those Who Defend Us | 127

her five twenty-dollar bills and told her to have a merry Christmas. I didn't know what to do. "Should we give it back?" I asked my wife. I had never been in this position before and wasn't sure of the protocol for such an amazing act of kindness.

We ended up deciding that the best way to honor the woman's kind intentions was to do just as she had instructed and use the money to have a merry Christmas. We picked out the tree of our son's dreams and headed to the checkout.

As we were paying, still in shock, my wife motioned to a woman standing in line a few lines over. "That is the woman who gave us the money," she said. I walked over and told her how much her help meant to me. She said it was not a problem, and before I knew what I was doing, I was giving the woman a big hug, too. She laughed and hugged me back. Afterward, I returned to my family, who were laughing and waving at the lady. My son was yelling "Thank you!" and the kind stranger was quietly mouthing, "You're welcome."

We went home and set up our new Christmas tree. While decorating the bright green tree with the glassy red ornaments we had in storage, we spoke about how unbelievably kind that woman had been. With Christmas songs playing in the background, I couldn't help but think that this is what that kind stranger had intended. There was no buyer's remorse to be found. We were not stressed out or worried about the expense. We were just… happy. We were together and smiling and enjoying what would turn out to be an outstanding first Christmas in that new place. Every year since, while setting up our Christmas tree, we tell the story of that kind stranger and how much her generosity meant to us.

~Vincent Olson

35

Angels Unaware

*Be not forgetful to entertain strangers: for thereby
some have entertained angels unawares.*
~Hebrews 13:2

There was a time in my life when I wasn't so sure that angels existed. Oh, I know that the Bible says they do, but since I had never had an angelic experience, I wasn't so sure.

Fast-forward to several weeks ago when my husband and I decided to buy a cabin at Pinecrest Lake. We had been looking for just the right place for a while and we liked that area, mostly because we had great friends who already owned a cabin there.

We were supposed to receive a telephone call from the real estate agent who was to show us a cabin. Cell phone coverage is sketchy in that area, so we had to drive to a main road in order to receive the expected telephone call. As it turned out, we sat there longer than we had anticipated. She never did call at the appointed time, so I eventually phoned another agent.

As we waited just off the main highway, an older-model car pulled up on the driver's side of our pickup truck. In it sat an old man who rolled down the passenger window of his car and asked my husband if we were okay. My husband told him that we were fine and were waiting for someone. The old man paused for just a second and then asked my husband if he had served in Vietnam. Since we have a couple of stickers on the back window of our truck that indicate he had indeed fought in that war, I didn't think it particularly unusual that someone would ask that question.

My husband told him that he had served in Vietnam, and he mentioned the dates of his service there. The man then said, "Stay right here. I have something for you." I don't know if it's because of the part-time work I do with the sheriff's department, or if I'm just naturally suspicious, but I told my husband to be careful in case the man had a gun. Now I realize it sounds pretty weird, but in that moment, my mind just went there.

The old man pulled in front of us and got out. He took something out of the back seat of his car, walked over to my husband's side of the truck and pushed forward an olive drab jacket that was neatly placed on a wooden hanger. He proceeded to tell us the story about a dear friend of his who had once owned the coat. This friend had told the old man that he should find a deserving person to give it to one day.

You're probably wondering why this jacket was hanging in his car. Well, I asked him that, and he said that local authorities had him and the rest of the community on alert to evacuate because of the Rim Fire that was raging at that time. What he did not realize is that the evacuation notice had been lifted two days earlier. But with the anticipation that he and his wife might have to flee at any moment, everything he valued most was in his car, including this jacket.

On that day, the old man found the deserving recipient his friend spoke of. As the man was speaking, my husband held the coat, and I noticed that the jacket was authentic Army issue. On the hooded portion, there was an insignia. It was the insignia of the division my husband served with while in Vietnam in 1968: The First Infantry Division; The Big Red One.

I began to cry.

This dear man, a seventy-eight-year-old veteran of the Korean conflict, told us about his life. He experienced a debilitating heart attack several years back and was currently recuperating from yet another surgery. He told us about losing his first wife to cancer when she was only in her mid-thirties, and his eyes misted as he recalled the heartbreak of that loss. He thought he couldn't go on, he said, that his own life was over as well. But he had three girls to raise, and somehow, by God's grace, he mustered up the fortitude to go on alone.

Alone, that is, until a woman appropriately named Joy came into his life. She was widowed and had six children. With a twinkle in his eye, he said they married, and together they raised nine kids. I don't recall how many grandchildren they have, but suffice it to say, they have a bunch.

"I believe in the biblical Acts where it says that it is better to give than receive," he told us. His words pierced my heart in the most profound way. I got out of the truck, walked around to where he was standing, and asked if I could give him a hug. He said something sweet and endearing while I very gently hugged him, remembering that he had only recently had surgery.

I got back in the truck and reminded my husband that we were late for our appointment.

The gentleman spoke for a few more minutes. We exchanged names and addresses, and then my husband and I sat there and silently watched him walk back to his car and drive off. We both had lumps in our throats and could hardly speak. I think I said something silly about there being no angel wings on his back. My husband smiled, but had tears in his eyes, too.

We both realized pretty quickly that something extraordinary had just happened.

Did we encounter an angel along the highway? I just don't know, but I do know that my husband received a treasured gift from a special person. But even more than that, our collective souls connected with someone extraordinary. And that is by far the best gift of all.

~Sunday Pearson

36

Seventh-Inning Stretch

There shall be eternal summer in the grateful heart.
~Celia Thaxter

O ut of all the seasons in the year, there's no denying that summertime holds a special kind of magic. It's the time when fireflies and fireworks light up dark, starry nights. A time when long, sunshine-soaked days are filled with trips to swimming pools and lakes, slip and slides, and snow cones.

But my favorite part of summer is baseball.

Baseball, to me, not only epitomizes summer, but also the heartwarming pride and patriotism of serving on active duty in this great country. And once you serve in the military, celebrations of patriotism and everything that comes with it will never be the same in your heart.

I had served on active duty for eight years and separated, while my husband had remained in the service. We had just been re-assigned to Maryland with the Air Force, and after waiting for months, summer finally came. We found ourselves at a baseball game in the Washington Nationals stadium.

I was not prepared for the overwhelming flood of emotion and pride that would come that day in the ballpark. You see, it was Military Appreciation Day.

The day started with a ceremony honoring World War II veterans. Some were on walkers, some in wheelchairs, but the pride radiating from these brave soldiers was unmistakable as their smiles and tears lit up the stadium on the big broadcasting screen.

Members from each branch of the armed services proudly marched out onto the field, each service flag held and presented with perfect precision.

Goosebumps shot down my arms as the Air Force Color Guard presented the nation's colors, and the National Anthem was sung.

During the fourth inning, the scoreboard lit up with an announcement for fans to stand and wave their caps in salute to veterans. That was quite a sight — everyone in the stadium on their feet and waving.

But it was the seventh-inning stretch that had me fighting back tears.

A long-time baseball tradition, the seventh-inning stretch is the time when the audience sways and sings "Take Me Out to the Ballgame." Often, "God Bless America" is played in addition to it, or sometimes replaces it entirely.

However, on this day, just before the stretch, the announcer asked all members who were serving on active duty and veterans in the audience to please stand.

I hadn't expected to be recognized, and was a little embarrassed actually to call attention to ourselves and stand. But we stood.

Scattered around the stadium, people got to their feet and stood, while the crowd roared around us. They didn't have to acknowledge us, and no one asked them to clap; they could have just as easily continued with their conversations and food. But they didn't.

Several people close to us clasped our shoulders or took our hands and said, "Thank you." Even people who weren't close enough to touch made eye contact with us and mouthed those two simple words.

As a service member, we don't often stop to think about what those simple, yet very heartfelt thank-yous mean. We aren't a group that tends to call attention to ourselves, and being recognized for acts of bravery, sacrifice, and heroism can actually be difficult to accept. "It's just what we do," we say. Or, "Anyone in my shoes would do the same."

But that day, the flood of a thousand thank-yous, both said and unsaid, wrapped around us in a blanket of gratitude. It was in the eyes of a little girl with a Popsicle-stained face. A teenager who stopped texting long enough to look up. A set of parents wearing the unmistakable look of hope, pride, and fear because they, too, had a loved one serving somewhere in the world.

There were looks that said:

Thank you for serving, to protect me and my family.
Thank you for volunteering, wherever the military takes you, to protect us.
Because you answered the call of service, millions of Americans can sleep safely in their beds, while someone keeps an ever vigilant watch.
Thank you for standing up and saying yes, while so many others cannot, or even will not.
Thank you for your sacrifice, and for the sacrifices your family makes, to preserve and protect our great nation.
Thank you, thank you, thank you.

One of the first things we learned in the military is that it is an honor to serve. It's why we adhere to customs and courtesies, protocols and tradition as deeply as we do. We honor those who have come before us; we honor each other; we honor our heroes and our fallen. We honor our country.

When the days grow long and warm, my mind often floats back to the overwhelming feeling of gratitude and honor we felt that day, as thousands of people we didn't know cheered for us: their service members and veterans.

The knowledge that I've served in the armed forces is always there, even if it's not always front and center. But the legacy of having served holds a special place for me during the summer.

That day, and that particular seventh-inning stretch, forever linked summertime and the honor of being trusted to serve deep in my heart.

~Kristi Adams

37

Filled with Kindness

The cheerful heart has a continual feast.
~Proverb 15:15

O ur monthly military pay never stretched to the end of the month. We were young newlyweds, expecting our first baby, and living in an old mobile home in Delta Junction, a rural, wilderness town at the end of the Alaska Highway. Large, wild animals roamed freely, and a closet-sized post office and equally small bank bookended the one general store in town.

I shopped on post at the Army commissary once a month, and because of our tight budget, I had to become a very creative cook. We purchased twenty pounds of ground meat, which I shoved into our built-in, dorm-sized fridge with a tiny, ice-crusted freezer.

I learned to prepare hamburger dishes thirty different ways. Often, I made one-pan meals of chili or soups and stews. Rarely did we have poultry or fish, unless you consider cans of no-name, smelly tuna packed in greasy oil a meal.

Mainly, we ate lots of pasta and carb-loaded meals with little meat and lots of tomato sauce. Most goods had to be trucked in from the lower forty-eight states. Dairy products, fruits and vegetables, prescribed as a healthy part of a prenatal diet, were especially costly and out of our price range. I was homesick, not only for my mom, but also for the variety of stores and farmers' markets back in Missouri, and the accessibility and affordability of fresh fruits and veggies.

Eighteen-hour days of winter darkness arrived in November. On our monthly shopping trip to the commissary, I planned ahead for our Thanksgiving dinner. I bought less ground beef and purchased one fat roasting chicken, which I stuffed into our tiny freezer. I also purchased a package of Pepperidge Farm dry stuffing mix and a can of cranberry sauce for our big meal. We invited our neighbors, Karen and Bob, a young military couple from Oregon.

All month long, I eagerly awaited our Thanksgiving get-together.

I rose early on Thanksgiving morning, pried the frozen poultry from the freezer, and thawed it. I washed and salted the hollow cavity and stuffed it with sage dressing. I smeared butter on the breast of the roasting hen and popped it into our twenty-inch, propane-fueled oven.

Half an hour into the baking, I peeked in. The light bulb illuminated a raw chicken in a barely lukewarm oven. I fiddled with the knobs and called my husband, who went outdoors to check the twenty-pound propane tank.

I knew before he announced it that the tank was empty. We didn't have enough money to refill it. Our friends and neighbors were as impoverished as we were, so borrowing money was out of the question. I dug deep into the bottom of my purse and rummaged through the couch cushions. Together, we came up with ninety-seven cents — not even a dollar. Three days before payday and flat broke, we drove to the service station on the main highway and asked the owner, an older gray-haired man who hustled out to greet probably his only customers, if he could please fill our small cylinder with just under a dollar's worth of propane.

"You kids stationed at Fort Greely? How long have you been up here? This your first Thanksgiving?" His exhaled words crystallized in mid-air, and he rubbed his hands together to warm them. The town's population was just over 500, and any newcomer was usually a military family. Many were young newlyweds, as we were, a year out of high school, and unfamiliar with the hazards of the large, free-roaming wild animals and the deep-freeze climate conditions. Spouses who joined their soldiers at the top of the world were required to take a survival training class on how to prevent frostbite and avoid serious situations.

At that moment, though, our most serious situation was having no way to cook our Thanksgiving meal.

The man tugged his fur-lined cap out of his pocket and pulled it down around his ears. He lifted our small propane tank from the trunk and said, "Hold on there a minute. See what I can do for you. Just under a dollar will get you through to payday, you say?"

I was so thrilled that I clapped my hands. "Oh, thank you, sir. I have the bird in the oven, and the oven went cold." I was too embarrassed to tell him our bird weighed less than five pounds and was a chicken, not a turkey.

He walked to the propane tank to dispense fuel. I watched the gauge register fifty cents, sixty-five cents, and when it surpassed a dollar, I panicked. "Tell him to stop filling!"

Before we could get the window rolled back down, the man turned to put our tank in the car. I dropped ninety-seven cents into his calloused hand and said, "I'm sorry, sir. You filled it, but we don't even have a dollar to pay you." I expected he would remove the small tank because there was no way to return the unpaid fuel.

With a genuine smile on his kind face, he said, "You kids have a nice Thanksgiving, and don't worry about it." If I had been outdoors, my tears would have frozen on my cheeks.

We thanked him for his generosity and promised to bring four dollars and three cents on payday to repay our debt. He waved us on our way.

I baked that chicken to a golden brown, whipped up instant mashed potatoes, opened cans of green beans and cranberry sauce, and proudly served a feast. As Bob, Karen, my husband and I bowed our heads to say grace, I was especially thankful for the generosity of a stranger with a heart of gold. I am forever grateful for his unexpected kindness as he demonstrated the true meaning of Thanksgiving.

~Linda O'Connell

38

The Least We Can Do

*Human kindness has never weakened the stamina
or softened the fiber of a free people.*
~President Franklin D. Roosevelt

The young soldier in line two customers behind us looked tired. His pregnant wife played hide-and-seek with a small boy buried under their purchases like a merry troll. While my husband, Dan, hummed along to "Jingle Bells" on the intercom, I watched the serviceman and his family.

Insignias on the chest and sleeve of the camouflage uniform identified the man as an enlisted National Guardsman. He bent and spoke to his little son, who giggled and dove behind a box of Frosted Flakes. Both parents laughed.

Growing up as a Navy brat, I knew firsthand the sacrifices required by military people and their dependents in defense of freedom. I remembered the frequent moves and the long stretches of time without my father. I still recalled the ache in my stomach every time he deployed.

My husband broke my reverie by speaking directly to the soldier. "Thank you for your service."

Startled, the man replied over the head of the woman between us. "It's my privilege," he said — exactly what my father used to say when someone thanked him.

"Are you home for a while?" my husband asked.

"Yes, sir, through the holidays. I ship out again in the new year."

His wife and son glanced up from their game, and their smiles faded.

Dan touched the tips of his thumb and his fingers together, making a circle like a pirate's telescope with his hand. He peered through it at the boy in the cart. "You be the man of the house when your dad's away."

The troll grinned and lifted his fist to look back at us through his own telescope.

"Be safe," my husband said to the soldier. "And thank you again."

I pushed our empty cart out into the lobby while Dan paid the bill for our few items. We met by the entrance, and he passed me the receipt to record when we got home.

As I tucked it into my purse, the total caught my eye — nearly two hundred and fifty dollars. I stopped midway through the automated doors, and the cold air rushed around us. "Dan! There's been some mistake. This can't be our bill."

He took my elbow and steered me toward the parking lot. The bags he carried bumped against the back of my legs. "There's no mistake. I'll explain in the car."

I waited impatiently while Dan opened my door, crossed to the driver's side and got in. He dropped the sacks on the floor behind me. As he fastened his seatbelt and started the vehicle, my husband confessed what he had done.

"I paid for their groceries," he said.

"What? For the Guardsman's family? How did you do that? They were two behind us in the line!"

"I told the cashier to ring up an extra two hundred dollars on our credit card for the cost of their purchase and to give the change to the serviceman. I asked her to tell him someone said, 'Merry Christmas.'"

My mouth hung open, and I stared at the man I married.

"I've been doing this for several years," he said. "When I see a military person in line somewhere, I try to pick up the tab. Most of the time, they never know it's me."

"You big elf!" I punched him lightly on the arm. "What a great gesture."

Dan's face flushed a warm, pink color. "It's no big deal. And please don't tell anyone."

He turned to look over his shoulder through the rear window. As he backed the car out of the parking space, he spoke again softly.

"It's the least we can do."

~Lynn Yates

39

But It's Our Rule...

*I follow three rules: Do the right thing, do the best
you can, and always show people you care.*
~Lou Holtz

"Excuse me." I tapped the back of his uniform.

He turned around with his wallet in his hand.

"Allow me to pay for your coffee, please."

"I'm sorry?" He stared at me like he didn't understand.

"I'd like to pay for your coffee. And thank you for your service," I added with a smile.

"Thank you, but I'm fine." With that, he turned back around.

I knew I needed to do something and quick. Only one woman was in front of the man. It would have been easy to say to myself, *Well, I tried*, and put my money away. It would be easy. But then I thought about John. No, it wouldn't be easy.

Three years earlier than this scene in a local coffee shop, my husband made a decision for our family. "Robbie, let's pay for that man's dinner." We were in a restaurant, and a man sat in a booth. His uniform identified him as Army.

John called the waitress over and told her to add that man's ticket to ours. And make sure not to tell him.

A few minutes later, the man in that booth was joined by three others: a woman and two teenagers.

The waitress came to us. "Do you want me to not add his ticket, sir? His family is with him now."

My husband didn't hesitate. "No, we'll pay for all of them."

On that day, John made a rule for our home. Whenever we see anyone who is in the military, and they are about to get coffee or a meal, we pay.

Another day, I watched John get huge eyes as a big group of Marines entered a Cracker Barrel. I giggled at him, but he said, "It's a rule."

On another occasion, John saw a waitress give a check to a table full of soldiers. There was no time to be anonymous, so he went to their table and asked for their ticket. He thanked them for their service and walked away with tears in his eyes.

His philosophy is that if anyone is willing to sign up for a duty that may require them to give their life, we are entitled to thank them. And one way to do that is to pay the tab.

As I stood in that coffee shop, I knew I needed to be assertive. I could almost hear John saying, "But it's our rule."

"Excuse me, sir." He was about to pay and turned around again. "Listen, sir, please allow me the chance to honor you and your sacrifice for our country by buying your coffee."

Then I grinned and whispered, "You don't want me to make a scene, do you?"

A smile lit up his face, and he took a step back and waved me in. "Thank you, ma'am." He took his coffee and left.

The woman working at the cash register said, "That was nice of you."

"It's a rule," I said.

~Robbie Iobst

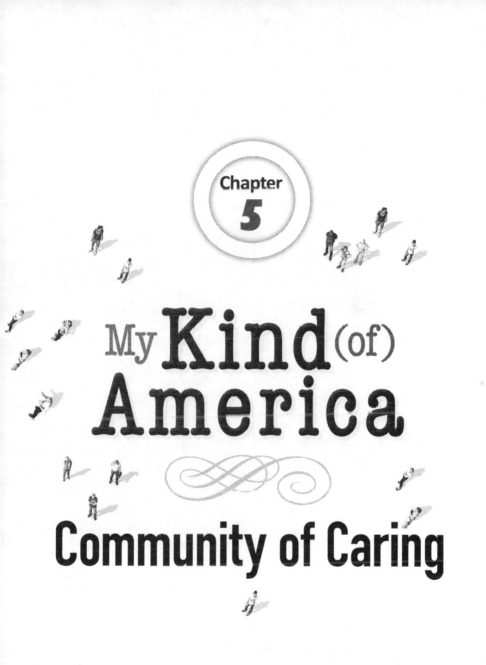

Chapter 5

My Kind (of) America

Community of Caring

40

My Ferguson

The life I touch for good or ill will touch another life,
and that in turn another, until who knows where
the trembling stops or in what far place
my touch will be felt.
~Frederick Buechner

The Jenkins family traveled all over the United States. Cathy and Jerome sat in the front seat, the three kids piled in the back, and off they'd go. Everywhere they went, they checked out the food that was popular. Fish tacos in New Mexico. Jambalaya in New Orleans. Vienna sausages in Chicago. Asian wings in California. Pulled pork sandwiches in Memphis. After some meals, Cathy got the chance to talk to the cooks, and sometimes she got them to share their recipes. Along the way, they'd swim in the ocean, spend a few days at Disneyland, go hiking in the mountains… whatever was on their to-do list for that year's trip.

So many fun-filled summers resulted in a little filing box crammed with new recipes, and Cathy and Jerome had a brilliant idea. Their kids' elementary school — the school where I taught — was full of hungry teachers. We never had enough time to visit a fast food drive-thru during our lunch period. The Jenkins lived only two minutes from the school. Cathy could start a catering business.

It was an instant hit. We teachers loved eating Chicken Divan and Beef Bourguignon at lunch instead of peanut-butter sandwiches.

Cathy loved getting the business, along with the compliments on her cooking. However, it wasn't enough. Cathy Jenkins had a bigger dream.

She and her husband started looking for a building. The two of them wanted to open a restaurant. They lived in Ferguson, and their children went to Ferguson schools. They loved the Ferguson community. What better place for a restaurant than Ferguson?

Once they found the perfect place, they had a huge hurdle to clear. Major renovations were needed before they could open the doors. Jerome and Cathy had a décor in mind, and it involved painting a highway above the booths, framing pictures of the dishes they were going to offer, and sharing their family photos and cute mementos as part of the décor. They also needed to include a bar, kitchen, and service counter.

Cathy said to her husband, "How can we rent this place and fix it up when we won't be making any money while we're doing it?" She and Jerome had three kids. Their family was their first priority.

Fortunately, their landlord believed in their dream just like he believed in Cathy and Jerome's determination. He told them, "Don't pay me any rent until you're open for a month. Then you can start paying on the place."

Then Cortez Thomas entered the picture. Cortez was a McCluer High School student and an aspiring chef. In the months that the Jenkinses worked on transforming the building into Cathy's Kitchen, Cortez showed up—sometimes several days a week.

"I'd like to work for you," he'd say as he stood there in his chef's apron and pants.

"We're not even open yet."

"I know, but when you are open, I'd like to be your pastry chef."

"Honey, I'm sorry, but I'm going to bake all the pies here," Cathy said.

On the first day that Cathy's Kitchen was open, Cortez was back. He was dressed to work, and he'd brought along his pastry kit.

Cathy invited him to audition. "Here's the recipe for my famous Dutch apple pie. Let's see what you've got."

When Cortez pulled the pie out of the oven, Cathy told me, "It looked prettier than my pie." Cortez was hired on the spot, and when he graduated from high school, his high school sent him to culinary school — and paid his tuition.

Immediately, Cathy's Kitchen became the spot for business lunches in the area. The teachers at my school — when we had an extended lunchtime — went to Cathy's Kitchen and enjoyed the smoked salmon, Philly sandwiches and Italian beef. I loved the fish tacos with the lime-infused slaw, along with the tables that were painted with chalkboard paint. Kids doodled on the table while families waited for their food.

Things were going well with the lunch and dinner crowd. Business was good. In fact, it was so good, they began opening up for breakfast.

But then, in 2014, Michael Brown got killed in an altercation with a Ferguson police officer. Protests, stand-offs, tear gas, and SWAT teams turned Ferguson into a boiling pot. The once-peaceful community's pain was splashed across the news every night.

After months of protests, the grand jury's decision was announced. The officer involved in the shooting would not be indicted. The city of Ferguson erupted.

Stores were broken into and looted. Shops had been set on fire, and windows were shattered.

Early the next morning, I went to Cathy's Kitchen. I knew they'd need help cleaning up. I just hoped the whole place wasn't destroyed.

When I rounded the corner, much to my surprise, all I saw was some broken glass. Only a couple of windows had been broken.

Jerome and Cathy told me the story.

There had been looters gathered that night. Feeling like their lives didn't matter, the protesters started taking their out-of-control rage out on the businesses in Ferguson. When they got to Cathy's Kitchen, they came up against a chain of people. The loyal customers were locked, arm in arm, in front of the restaurant.

"Not here," they said. "The owners of this place are good people." They deterred the looters with a firm but positive message. Their clasped hands and connected hearts were more powerful than the mob's anger.

In 2014, Ferguson got a reputation for being a dangerous city. During the 2016 election campaign, Donald Trump even called it one of the most dangerous cities in the world. I just wish everyone knew the Ferguson I know.

In the Ferguson I know, a family invested their sweat, time and money into a restaurant that's bustling all day. In the Ferguson community I'm familiar with, a landlord lost out on some revenue so a dream could come true. In my Ferguson, a young man was given a chance to succeed. In the city of Ferguson that I love, people from all over came and swept up glass, cleaned up debris, and protected businesses from looting and destruction.

People are kind in America, and there are especially kind folks in Ferguson....

~Sioux Roslawski

Carmen's Gift

Freely you have received; freely give.
~Matthew 10:8

It was a snowy winter, bitter and cold, but not even that could wipe the smile off my face. I was in the United States of America. A twenty-year-old African girl was finally getting a chance to fulfill her dreams, and going to college was a good way to start. I was going to make my mama proud. My fifteen-hour Greyhound bus ride from Atlanta, Georgia, to Arkadelphia, Arkansas, was finally over. It was 9:00 p.m., and I had no idea where I was. I stood in the cold night air and hoped someone would stop so I could ask for directions. A few minutes later, a car pulled up.

"You're about an hour away," one of the girls in the car told me. My heart dropped and my face fell. It was a Sunday night, and I was due at school Monday morning. I hated being late for anything, especially for the first day of the rest of my life. Plus, I was extremely hungry and tired.

"We can take you there. Hop in!" They must have seen the defeated look on my face. I barely had time to wonder if they'd take me into the forest and chop me into bits like in some horror movies. I was getting into that car even if my life was at risk. I settled in the back seat, gratefully yet fearful, and said a little prayer.

The first day of school was chaotic. I managed to register for classes and find a few people from my country. We decided it was cheaper to rent an apartment together. There were five of us. The two boys shared a room, and so did the two female cousins. I had a room all to myself. I had spent all the money Mama sent from home to pay for my tuition for that semester. I was literally broke, and my roommates had no idea I didn't have my share of the first month's rent.

I borrowed textbooks from every class I attended and stayed up all night to read four to five chapters ahead of each class. I made tons of notes since no one would be lending me their textbooks during test periods. It was no surprise to me when I got an A+ in every class. I was extremely determined but, most importantly, I was grateful to be in school.

As time went by, I received help from some generous friends who chipped in to help me cover my rent. I ate what I could and when I could. Most days, my stomach ached with pangs of hunger, but I did not let it show. One of my roommates had landed a job at a fast-food restaurant. Whenever he could, he would bring me a little burger from the leftovers that were going to be trashed.

"Thank you so much, James," I would say.

"Ah, you know it's nothing. They were going to throw it away anyway." He would hug me and sit with me for a while, telling me jokes to make me smile.

"My Mimi," he would say lovingly. He was more than a friend, more like an older brother.

I was super grateful for those days when I had food to eat.

Interestingly enough, before I came to school, there was another James, my young cousin, who had heard about my financial plight and decided to do something marvelous about it. James worked as a waiter in a restaurant in Atlanta, and before I made the trip to Arkansas, he had saved weeks of his pay as a gift to me for college. It was such a kind gesture because I knew how hard he worked and how many long hours he put in to come up with such a sum of money. I used most of it to pay for a few school supplies, utilities and some furniture at Goodwill for my room.

As weeks passed, I got into the routine of borrowing textbooks. Soon enough, people took it upon themselves to ask, "Do you need to borrow my book for a while?"

Even though my grades never faltered, my weight was dwindling.

We were far from wealthy back home, yet somehow we never really starved. It was hard for my mother to raise five children on a meager salary, but her kindness was always returned. Mother always shared her groceries with two of her other friends who were financially worse off than we were.

"What if we don't have enough?" we'd ask, but she would always say, "Freely you give, freely you will receive." And like magic, someone always dropped by days before we ran completely out of food to drop off some kind of staple. It never failed to happen!

But now, it was beginning to get hard to read, to study, and to smile. There were no more free burgers from my friend James's job. Someone had reported seeing him take leftovers home. But James knew how to make me laugh, and for a while I would forget that my insides were burning with hunger.

I'd come home every day from class, drink a large glass of water, and make myself fall asleep to forget the pain and make the day go faster.

Carmen, a woman I used to help with studies, offered me a ride home from class. It was unusual, but I wanted to get home quickly to drink some water and sleep off my anguish.

"I'm going to Walmart. Do you want to come?" she offered, but I declined. I had no business going to tempt myself with food when I couldn't afford it.

And so she dropped me off, and as usual I performed my ritual of water drinking and sleep. It was 3:00 in the afternoon, and I'd hoped to sleep long enough to wake up the next day. But a disturbing, consistent honking woke me up. I went to the door to see who the lunatic was, only to find that it was Carmen.

She started to unload bags of groceries from the trunk of her car and drop them into the house. It took me a while to register what was going on or how she even knew that I needed food! I never mentioned anything to her, let alone showed anyone that I was in any kind of trouble.

When she was all done, she came back to the spot where I stood transfixed, wiping away my tears.

I wanted to ask her why, but I could only say her name. She gave me a tight big hug and whispered in my ear, "I am your friend." Then she got into her car and drove off, leaving me on my knees, sobbing gratefully.

~Bernice Angoh

The Biggest Hearts

What do we live for, if it is not to make
life less difficult for each other?
~George Eliot

ll three of my children were sick with the flu. Six-month-old Ann was feverish and miserable. I rocked her and sang to her softly, but nothing seemed to comfort her. My husband had our sole car and was working long hours for low pay, and I was alone and worried. There was no money to bring her to a doctor.

Four-year-old Billy's fever had gone down a little, and he followed me around all morning, trying to help. "It's okay, Ann," he said, handing her a soft baby toy.

The night before had been devastating. I had slapped some peanut butter and jelly on some bread for the kids and poured them each a half-cup of milk. All we had in the refrigerator was a quart of milk, grape jelly, and a couple of eggs. There was no fresh orange juice, fresh fruit, or soup to feed my children.

Then my two-and-a-half-year-old, Michelle, had asked me for a coloring book, and I didn't have a single unused one in the apartment. That was the last straw. I had locked the bathroom door and turned on the shower so the kids wouldn't hear me crying.

I had friends who were in the same dire straits as I was, but somehow they were handling it better. My friend Elaine lived in the apartment across from me. Her baby girl was the same age as Ann, and people from their church helped her with everything. When she arrived home from the hospital after giving birth, her church friends came over to clean and brought over flowers, huge casseroles and an endless parade of gifts. I secretly wished they would visit *me*.

My friend Dale lived in the apartment complex too. She didn't have much, but was always smiling. I could have really used some of her cheerfulness that day.

Elaine and Dale wanted me to join them at their Bible study. "Why don't you come with us?" they asked. "We'll drive you. They have a babysitter there."

I always had some excuse not to join them. Most days, I could barely function.

Dale couldn't wait to tell me about a family with small children whose car was destroyed by a fire. "You wouldn't believe what a woman from our church did," she said as I folded a huge mountain of laundry.

"What?"

"A lady from church donated her car. Can you believe it? People can be so kind."

Dale's family struggled as much as ours, but she had a grateful spirit.

I thought about that as I sat there, rocking Ann, and marveling at my friends' good spirits. And then the doorbell rang.

People rarely came over, and most of my friends worked. I wondered who it could be.

Billy opened the door.

"Who is it?" I asked. The room around me was scattered with used, germy tissues and I wasn't dressed for company. I didn't want to invite anyone in.

"Nobody," Billy said, looking around. "But there's a big bag on the doorstep."

"A bag? I wasn't expecting anything." Wearily, I rose from the rocking chair, cradling the baby.

Right outside there was a brown paper bag stuffed with groceries.

"Where did that come from?" I asked. Billy shrugged his shoulders. He dragged the bag inside.

We were amazed at what we saw. Inside the bag were a couple

of big cans of chicken noodle soup, jars of baby food, a container of rainbow sherbet ice cream, a box of fluffy tissues and animal crackers. Tears filled my eyes. *Who could have done such a wonderful thing for us?*

"Look, Mom," said two-year-old Michelle, clapping her hands in delight. "There's a coloring book and crayons!"

I stood in silence, overcome with gratitude, yet completely bewildered.

First, the children feasted on warm chicken soup and were delighted with the dessert of cool rainbow sherbet that soothed their throats. They scribbled happily in the coloring book. Yet still I wondered. *Where did that mysterious bag of groceries come from?*

Elaine called to ask how we were doing.

"Listen, please don't tell her I told you this, but I know who left the groceries at your house."

"Who?"

"It was Dale."

"But that's impossible. How did she do that? She's struggling, too."

"With her food stamps," said Elaine. "And we qualified for a program that gives the children food. We have lots of extra cereal for your kids if you want it."

I was speechless and forever changed by their kindness. To this day, I strive to pass it on. There are people in America who don't have much, but they have the biggest hearts. And that makes all the difference in someone's life.

~L.A. Strucke

Please Don't Leave

The best way to find yourself is to lose
yourself in the service of others.
~Mahatma Gandhi

I'd done it before, and so I had no reason to believe that this time would be any different. I was sure that when I returned home from my mission trip, as always, I'd bring back nothing more than some mud on my boots, a hole or two in my jeans and, of course, a lot of great memories. Little did I know that this time it was going to be different.

The summer before my high school graduation, I went to West Virginia with others from my church as members of the Appalachia Service Project. Our goals included refurbishing the homes of those in need, and where we were heading, there was no shortage of need. Along with volunteers from several other churches, we arrived at our destination much like an invading army in miniature, and we arrived ready to do battle. The tools we brought from home would serve as our weapons as we prepared to wage war against an all-too-familiar enemy—substandard living conditions. Our mission was to make the homes of those we served warmer, safer and drier, and with only five days to accomplish as much as we could, we were anxious to get started.

My group was assigned the task of rebuilding sections of a home that had been damaged by fire. No sooner had we parked on the home's dirt driveway than we saw an excited little girl, no more than six years old, standing in the doorway of the family's temporary trailer home.

Shoeless and wearing dirty clothes and the biggest smile I'd ever seen, she yelled, "Ma, Ma, they really came!" I didn't know it then, but her name was Dakota, and four more days would pass before she'd say another word near me.

Behind Dakota was a woman in a wheelchair—her grandmother, we'd soon learn. I also discovered that my job that week would be to help convert a fire-damaged dining room into a bedroom for this little girl. After meeting several more family members, we got down to the business of making a difference in their lives.

Grabbing our tools, we went to work. Walls were torn down and replaced. Hammers and nails, saws and electric screw guns, drywall prepping and painting—we moved at a fast pace. Over the following days, I noticed Dakota peeking at us every now and then as we worked. A few times, I tried talking with her, but she remained shy and aloof, always fluttering around us like a tiny butterfly but keeping to herself.

By our fifth and final day, however, this was about to change.

Before I went to work on her home on that last morning, I spoke for a moment or two with the grandmother. I was especially pleased when she told me how much Dakota loved her new room—so much, in fact, that she'd begged to sleep in it the previous night, even though it wasn't quite ready. As we talked, I noticed something I hadn't seen before—Dakota was hiding behind her grandmother. Cautiously, she stepped into view, and I could see that just like her clothes, her face was still dirty. But no amount of soil could hide those bright blue eyes and big smile. She was simply adorable. I wanted so much to hug her, but respecting her shyness, I kept my distance.

Slowly, she began walking toward me. It wasn't until she was just inches away that I noticed the folded piece of paper in her tiny hand. Silently, she reached up and handed it to me. Once unfolded, I looked at the drawing she'd made with her broken crayons on the back of an old coloring book cover. It was of two girls—one much taller than the other—and they were holding hands. She told me it was supposed to be me and her, and scrawled on the bottom of the paper were three little words that instantly broke my heart: *Please don't leave*. Now almost in tears, I surrendered to the impulse that I'd suppressed only moments before — I bent down and hugged her. She hugged me, too. And for the longest time, neither one of us could let go.

By early afternoon, we finished Dakota's bedroom, and so I gladly used the rare free time to get to know my newest friend. Sitting under a tree away from the others, we shared a few apples while she told me about her life in the hollow. As I listened to her stories about the struggles she and her family endured daily, I began to realize how frivolous various aspects of my own life were.

Suddenly, things like deciding what to wear on a Friday night or which wannabe celebrity was starring in the latest reality television series seemed trivial. I refocused on my friends, family and faith, all because of one special little girl living in the mountains of West Virginia.

I left for home early the next morning. I was returning with muddy boots and holes in my jeans. But because of Dakota, I brought back something else, too — a greater appreciation for all of the blessings of my life. I'll never forget that barefoot little butterfly with the big smile and dirty face. I pray that she'll never forget me either.

~Tracy Rusiniak

It Will All Work Out

It is not what life brings us, but the manner in which we receive it, that shapes our destiny.
~Marie Dubsky

"You want me to do what?" I was in a wheelchair dance lesson with Brandon, my instructor, and that day he was choreographing a new routine. I wasn't sure I had heard him correctly.

"I want you to let me get you out of your wheelchair during the routine, then let me guide you while you walk for a few steps. Then I will lift you and spin you around, and carry you back to your wheelchair," Brandon repeated.

Upon seeing the flash of fear in my eyes, he said, "C'mon, Lorraine. Trust me. It will all work out."

I had known Brandon for a few years at that point, and one of the things I loved about him was that he was continually pushing me outside my comfort zone. I was used to people focusing on what I couldn't do. Brandon never did. In the time we had worked together, he had come up with numerous dance moves I didn't think I could execute. But with his faith and patience and my trust in him, we always found a way to make them work.

A few weeks later, my next-door neighbor told me that a tree in my back yard had been struck by lightning in a recent storm and was almost completely split in two. Part of the tree was in danger of crashing into his kitchen.

The next morning, I started to get bids to remove the tree. It was the biggest hedge tree anybody had ever seen, and I could say the same about the size of the bids to take it down. They ranged from $4,000 to $6,500.

I was lost. There was no way my limited income from Social Security Disability could cover an expense like this.

I called Brandon. After explaining the whole situation to him, I told him how stressed out I was, and he suggested we pray. Faith was something Brandon and I shared. "Hang in there, Lorraine," he said. "Nothing is impossible with God. It will all work out."

Over the next few days, the cloud of worry weighed me down. I called every tree guy who had been recommended to me, and every bid was out of my reach. It was hard, in this situation, not to let the stress snuff out my faith. Usually, when things come up in my life, it is fairly easy to devise a plan I can break down into baby steps and tackle slowly. I had never had to deal with anything like this before. It felt bigger than I was and more than I could do.

Then one evening, Brandon called. "Hey, Lorraine. Rachel and I sponsor the youth group at our church. We have been looking for a project we could do with the kids, and I think we may have found it. Would it be okay if we organized a fundraiser to get your tree taken down?"

I hesitated. I need to have people help me with many things in my life, everything from getting dressed to getting around town. Because I have to get help for physical things on a daily basis, getting help taking my tree down seemed like too much to ask of anyone.

When I expressed my concern to Brandon, he said, "Lorraine, I have one question for you. If the situation were reversed and I needed your help, what would you do?" The answer was easy. I would do whatever I could.

"I don't know if we can raise fifty cents, but I would like to try and raise this money, okay?"

I couldn't say no.

Within days, Brandon posted a fundraising video on YouTube.

The video showed clips of us dancing together, along with text explaining my need to take a tree down in my back yard. Brandon put the video up on Facebook and encouraged me to do the same. He set up a PayPal account for donations. Brandon spent an evening teaching dance lessons in exchange for people contributing to my tree-removal fund. The youth group got sponsors to donate as well.

By using social media and word of mouth, donations came in from family, friends, and even strangers. After the church service one Sunday, Bill, the senior pastor at my church, told me that the elders of my church had voted to make up the difference to cover the cost of taking down the tree if the fundraiser did not bring in enough money for the entire expense.

But that was not necessary. Brandon called the next day and gave me incredible news. In two weeks, the community raised five dollars more than the amount I needed to remove the tree.

Through tears of gratitude, I shared the news on Facebook. The post read: "I just got the official word that enough money was raised through the fundraiser to cover the entire cost of removing the tree from my back yard. I am completely overwhelmed by the generosity of people, some who didn't even know me, who contributed in order to meet this need. I cannot even begin to explain the impact that this kindness has had in my life. I am abundantly blessed!"

One response stuck with me. My friend Katharine said, "That is great news on many levels. The tree is one. Your feeling loved is another."

This act of kindness by one of my best friends had some unexpected outcomes. The main goal of removing the tree in my yard was accomplished, but in the process I felt the compassion and caring of my community surrounding me in ways I never had before. I learned that I don't always have to handle things in my life on my own. It's not only okay to ask for help, but also to draw strength from others when I don't have much strength left.

Several weeks later, I was back in the dance studio with Brandon. The music we were dancing to swelled in the background, and after several attempts, we successfully executed the complicated dance move he had suggested a few weeks previously. Raising his hand to give me a high-five, he said with a smile, "See, Lorraine, I told you it would all work out."

He was right.

~Lorraine Cannistra

45

The Escape

Courage is being scared to death...
and saddling up anyway.
~John Wayne

The wobble in my legs was so severe it was a struggle to press the gas pedal. No matter how hard I worked to push away the events of the last several hours, they kept creeping back. The gun, the screaming, the crying. Overwrought and numb, I pulled onto the interstate. I had no destination in mind besides going somewhere my husband could never find me. That meant not heading to friends or family. With my two girls in the back seat, I followed the freeway in the opposite direction, leaving the city as far behind as possible.

I pulled off in Council Bluffs, Iowa, searching for a place to settle for the night. The only things on this exit were a gas station and a church surrounded by cornfields. After a brief hesitation, I slid into a parking space in the crowded church parking lot. I remembered my friend Polly's advice when we left Kansas City. "Go to the churches! They will help you!"

I scanned the parking lot for signs of danger. I swallowed hard, breathed a prayer for help, and said: "Come on, girls, let's go."

I stepped through the door with shaky legs as another wave of tremors coursed through me. A hand gripped my elbow before I succumbed to the panic. An elderly gentleman pulled me aside into an adjoining room, and I heard him tell someone to "go get Pam."

By this point, I was feeling foolish for coming here, as I was incapable of uttering a simple sentence. A lady hurried into the room, swinging the door wide. She paused for a second, and then walked straight toward me. As she drew me into her arms, she proclaimed, "Someone has hurt your heart!" She radiated love, peace, and a sensation of calm, and at her encouragement, my story spilled out. I told her how my husband had held us at gunpoint for hours, terrorizing us, refusing to let us leave, threatening to shoot me first, then my daughters.

Bewildered and in disbelief, I strove to comprehend the personality change he'd undergone. The man I'd married would never act this way. Since he'd lost his job, he'd become a complete stranger.

I confessed that I had no particular destination and asked her to recommend an inexpensive motel. Pam leaned back and looked me square in the eye. "You'll not spend the night in a motel room," she declared. "You're coming home with me!"

I blinked in astonishment and stammered, "But I have two daughters!"

"Don't worry about space; we have plenty of room." She turned and appealed to the man standing behind her. "Russ, tell her we have plenty of room."

He stepped forward, extending his hand. "Hi, I'm Russ. I'm Pam's husband, and I want you to know that you and your girls are welcome to stay with us. Don't worry you'll be putting someone out. You won't. We have a huge house."

Pam put her arm around my shoulders and steered me toward the door. "Why don't we go find your girls, and we'll go home so you can get settled in for the night. Have you eaten?"

"Yes, we stopped at Taco Bell earlier."

"Okay. Are those your girls over there?" She pointed to my daughters sitting with two blond girls close in age.

"Yes, those are mine."

Pam and I collected our children and went outside to meet Russ in the parking lot. I followed them to a sprawling two-story house. They provided me with a bedroom of my own, and my girls an alcove they used for TV watching. Soon, everyone settled in, and minutes later I was telling my girls goodnight. This resembled a dream. It surely couldn't be real. People don't open their doors to complete strangers and set them up in their houses, do they?

In the coming weeks, I found out they do. At least, some do. Over the next few days, Pam spent hours talking with me, listening as I relived the events of that night. I explained that my husband had always been an alcoholic, but he'd never been violent before. The man I once trusted with my life now terrified me. She shared her own stories of growing up with an alcoholic father.

There was an ease with Pam that I'd rarely had with anyone else. She instinctively seemed to know when I needed to be alone, yet was always available if I wanted to talk. She hugged me, laughed with me, and cried with me. One day, she laughed and said, "He has no idea where you are. He wouldn't know where to search for you."

Her confidence broke through the fog of trepidation, dread, and apprehension that surrounded me. The fear, anxiety, and tremors diminished, and I could turn my thoughts to the future. I turned my attentions back to the care of my daughters and providing them a home. Pam helped me navigate an unfamiliar town, enroll my girls in school, and locate a new job. Russ took me to shop for apartments. They took my girls swimming with them on the weekends. I stayed in Pam and Russ's home over three weeks, and their generosity and support never flagged.

Moving day was momentous. I found the prospect of life as a single mother daunting. Life in the city had left me cynical and mistrustful. Most of the time, I didn't even trust myself. I was nervous being on my own. What if I messed up? When I confided my fears to Pam, she gave me this advice: "Trust your gut. That little voice, that feeling you get… listen to it." Could it be that simple?

It wasn't easy those first few weeks. There were bumps and mishaps as we adjusted to our new life.

But due to the love and generosity of strangers, I was learning to trust again. Pam and Russ lived their life with such grace, and I became determined to emulate their example. I vowed to be more optimistic, courageous, and trusting. To extend my hand when I see a need. And to teach my daughters to do the same.

I took Pam's advice and learned to trust my gut. I found that whatever situation I find myself in, it's best to stop, take a breath, and listen. And it's never steered me wrong. It's something I might never have learned were it not for the kindness of strangers.

~Karen Cooper

46

Circle of Kindness

*I learned that courage was not the absence of fear, but
the triumph over it. The brave man is not he who does
not feel afraid, but he who conquers that fear.*
~Nelson Mandela

The instant I put down the phone, I regretted my decision. I'd just promised my daughter Karin that I would fly from northern Minnesota to Chicago to spend Thanksgiving with her family and my two sons. While I was on the phone, I was excited. Then, one minute later, I was terrified.

Soon, things got worse. Karin called back. "I got a good deal on your ticket, Mom. You fly out of Duluth at 6:00 a.m. and then change planes in Minneapolis."

Change planes?

The airplane trip scared me for two reasons. My late husband Ernie wouldn't fly, so I hadn't been on a plane for many years. Secondly, Ernie had only died three months ago and my grief had truly damaged my memory. My doctor assured me it would come back, but right now I had difficulty performing routine tasks and I got lost easily.

I couldn't face my empty bed unless I took a sleeping pill, and I caught every bug that came within a one-hundred-mile radius.. During the last seven months of my husband's illness, my main contact with the world outside our forty isolated acres was by e-mail. When he was able to sleep for an hour or two, I would write to our friends and family sharing little stories about our struggle. Two of the friends on this list,

Frannie and Larry, were neighbors we'd known for only a short time.

After Ernie's death, Frannie, a teacher, used her precious Saturdays to stop in and check on me. She'd haul me off to the farmers' market or invite me to a local concert. Above all, she listened without judging.

I was supposed to fly the day before Thanksgiving. The television increased my panic, reminding everyone that Wednesday was always the worst travel day of the year. On Tuesday, Frannie stopped in on her way home from work. I confessed that I'd promised to go to Karin's, but then, to my horror, I burst into tears. My new friend listened, hugged me patiently, and hurried home. I scolded myself. *Lou, you are going to ruin that friendship. You have to stop being so honest.*

A few minutes later, my phone rang. It was Frannie. "Lou, Larry will pick you up at 4:00 a.m. He'll drive you to the airport and help you check in."

I started a weak protest.

Frannie continued firmly, "Don't argue." She hung up.

As promised, Larry knocked at my door at 4:00 a.m. At the ticket desk, the harried clerk quickly checked my driver's license, and then moved me on to a check-in computer. Ignoring the confused look on my face, she turned to the next person.

The computer refused to cooperate. Larry studied the problem and then typed in the information it asked for. Once we were past that hurdle, Larry explained how to get through security.

My fears took over again as I sat waiting for my plane. A confident young mother with a teenage daughter, a new baby, and a busy toddler sat next to me.

She smiled. "My husband has to work, so the children and I are going to spend Thanksgiving with my parents in France."

"You're going alone?" I was astonished.

She looked so confused by my surprise that I felt I had to explain. Again, I was embarrassed. "I'm just going to Chicago, and I'm scared. My husband just died, and my memory won't work."

To my surprise, she hugged me. Then she pointed to her teenage daughter. "When she was six months old, my first husband was killed in a car accident. I couldn't function. I had to live with my parents for more than a year before I was ready to be on my own."

My new friend and I talked until I boarded the plane. Then, as I sat quietly in my seat, another worry hit me. I turned to the man next to me, already buried in his book. I felt foolish. "Excuse me, sir. I'm sorry to bother you. My husband just died, and my memory isn't working very well. Would you help me remember to take my things out of the overhead compartment when we land?"

He smiled. "I'd be happy to. My mother was so distraught when my dad died, she never would have attempted a trip by herself."

His kind words gave me confidence. We talked all the way to Minneapolis, and then he walked me across the airport to the gate for my next connection

Fear didn't hit again until I stepped off the plane in Chicago. Karin had told me to meet her in front of the airport. I hadn't been prepared for the size of O'Hare. My knees shaking, I started down the escalator wondering how I would find my bag and my daughter.

At that moment, I heard a child's voice yelling, "Grandma Lou!" Once again, I was saved.

Our Thanksgiving visit was wonderful but, before I knew it, it was airport time.

My busy son-in-law took the time to help me check in. Then, more panic. I turned to the man sitting next to me and asked for help. He nodded. Next, he told me that his wife's twin sister had just died. Throughout our flight, and all the way to my next gate, he talked of his wife's pain. When we parted, he reached for my hand. "Thank you for listening," he said. "I needed to talk."

Now, instead of panic, I felt joy.

On my final flight, the woman next to me sat staring at the window. Then her shoulders began to shake.

"Excuse me," I said, gently touching her arm. "Can I help?"

"No."

She was quiet for a while, and then said, "Sorry. I didn't mean to be rude. My husband died last month, and I don't want to return to my empty house."

I passed on one of the many hugs I'd received on my journey.

She wept harder. Then I told her about my husband's death, and we shared our stories.

"Thank you," she said. "This is the first time I've talked about my pain. I thought it would make things worse, but it helped."

When I got off the plane, I told Larry about my amazing conversations.

He didn't seem surprised. "Your courage in sharing your fears created a circle of kindness. When you open your heart, life gives you what you need."

Openness creates kindness?

The years have shown me that Larry was right. Today, I'm happily remarried, have traveled extensively, became a certified grief counselor, and started a grief support group at my church in sunny Florida.

And every time I'm brave enough to open my heart, I find a new circle of kindness.

~Lou Zywicki Prudhomme

47

The American Thing to Do

All great change in America begins at the dinner table.
~President Ronald Reagan

H e stood by the entrance of the grocery store looking ragged and weary. His clothes were dirty and tattered. His beard needed to be trimmed, and his long, greasy hair was sticking out underneath an old black ball cap that said "Vietnam Veteran."

I'm ashamed to admit that I only noticed him because there were three teenage boys harassing him. They were calling him names and telling him to get a job. One of the boys knocked the hat off his head. I walked over, picked it up and handed it back to the man. The boys scattered the moment I intervened. I had given them my best angry mom scowl. The man gave me a shy smile and put his hat back on his head. Immediately, I noticed how frail and thin he looked. He asked me if I had a couple of dollars to spare. Unfortunately, I always use my debit card, and I didn't have any cash on me.

I started to walk away, but something inside me made me go back. I asked him if he was hungry. He looked at me puzzled. I told him that I lived a block away. We were having a barbecue, and I would love for him to join us. He stared at me in disbelief. I promised him that I wouldn't hurt him and told him that I just thought he could use a hot meal. He joked that most people were afraid he would hurt them. He tried to turn down my offer, but I persisted, and eventually he got into my car. He told me that his name was Joe, and I told him that my name was Tiffany. After that, we sat in silence for the three minutes it took to drive to my house.

When I parked the car, he still looked a little uneasy. He insisted on carrying my groceries into the back yard. My husband was standing at the grill, and my sons were running around in the grass with their friends. Everyone stopped to look at my dinner guest. Joe clammed up and stood there uncertainly at the gate. I beckoned to him to come and meet my husband. My husband told him to make himself comfortable, so Joe set down the groceries and had a seat at our picnic table. He asked if there was anything he could do to help. I told him to just relax and brought him a glass of lemonade.

My younger son immediately came up to the picnic table, sat down and started to ask Joe a bunch of questions. He wanted to know his name, his favorite color, if he had any kids, what his hat said, and if he liked hamburgers or hot dogs better. My son never asked him about his appearance. Kids overlook things like that. In the kitchen, my husband questioned me about where I had found my new friend. I told him what had happened, and he agreed that Joe probably needed a hot meal.

When the food was done, everyone squeezed around the picnic table. The children continued to ask Joe questions, and he seemed genuinely happy to answer them. He told them how he had three sons who were all grown up now. He told them about a tire swing he had set up for his sons when they were the same age as they were. As he ate and talked, his uneasiness lifted. He really appeared to be enjoying himself, and everyone at the table was enjoying his company. I noticed him jump when a trashcan got knocked over by the neighbor's dog, and he avoided being touched by other people as much as possible. When everyone was done eating, he helped carry dirty plates into the house and thanked us for having him over for dinner.

He told us that he needed to leave and started to walk out the door. My husband told him to wait. He went and made a backpack with some clean clothes and food. He brought it to Joe. When Joe looked inside, he started to cry and told us that he couldn't take it. He said that we had already been so kind by sharing a meal with him, and he didn't want to take advantage of us. My husband insisted that he take the backpack. Joe thanked us again. I offered him a ride, and he turned it down. He said that it was such a beautiful summer night that he really would rather walk. Joe walked out the gate and into the night, and we never saw him again.

Friends and family members were horrified that I invited a homeless man to our home for dinner. They told me that he probably had some sort of mental illness, and he might come back and rob and kill us. In reality, he was a very nice man who for some reason was down on his luck. I believe that one of the most wonderful things about America is that there are so many people who feel a sense of community. They help other people when they are down, simply because it is the right thing to do. All the time, I see people doing random acts of kindness — paying for the coffee of the person in line behind them or putting change in an expired meter to help someone avoid a parking ticket.

My favorite holiday movie is *It's a Wonderful Life* because I love how the community bands together to help George Bailey. Things like that still happen all over America. Communities work together to help families stay out of foreclosure when a neighbor's child is going through cancer treatments. Strangers will pay for diapers for a single mother when she comes up short of money at the grocery store. And amazing men in uniforms put their lives on the line every day to protect people they have never met before. The kindness and compassion of the American spirit can't be beaten by fear, cynicism, and hatred. Even when bad things happen, we rise up together and continue to help each other — because that is the American way.

~Tiffany O'Connor

48

Turn-About Thanksgiving

Tell me and I forget, teach me and I may
remember, involve me and I learn.
~Benjamin Franklin

My daughter, Katie, was in third grade when she became an American. Oh, she may have been a legally born citizen for nine years, but this was when her heart became quintessentially "American."

Katie's class had been studying the Pilgrims and how they had only survived through the friendship of the Native Americans. My daughter was fascinated by how the Wampanoag people had taught the English how to use fish as fertilizer and grow native corn. Her imagination was stirred by the additional suffering and hardship averted by this act of kindness from the original Americans. She also learned Thanksgiving was a feast of appreciation that we repeat every year in honor of this act of kindness.

To celebrate their studies, the class was going to create their own Thanksgiving feast and had agreed to try some of the recipes from that first celebration. Katie and her best friend, Vera, were on a team together. Their job was to make corn on the cob. Best friends since kindergarten, they were a study in opposites. Vera was a tiny, black-haired beauty with dark eyes and a rich, brown complexion.

Katie was tall and blond, reflecting her English heritage, with hazel eyes and golden skin.

As the girls worked, talk turned to family feasts and what everyone was doing for Thanksgiving. Vera was silent in class, but later confessed that her mom "wasn't sure" about Thanksgiving.

Vera's mother had come from Mexico and was part Native American. After working as a veterinary assistant for decades to raise her large family as a single mom, Vera's mother was going blind, had consequently lost her job, and was struggling to provide for her youngest three kids. Decades of giving to others and sharing all she had had created a large network of supporters who felt honored to give back to this remarkable woman and her children. But despite their help and her church's help, times were hard. Vera confided in Katie that not only would she not be having a feast for Thanksgiving, but she might not even be eating.

Katie was appalled and came home determined to do something about it. She emptied her piggybank while her sister and brother chipped in as they could. Too often our family had been the recipients of others' charity; now it was our turn to give back.

We bought a turkey and fixings for mashed potatoes, gravy, stuffing, and sweet potatoes. In honor of their class project, we bought corn on the cob. We baked pumpkin pies and made cranberry sauce.

The Wednesday before Thanksgiving, I made our family feast (except the turkey), packed it in aluminum tins and stacked it all in the refrigerator.

Thanksgiving morning, we were all up at the crack of dawn to create a new feast for Vera's family. We put their turkey in to bake and began making all the sides so they would be warm and fresh.

With her brother, sister and me, Katie directed the cooking as we sang and danced and played in the kitchen, so pleased at the wonderful surprise we were preparing for Vera's family.

"You know what's funny?" Katie asked as we chopped and measured and stirred.

"No, what?" I asked.

"It's turn-about," she said.

"What do you mean?"

"Well, the Native Americans helped the English Pilgrims on Thanksgiving, right?" Katie ventured.

"Right…"

"Well, now the English get to help the Native Americans!" Kate said, laughing at her own joke.

Soon, we had beans and corn, sweet and mashed potatoes, pie and cranberry sauce all packaged up and smelling of sweetness, spices, and love. The beautiful, hot turkey was centered on a plastic platter and surrounded by carrots and onions. We'd replaced Vera's turkey in the oven with our own and set it to roasting while we headed over to Katie's friend's house.

Everything had been put in cardboard boxes so we could play a game of "Ding-Dong Dash" to deliver it. And, with her brother and sister, Katie quietly sneaked up to Vera's door, going around the side of the house so as not to be seen from the picture window in the living room, and silently set the boxes on the stoop.

Her brother and sister circled back and got into the car. We started the engine with the passenger door open so that Katie could jump in, and we could drive off.

Then Katie looked to the car for the "high-sign" that we were ready to go. She'd been hunched down on the stoop to make sure no one could see her standing at the door.

As we signaled, Katie reached up, rang the bell—and ran! She jumped in the car, and off we drove. Just as we turned the corner, Katie's brother called out, "They've opened the door!"

And our deed was done.

We never told a soul. And, in fact, I changed Vera's name here so as to not give us away.

When Vera came back to school, she did ask Katie if she knew anything about her special delivery.

"How could we help you, Vera?" Katie replied. "You know we can barely take care of ourselves."

And, with that, Vera dropped it.

But what I can't drop is what happened to my daughter that day.

For that was the day she exhibited all the best traits of Americans — caring, compassion, loyalty, resourcefulness, and kindness… above all else, kindness.

Yes, Katie may have been born a citizen, but it was on Thanksgiving of her ninth year that my child really, truly became an American.

~Susan Traugh

49

Dinner and a Movie

Here are the values that I stand for: honesty, equality,
kindness, compassion, treating people the way you
want to be treated and helping those in need. To
me, those are traditional values.
~Ellen DeGeneres

Katrina crammed through the front door of our brick ranch home. Her arms were wrapped around three large foil baking trays and she had grocery bags hanging from her elbows the way pears dangle from tree limbs.

I didn't really know Katrina. She was an old friend of my wife's. They hadn't spoken in years, but she instant-messaged my wife one evening and asked if she could cook dinner for us and our three daughters. She even listed a few menus to choose from.

Her gesture was unexpected.

She explained that after suffering a miscarriage and then losing her job at a local private college due to a funding shortage, she had decided to perform one act of kindness a week to pull herself through a time of darkness and grief.

She insisted the purpose for her offer was actually selfish.

"If I can stay focused on others, I don't have time to crawl on my couch and cry," Katrina wrote.

Although it is human nature to feel good when we do something nice for others, I felt there was more to her kindness than that. She could have chosen some other form of distraction, like scheduling a massage three times a week, taking an art class, or another type of solitary and self-serving activity to combat the depression of her circumstances. Nothing is wrong with any of those choices. Instead, she chose to do good deeds for others. In and of itself, her choice was selfless.

She chose our family to receive this act of kindness for the week because she had heard of our struggles to find acceptance in our community as a two-mom family. My family is unique in our corner of Kentucky. Word spread that our daughters were being bullied at school. One was called gay slurs. Another was told that her moms would one day be kicked out of the country for being lesbians. Like our children, my wife and I had also been taunted, ranging from being told that we should go "back into the closet" to that we deserved to die.

Although such harsh words did not weaken our family's strength and bond, they did make us feel unwanted, unloved, and hopeless. We didn't know if we would ever be allowed to live peacefully while shuttling our daughters to afterschool activities, enjoying dinners around the table in our warm home, and going about our lives that same way as other American families.

Katrina sought to inject some positivity back into our lives with her perfectly baked and seasoned spaghetti, cheesy garlic bread, side salad, and cheesecake topped with caramel on a cookies-and-cream-crust dessert. She had even thought to supply us with paper plates to minimize the cleanup afterward. As if dinner weren't enough, Katrina surprised us with gift cards to the movies so we could enjoy a night out together. She refused to stay and eat with us, insisting that we deserved time together as a family.

"I really wanted you all to know that there are people who care," she wrote of her reason for choosing us. "My faith is deep, and the God I serve says the greatest commandment is to love your neighbors as yourself."

I, too, was raised to believe that this was God's greatest wish, and my belief to treat all humankind with love, respect, and equality drives so much of who I am. I do not see people on levels or in categories by status, wealth, health, age, race, religion, or any of society's other invisible boxes in which we place each other. This belief factored into my decision to slowly pull away from my community because I was finding it harder and harder to continue exuding love and respect living among people who did not return either. The return I received instead was intolerance and, sometimes, far worse.

But the night Katrina made us dinner, I watched as our kids smiled and ate, discussed how great everything tasted, and asked if we could hang out with Katrina and her family soon. After we dined, we sent Katrina a note thanking her again for cooking our family a tasty meal, and for showing us such kindness and love.

"Please don't quit giving some people the opportunity to get to know you all," she wrote in response. "You have a beautiful family, and your girls are precious. Please don't hide in fear. Show the world the love and happiness that you all have as a family!"

Katrina's words and act of love renewed my spirit and sense of belonging in our community. She taught me that by extending the love and bond of my family, we can help heal not only our own broken hearts, but also the cracks in the hearts of others.

~Mary Anglin-Coulter

50

The Gift of Wisdom

Be a gift to everyone who enters your life, and
to everyone whose life you enter.
~Neale Donald Walsch

I was twenty-nine, single, and had never lived on my own. Right after college, I'd moved into a house off campus with a dozen of my closest friends. The rent was cheap, and there were other advantages, like learning how to cook a three-course dinner for twenty people in less than two hours, or how to agree on a paint color for the kitchen when everyone had a different opinion.

But there were drawbacks. I was working as a freelance writer, and it was difficult to get work done with all the noise that living with so many people entails. Plus, I'm an introvert. Other single people fantasize about coming home to a partner and a warm meal. I fantasized about coming home to an empty house.

I looked at my financials and realized I could move out on my own if I wanted to. I was making just enough to cover rent on a one-bedroom apartment, plus other monthly expenses. Hopefully, the added quiet would help me write — and earn — more.

But I'd have to do without much furniture for a while. The only pieces I had to my name were those that fit in my bedroom — a bed, desk, chair, and dresser — and I couldn't blow a lot of money on stuff for the apartment up front. Most of my reserves were going to the security deposit and basics like knives and forks.

That was fine, I told myself. I'd just have to set aside a little each month and furnish the place as I went. Packing crates could do double-duty as a kitchen table until I saved up enough to buy one. I just wouldn't be able to invite anyone over for dinner, unless they were okay with sitting on the floor.

"Wait," a friend said to me one Sunday after church. "You're a writer, and you don't own a bookshelf?"

I shook my head. The bedroom I'd had for the past few years had a built-in. All the books I'd kept on those shelves would have to stay in their moving boxes for a while.

My friend's eyes lit up like a bulb had just turned on in her head. "You know, I have an old one I'm not really using. It's yours if you want it. And I bet other people have stuff they could give if you asked. You could post something to the church e-mail list."

"Maybe," I said.

"Too proud to ask for help?" she said with a knowing smile. "I have that problem, too."

I laughed. I sent an e-mail out a couple days later, but didn't expect much response.

The next Sunday after church, a longtime member named Sandy tapped me on the shoulder. "Can you come to the fellowship hall for a minute? I need help with something."

I said "yes" without giving it much thought. A potluck was scheduled for that week. I assumed she wanted help setting up chairs.

"I saw your e-mail about moving," Sandy said as we walked toward the hall. "Do you still need stuff for your apartment?"

"Not really," I said, trying to be stoic about it. I thought I should be more like the lilies of the field I'd taught my Sunday school kids about — the ones that don't worry about clothing or shelter, but do just fine anyway. "I have the furniture I need to sleep and do work. That's the most important thing."

"Do you at least have stuff so you can cook?" she said.

I blushed. "Not yet. I guess I'll have to do a little shopping once I move."

"Or not." She smiled mischievously as she pushed on the fellow-ship hall's door.

"Surprise!" Several dozen voices shouted in unison as the door swung open. I looked at Sandy in confusion. Apparently, there was a surprise party being thrown for her that I'd forgotten about.

But then I got a closer look at the room. Two of the long tables usually reserved for potlucks were piled neatly with assorted necessities of apartment living: toasters and dish racks, towels and sink scrubbers still in the package, pots and pans, brand-new shower curtains and measuring spoons. Next to the tables sat various pieces of furniture: a table, rocking chair, TV stand, kitchen stools, and more.

"Happy apartment-warming!" someone said, stepping out of the crowd. "It's all for you."

I turned to Sandy in shock. "I can't take all of this."

"You don't have to. Just decide what you want, and we'll set it aside for someone to bring over the day you move in. Anything you don't want, we'll give to other folks who need it. Enjoy your shopping!"

A kid I'd taught in Sunday school ran over with an empty Macy's bag. "Go on. Fill 'er up!" Then he led me over to the table and pointed out a rubber duckie he'd asked his mom to buy for me.

I smiled so wide that the muscles around my ears started to hurt. I couldn't believe that people would have gone to all this effort just for me. As much as I'd shrugged it off, the prospect of furnishing an apartment from scratch had been daunting. I'd lost sleep worrying about the finances of it as well as the logistics. It was such a relief not to have to worry about it anymore.

And I felt incredibly loved. I might be moving out on my own, but I still had a community of people I could rely on.

"I can't believe you guys would do all this for me," I said to one of the men who had helped haul in the furniture.

"I just carried furniture," he said. "It was really Sandy's idea."

I was perplexed. I had known Sandy for a while and I liked her, but we'd never been very close. We were from different generations, and our social circles didn't really overlap. We mostly just said hello to each other at church. It touched me that she would go to such lengths for someone she barely knew.

I found Sandy and gave her a hug. "I keep trying to thank people, but they say it was all you."

Sandy shrugged it off. "Oh, all I did was shoot off a few e-mails." She explained that she'd been at home that week recovering from the flu, and she'd started to go stir-crazy with boredom. When she saw my e-mail, she decided to pass the time by organizing the surprise apartment warming for me. "I could be sick and still feel productive," she said. "So really, it's your gift to me."

That apartment became a sanctuary to me. Even though I lived alone, I never felt alone. The friendship of others was always present in tangible ways, from the rubber duckie in my shower to the toaster oven where I heated my dinner.

But maybe the more important gift was the wisdom Sandy had shared with me: Sometimes, the best way to help yourself is to make life a little easier for someone else.

~Kathryn Kingsbury

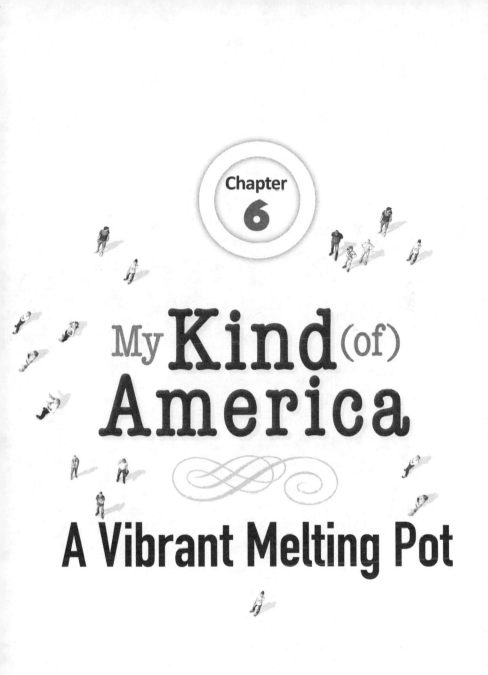

Chapter
6

My Kind (of)
America

A Vibrant Melting Pot

51

Ode to Buffalo

The best way to predict your future is to create it.
~President Abraham Lincoln

My boyfriend and I were talking about getting married. I was crazy about this man, and now we were planning a life together. "We need to talk about something that's very important to me," Vishal said seriously. "It's about the way we raise our kids."

We were both spiritual people, but not terribly religious. I was raised Catholic, and he was Hindu. I did want to baptize our future children, and I hoped that he would be supportive. I was a touch concerned about the impending conversation.

"It would really mean a lot to me if we could raise our children to be... Buffalo Bills fans."

"Wait, what?" I asked.

"I'm not joking. Buffalo all the way."

"You're serious? This is your important talk?"

"Totally."

"Ummmm, okay? Can I baptize them?"

"Sure. We can teach them about Hinduism, too, though, right?"

"Of course."

That settled that. A decade of marriage and two sons later, we have both made good on our compromises. Despite living in solid New York Giants country, my husband has season tickets to Bills games, and during away games, our special-order cable sports channel is on the ready so he and our boys can tune in. "Let's-Go-Buff-a-lo," echoes through my house.

Vishal is truly one of a kind. He immigrated to Buffalo from India when he was four years old. There were several reasons why his parents chose to do so, but chief among them was care for his disabled older sister, Anjali. She has cerebral palsy and is deaf due to G6PD deficiency, a genetic disorder. If she were born here in America, she would have probably received a blood transfusion and been fine. In India, they thought she had a case of yellow fever, and her mother watched her newborn daughter drift away each day.

St. Mary's School for the Deaf in Buffalo, New York changed her life. Vishal and his family learned sign language, and Anjali excelled. However, their mother worked tirelessly to care for her, Vishal, and Vishal's younger sister.

His father started an imported auto parts business, which failed and left him bankrupt. They were poor. When Vishal was in middle school, he took on a paper route to help support the family.

Despite all that his family suffered, his memories are happy. He recalls his family sitting around the TV shouting for the Bills while his mother cooked Indian food. There weren't many Indian kids who lived in his public housing project. He didn't have much in common with the American boys, but the Bills connected him to his classmates and community. Their sports team transcended class, racial, and religious differences. Vishal wasn't the foreign Indian kid. He was a Bills fan.

He was also valedictorian of P.S. 81. His parents pushed him to excel, as many hungry immigrant families do. His dad often recited, "Standing at the foot of the mountain, looking up at the sky, how will you ever get there my dear boy, if you don't try?" There was a fire in his belly, and it sparked in Vishal. His parents knew he was special; they believed in him. Vishal understood that his shot in America would be through his education.

He won a work scholarship to Canisius High School, the premier boys' private school in Buffalo. After his classmates went home for the day, he would mop the floors with the custodians. When Vishal told me these stories of sacrifice as a kid, my heart sank for him. But he always assured me that they provided him with everything he needed to learn in life: hard work, the value of education, and the knowledge that there is always a way and you can never give up.

This all coincided with the time the Bills made it to the Super Bowl a record-breaking four times in row. Just when everyone thought they were done, they would claw their way back. The spirit of hope, hard work, and faith in a team saturated the city of Buffalo.

Once, Vishal mustered up enough money for a nosebleed seat in the back of the stadium. That game happened to be when the Bills beat the Oilers for the biggest comeback in NFL history, advancing them in the playoffs. They were so far behind that people started leaving. The stadium was empty, but Vishal stayed. Perhaps because that ticket was such a treasure, he stayed and witnessed that miracle game. That teenager, in the back of the stadium had something planted in his soul that day. He never, ever stops believing in what is possible.

Vishal attended the General Motors Institute (now Kettering University), an engineering college in Flint, Michigan. He chose GMI in part because it operated on a quarterly system, one of which allowed for paid work experience. When Vishal's fraternity brothers were partying, he was studying. He had a big dream to attend Harvard Business School.

He wanted to apply as a senior in college. He met with a Harvard admissions counselor, who advised him not to apply that way. She told him he had "no chance" of getting accepted. They wanted a few years of work experience first. But Vishal felt he had already gained that experience through the work quarters. That fire in his belly was stoked ("standing at the foot of the mountain..."). He applied for immediate acceptance.

The application for Harvard Business School involved a series of essays. He included the story of his disabled sister, Anjali, in one of them. Again, an advisor warned him not to, saying it was too personal. But Vishal, like the 1991 Bills holding hands on the sideline for that final infamous kick that lost them the Super Bowl, was all heart. He wasn't ashamed of that heart; it was his power ("looking up at the sky..."). He included the essay.

This time, the winds of fate blew in favor for Buffalo. He got in! He was one of the youngest students to be accepted in his entire class. His fifty-two-year-old mother passed away from cancer when Vishal was just twenty-one years old. She died knowing her son got into Harvard. He would have to take out more than $100,000 in student loans ("how will you ever get there, my dear boy…"), but he bet on himself.

Vishal has made *Barron's* "America's Top Financial Advisors" list five times ("if you don't try…"). He's made the *Financial Times* list twice. He is a major charitable donor supporting organizations for people with special needs, cancer research, and education. He is in a prime position to grow his business, but instead he chose to restrict his client list. He is loyal to the people who signed with him on his way up—those who believed in him. He could easily take on more, but he would rather focus on them and our family. Now, he's the one cooking us dinner, yelling at the Bills game on TV!

So, thank you to the city that never gives up for being a key ingredient in the recipe for an American dream. It was the perfect storm. Let's-Go-Buff-a-lo!

~Kelly Bakshi

52

Truly America

*What is shared in common is infinitely more
significant than what apparently divides.*
~Dave Mearns

It was the first time my mother dragged me to her work — but only because it was the first time I ran out of excuses. As a sixth grader, I was already upset that I had to spend my Saturday afternoon in the basement of a church instead of hanging out with my friends. I never really understood the nature of my mother's work beyond the fact that she was called an "interfaith activist." To me, it was just a label. But little did I know that it would change my outlook on life.

As I lugged posters from our car down the old church stairs, I saw my mother already eagerly placing chairs in a circle. She set up the posters containing information about various religions around the circle of chairs. Like a machine, she did all this work within seconds, while keeping a huge smile on her face. Her excitement got me curious. I wondered, *Who are these chairs for? Why are there so many posters about different religions I have vaguely heard of?* A few minutes later, I heard the sound of the basement stairs creak and got the answers to my questions.

The chairs were meant for teenagers and young adults of various faiths and backgrounds. I sat in awe as I observed the room full of teenage boys wearing turbans and yarmulkes, and women and men wearing traditional clothing. I was surprised to see everyone confidently take a seat within the circle, and I was even more shocked to see my mother getting ready to start a conversation among this diverse group of people.

My mother began by asking everyone to introduce themselves. It was a bit awkward, as everyone, one by one, recited their name, school, and age in a monotone pattern. I was worried that the rest of the time would be just as dull. However, my mother then proceeded to ask us to stand by the poster we identified with most closely. Everyone got up immediately, running in different directions. I stood by the poster that read "Islam" and was greeted with warm smiles from others standing there, too. I saw others standing by posters with the words "Sikh," "Judaism," "Hinduism," "Catholicism," etc. Then we were instructed to break into smaller groups, with each group having individuals from various faiths. My mother instructed us all to share the knowledge we had about our religion with the members of our groups. The room went from silent to loud, as everyone started asking questions and actively engaging. I was intrigued by the discussions of each religion, which made me eager to discuss Islam when it was my turn.

As we regrouped into the big circle of chairs, my mother asked us all to relay information that we gained about a new religion. I was proud to present what I learned about the Sikh faith and smiled when my fellow group member shared what she learned from me about Islam. My mother then asked us to share what we liked about our religion and some struggles we might face. We all realized as everyone went around the room that we shared even more commonalities than differences in our everyday struggles and experiences. In that moment, as I scanned the room and its diverse group of people, I saw what it meant to be an American.

This room not only represented people of different colors, but people of various backgrounds and religions who were able to look beyond their differences to discuss their everyday lives while sharing smiles and laughs. That Saturday afternoon, in the basement of a church, I was proud to be an American.

~Zehra Hussain

53

The American Team

America is a tune. It must be sung together.
~Gerald Stanley Lee

If we are fortunate enough to have good teachers, we discover at any early age why America is so great and unique among the world's nations. In elementary school, I had only a vague sense of this greatness from memorizing the names of our founding fathers, significant historical events, the names of documents, and so on. I knew America was special somehow, but the true magnitude and originality of what the founding fathers created didn't hit home for me until the seventh grade, thanks to a teacher by the name of Dr. Stock. He wasn't a history or political science teacher as one might expect; he was a Physical Education coach.

Dr. Stock was a kind and soft-spoken man with an easy laugh who usually stuck with the P.E. curriculum. But one sunny afternoon, he pulled us all away from a volleyball game fifteen minutes before class ended and asked us to sit down on a patch of grass near the court.

The Olympic Games were in full swing at the time, so he asked us what events we were most interested in. Everybody yelled out something different, of course. He then asked if we had noticed anything different about the American teams compared to the teams from other countries. We all looked at each other, as kids often do, wondering who was going to come up with the right answer. The fact that nobody did demonstrated how much we all took America's uniqueness for granted.

Dr. Stock smiled, waiting for the penny to drop, but it still didn't, so he looked at my friend sitting next to me and said, "Matt Moller, your last name is German." Then he looked at me and said, "Mark Rickerby, your last name is English." (Actually, my parents immigrated to America from Northern Ireland, but he was right: Their ancestors started out in Northern England.) He then looked at the boy on my left and said, "Jeff Napoli, your last name is Italian."

And on down the line he went…

"Sunti Singhanate, your last name is Thai. Rosaleen Andersen, your last name is Swedish or Danish. Alex Osorio, your name started in Spain, but from meeting your parents, I know they came here from Mexico." Alex smiled and nodded as the teacher continued through the rest of the class and covered just about every nationality under the sun.

He then looked at a black girl named Cindy Jackson and said, "Cindy, I wish I could say your ancestors came to America from Africa by choice, but they were brought here as slaves, and one of them was probably named after President Andrew Jackson."

Cindy said, "I know. My mama told me that."

This was a revelation to me. Until then, I had never made the connection between slavery and all the black kids named Jackson, Washington, Jefferson, etc. I liked Cindy and felt sad to know that the ancestors of such a nice girl had suffered so much. I also had never really thought much about the variety of racial and national backgrounds of my fellow students. They were just other kids to me. Having been born in America, I took our diversity for granted.

As I was lost in thought, Dr. Stock continued, "My last name is English, but my mother was from Poland. My point is that even though most of you were born here, your parents, or their parents, or some ancestor of yours you've never met, came here from somewhere else in search of a better life. Even our class here today represents Germany, England, Italy, Israel, Denmark, Mexico, Thailand, Africa, and many other countries. The same is true of our Olympic teams. But that's not the case if you look at the names of players on teams from other countries. The German players have German surnames, the Italian players have Italian surnames, and so on, with very few exceptions. We are a nation of immigrants, the great grandchildren of slaves, descendants of Native American tribes, and the sons and daughters of exhausted refugees, fleeing faraway places with nothing but a dream and the clothes on their backs. Our families all started out somewhere else, but we're all one team now, joined by the dream of a better life, a dream that America makes possible."

He looked at our young faces one by one and then asked, "Do you understand what I'm saying?" Again, we were silent. But this time, it wasn't a thoughtless silence. Our minds were swimming with what it meant to be American. He continued, "Let me ask you this: Considering everything I just told you, what word would you use to describe America?"

This is why he was such a good teacher. He knew how important it is to engage children, not just give lectures. Galileo said, "You cannot teach a man anything; you can only help him to find it within himself." If it's true of men, it must be doubly true of children.

Slowly, one by one, our hands went up. We said words like "unique," "original" and "revolutionary." He smiled, proud that we had understood his lesson. We were proud, too — some for the first time, like me, to know that we were part of such a wonderful place, that people flock to from every corner of the world to make dreams come true. We suddenly felt like we were all co-owners of Disneyland.

In my memory, I mark that day as the real beginning of my deep patriotism and love for America, and the knowledge of how very fortunate I was to be born in the greatest country mankind has ever conceived. Decades ago, one very wise but humble P.E. teacher succeeded in making the terms "melting pot" and "noble experiment" alive and personal for me, and I never again took for granted how lucky I am to be an American.

~Mark Rickerby

An Immigrant's Daughter

Prejudices are the chains forged by
ignorance to keep men apart.
~Countess of Blessington

I sat in a chaise lounge watching waves crash along Hawaii's Big Island coastline. Turning to my sister and brother-in-law, I said, "Dave and I are learning Spanish."

My husband Dave nodded and smiled from the pool where he floated on an inflatable mat.

"Really. Why?" Conversation came slowly and easily between my sister and me as she sipped her drink. I glanced out to sea and considered my reply. Multiple reasons enticed me to study another language, making it difficult to explain. I blinked, scenes from the morning spent downtown twinkling in my memory... the Portuguese man serving Scandinavian-style shaved ice, the African American woman selling Kona coffee, the Japanese server at the Italian restaurant where we enjoyed lunch. So many individuals working together, muddying nationalities and cultures to create an incredible mosaic of life.

Then I thought back to my childhood. I saw myself sitting in my mother's lap, every need met, unaware of the drama entwined within my family's roots. As I grew, I had no clue that another story waited beneath the surface, one filled with hardship.

Like many babies, I was unplanned. A late, but as my parents assured me, much adored surprise. Living within the glossy bubble of a childhood spent in 1960s California, I never imagined anything beyond sun and fun. But one day I'd asked my mother an adolescent girl's favorite question: "How did you and Daddy get together?" I'd expected the usual vague response, something involving moonlight and birdsong.

Instead, the answer Mom chose to share that evening was steeped in sadness. It wasn't the fairy tale I'd imagined — not by a long shot.

Maybe she considered me mature enough to hear the truth. I sat quietly, leaning closer on the old damask couch to grab every bit. Each scent, texture, and sound from that moment is ingrained in my memory.

She'd grown up in Germany in the 1920s. A bookkeeper for the local government when World War II broke out, she didn't support Hitler's regime. Because of their political leanings, her family was under constant watch by the Nazis. After the war, a wounded German soldier moved into the apartment below them.

My father, an American soldier, was stationed in Germany to take part in the de-Nazification process. His duties included keeping an eye on German ex-military, to make sure nothing was brewing beneath the surface.

One day, as my father was visiting with the soldier downstairs, Dad spotted my mom and sparks kindled. He tried to strike up a conversation with her, but since neither spoke the other's language, they struggled. Months passed, and through their painstaking efforts, friendship evolved into love. As soon as it was possible, they eagerly married and moved to America.

But the United States didn't accept her with open arms. Thousands and thousands of our men had died as a result of Hitler's murderous insanity. A lot of the people my parents encountered saw all Germans as culpable.

Yet there were a few who chose to forge friendship with her. They listened, really listened — not only to the words spoken, but also to those unspoken. They accepted my mother's differences and embraced them, from her cooking to her unique and earthy sense of humor. They forgave her for her country's sins. The kindness they showed helped my mother to find a place to fit into our society, her own way to belong and make a difference.

Years passed, and my mother taught herself how to read English. She felt confident enough to study for and receive her citizenship. As proud as I'd been of her prior to that time, my pride doubled.

Now, as a bicultural adult, I realize that my perspective is different from many of my friends. Wartime atrocities in my mother's native land shrouded her in unwarranted guilt that took her decades to overcome. But the post-war shunning she endured at the hands of my fellow Americans shames *me*.

I'm aware of the way those without a voice are treated and mistreated. Studying Spanish so I can better understand my new countrymen, I'm hoping to share in their joys and sorrows, and maybe replace bad memories with happier ones. Mom was proud to be a citizen. So am I. And I welcome every mother, father, and child who wants a seat on this kaleidoscopic ride.

As the daughter of an immigrant, I'm doubly blessed. I see both sides, and I know where I belong: right here in America.

~Heidi Gaul

55

Nine, Twelve, and Fourteen

*True friendship comes when the silence
between two people is comfortable.*
~David Tyson

Wheeling, Illinois, summer of 1997. It didn't seem that unusual when my mother told us a Somalian family was going to stay with us for a few weeks. My mother liked taking care of people. Not only did she make cookies for the school bake sale and help us with homework, but she also took in foster children from time to time. They'd stay for a few days, even a month, and then move on.

Like most fourteen-year-olds, I knew Somalia was a country in Africa where no one had food, but I couldn't point it out on a map. I asked my mom some questions about the whole situation, and I learned a few things:

- *The family consisted of five people: mother, father, and three kids — a little boy about five, and two girls about nine and twelve.*
- *They spoke mostly Arabic. The dad spoke a little English.*
- *No, I didn't have to share a room with the girls. They were all going to sleep in the guest room.*
- *Yes, she was positive I didn't have to share my room.*

A Vibrant Melting Pot | 203

When the family showed up, I watched them from down the hall. The father had a large mustache. He shook my stepfather's hand with a firm grip. The females had scarves covering their hair and necks. The little boy and nine-year-old girl clung to their mother's skirt, but the twelve-year-old girl peeked around at everything. She was scared, though. They were all scared.

I asked Mom about it later. She told me they were escaping a war in Somalia. Some of their family members had been killed, and they were scared for their lives. They ran away first to Russia, and then to America.

A few days after they arrived, I found myself in the living room trying not to make eye contact with the sisters. Mom had told me their names, but I didn't remember them, and I felt stupid asking. In my mind, the older one was Twelve, the younger was Nine. I didn't know what to say; I didn't speak their language anyway. I couldn't stop thinking about how hot they must be in long sleeves and headscarves in the summer. They sat on the floor next to each other, talking quietly. It was odd to me to see siblings who were so gentle with each other. My brother would yell at me if I put my pinkie on his side of the couch.

Mom told me they could use a friend and suggested that we all play a game together while she was in the kitchen doing kitchen things. I rooted through the pile of games in the corner, finally settling on *Connect Four*. I sat on the carpet by Twelve, dumped the box out in front of us, and started sorting the reds from the blacks. Twelve saw me sorting and shooed Nine away so she could help. Once we were done, I scooted in front of her, set up the stand, and dropped my first black piece in. She looked at the faded box cover, saw the illustration, and dropped in a red one.

We played for a few minutes, making patterns, until I made four in a row. I pointed with my finger and wordlessly counted one, two, three, four markers before hitting the switch to release them. Twelve looked at me with a gleam in her eye as I set up the game again. Nine scurried over and tried to push Twelve out of the way, but Twelve said something to her, and Nine sat down next to us, huffing. Nine watched very carefully as Twelve and I played another game. By the end of that second game, Nine kept pointing at places for Twelve to drop her chip. Sometimes, Twelve would put her piece there, sometimes not. After a third game, Nine scooted in to try. She wasn't as deliberate as Twelve, but she played with the enthusiasm and drive that only a nine-year-old can.

About a week into their stay, it was stiflingly hot. Twelve, Nine, and I had been chugging water while we played. After three games, I grabbed a ponytail holder and threw my hair up into a messy bun. Twelve nodded empathetically and carefully unwrapped her headscarf. She laid it on the floor next to her. Mom had told me they wore those scarves for modesty, so I felt awkward looking at her. I looked down and touched the scarf; it was lighter and more delicate than I thought. Twelve said something to Nine, and the sound of her voice made me look up. I saw her hair. It was... hair. There was nothing interesting about it, other than that it was hers, and she chose to share it with me. Nine also unwrapped her head and dumped her scarf on the ground next to her sister's. Twelve glared at her. Nine sighed and straightened it out, like making a bed.

An hour or so later, we heard keys scraping in the lock at the front door, most likely my brother coming home from summer school. Nine and Twelve took their scarves and gently wrapped them around their hair. They did it as smoothly and calmly as I put on socks.

When it was time for the family to leave, there wasn't much preparation or ceremony. As they pulled on their shoes, I gave my *Connect Four* game to Twelve. She looked down at the faded box cover for a few moments before reaching under her scarf and pulling out a barrette. It was a white and gold plastic clip with flowers all over it. Twelve pressed it gently into my palm and smiled at me. Her gesture said, *Thank you for being my friend.*

I clipped the barrette in my hair and smiled back.

~Lauren B. H. Rossato

56

Education for Everyone

*Education breeds confidence. Confidence
breeds hope. Hope breeds peace.*
~Confucius

"I have a student who needs a little extra help." The teacher at the charter school where I worked as a reading tutor looked at me with worried blue eyes.

"What's the problem?" I asked.

"It's her basic grammar skills. Her family has moved around so much that she's never really had the opportunity to learn things like what are verbs, nouns, pronouns — all those things other students learn in grade school. She told me she's embarrassed not to know what the class is talking about during English class. Would you work with her?"

Of course I said yes, and the next day Victoria appeared in the library where I tutored students. Pretty, with long black hair and huge dark eyes, Victoria looked nervous. Before tackling the basics of grammar, I tried to help her feel more comfortable by getting to know more about her and her journey so far.

Nineteen years old and a senior in high school, Victoria had been moved through the school system almost as much as her family had moved around the country. Born in Texas, Victoria and her parents followed seasonal jobs from the south to the Canadian border and east to Pennsylvania. When we met, Victoria and her parents were living in Minnesota. Her father was working at a small factory while her mother worked as the cleaning woman for the owner of the factory.

Victoria wanted nothing more than to get her high school diploma so she could work full-time and help her family. But she had a lot of ground to cover, and it was my job to help her.

I found some middle school–level grammar books, and Victoria and I got to work. As we studied grammar together, I learned more about her. Some of her stories made me smile, but some made me want to cry—like the story she told me about being targeted by a teacher as an example of a student who "couldn't" learn. Or the stories she told me about other students who assumed, since Victoria was Hispanic, that she was in the country illegally and should go back to the country they assumed she was born in.

"I was born in America," Victoria told me. "Why would anyone think I wasn't without bothering to ask me first?"

It was a good question, and I didn't have an answer. But as I worked with Victoria, I wondered how many times I'd made the same assumptions about people myself.

Victoria sailed through her assignments, and by the end of the school year, she was much more comfortable with grammar and high school literature. Together, we read some of the classics, including *A Tale of Two Cities*, our favorite. Although the book was set in Europe, Victoria told me it reminded her of America.

"There's more than one America," she commented when we finished the book. "There's really a lot of Americas just like there are a lot of Americans."

"What do you mean?" I asked.

Victoria thought for a moment before answering. "There's the America we see on TV where everyone looks the same and thinks the same way, like in an old movie. Then there's the America of now where we all look different and think different, but we don't really notice how different we are once we get to know each other."

I agreed with her. "And then the differences really don't seem to matter."

"Exactly," Victoria said with a smile.

The day Victoria graduated from high school was one I will never forget.

The girl selected to give the graduation speech had a last-minute moment of anxiety and couldn't bring herself to get up on the stage and speak. Desperate, the principal asked Victoria if she'd be willing to read her classmate's speech. Victoria agreed.

From my seat in the audience, I watched in amazement as the shy, withdrawn girl I'd met in September walked onto the stage with the poise of a movie star. She read her classmate's prepared speech with ease and then, looking up at the audience, added a few thoughts of her own.

"I came to this school as an American citizen," she said, "but an American citizen who never stayed in one school long enough to really learn anything. Today, I'm graduating knowing that I've learned so much over the past year. I've learned about things like nouns and adverbs, but I've also learned how people care about each other and will help if you ask — or even if you don't. Sometimes, they can see you need help, and they do what they can to make sure you get it. Thank you for helping me when I wasn't sure how to ask."

Victoria smiled at me, and I felt my eyes fill with tears. We've lost touch over the years, but I think about her often. I may have helped her fill in some gaps in her education, but she helped me remember what a truly awesome country we live in, one where education is free and available to everyone — whether you ask for it or not.

~Nell Musolf

An American Wall

It is the flag just as much of the man who was naturalized yesterday as of the men whose people have been here many generations.
~Henry Cabot Lodge

According to my family legend, my paternal great-great-grandparents emigrated from Germany and settled in upstate New York near Lake Ontario in the late 1800s. Supposedly, the region was popular with farmers who claimed the area's long, frozen winters permit the earth an extended rest, which then produces incredibly bountiful harvests each autumn. I don't know about the validity of that theory, but I do recall, as a kid, we always had a white Christmas. The white Halloweens and white Easters were equally impressive.

By the time I came along in the 1960s, my family's farming days were long over, but my grandparents continued to reside in the old family farm homestead. It was a five-bedroom colonial with unreliable plumbing, windows that rattled in the wind, and a roof that leaked. Every floorboard in the house creaked, except the basement, which had a dirt floor. When the house was finally sold after my grandparents passed away, the real estate agent listed the property as having a unique antique charm.

I remember my father repeatedly urging his folks to sell the ancient, outdated house. "Living in this worn out place is like you're living in poverty," he insisted.

"We do not live in poverty," snapped Grandma, offended by her son's implication. "We're… well, we're the working poor."

"Being poor ain't no work for us," Grandpa added. "It just seems to come natural."

When I was a kid, I loved to wander the acres of old farmland with Grandpa. On the way back from our walks, we would always encounter an old, hand-built stone wall that paralleled the west side of the property. It was about three feet high, a couple of feet wide, moss-covered and ruggedly sturdy. We'd always stop there and take a rest.

"You know," Grandpa said as he sat down on the wall, "my grandfather — I called him Opa, which is German for grandfather — built this almost a hundred years ago. He used to tell me this wall was strong and made to last because it was his American wall."

"Because it's in America?" I asked, sitting beside Grandpa.

He shook his head. "Opa said it was his American wall because it was built just like the USA — lots of different pieces locked together, holding each other up, each one supporting the other."

I shrugged. "I don't get it."

"Well, you see," Grandpa explained, "the stones in this wall are all different. They're big, little, round, square, light, dark, but they're all stones. Opa said the people of America are like that, too. There are Italians, Irish, Chinese, Polish, Spanish, Egyptian, and English, but they're all Americans."

"And German like us," I added.

"And German, that's right," replied Grandpa, smiling. "Opa told me it ain't important if you're an Italian baker or a Polish doctor or a Chinese grocer or an Irish teacher. What's important is that we're all Americans and, just like this wall, if we stick together, give support and hold each other up, we'll be so strong that nobody can ever knock us down."

That all happened years ago, but one sunny Saturday afternoon in the fall of 2016, I took a walk back onto my grandparents' old property. Most of the fields lie fallow now, and quite a few pine trees have grown up over the years. In 1999, a major portion of the farmland was sold off to build a housing development. But after a bit of searching, behind a thick overgrowth of weeds, I found my great-great-grandfather's old American wall, still so strong and sturdy that no one has ever knocked it down.

~David Hull

A Melting Pot Wedding

We become not a melting pot but a beautiful mosaic.
Different people, different beliefs, different yearnings,
different hopes, different dreams.
~President Jimmy Carter

It had rained like a monsoon for two days after Christmas, palm fronds littering the Pacific Coast Highway from the whipping winds. But the morning of our wedding, the sky was a striking blue and cloudless, with a crisp chill in the San Diego air. It was a perfect metaphor for this peaceful marriage-making day, after the stormy ones our own parents had experienced decades before.

In 1969, my parents faced hurtful words and declined invitations from family members who were against their marriage: a Catholic girl to a Jewish boy. In 1972, my fiancé's parents raised eyebrows and hackles as well: a white Jewish woman marrying a second-generation Japanese-American man.

But that late December day in the new millennium, our clear-sky wedding was a symbol of all that our families — and our country — had overcome in nearly forty years. Those old clouds of intolerance had parted for our generation's union. Nobody batted an eye at us marrying, though my soon-to-be-husband's skin was several shades darker than mine. Nobody thought twice about the mix of religious traditions we included in our wedding ceremony.

Our female celebrant invited up my family's honorary rabbi to give us a Jewish blessing, his hands raised above our bowed heads.

Then the rabbi pulled from his pocket a surprise he had solicited — a letter written in the impeccable script of my Catholic grandfather (who'd become his dear friend over the years), with blessings for our marriage from my grandparents, who were too frail to travel. My soon-to-be-husband's brother read aloud the favorite poem of their Japanese grandmother, a Shinto-sounding ode called "God of the Open Air."

Looking out into the audience, we saw the smiling faces of family members who had fought for the Allies in Europe during World War II, and others who had spent that war in Japanese-American internment camps. As they arrived at the rehearsal barbecue the night before, they had all welcomed each other "into the family." Our friends, who covered the spectrum of beliefs and identities — Christian, Jewish, Mormon, Buddhist, agnostic, atheist, New Age, various ethnicities, politics and sexual orientations — sat together, laughing and sharing stories of their mutual connections.

It was a simple wedding, really. After the outdoor ceremony, we had a light brunch buffet of bagels and salads on paper plates, then impromptu speeches and a slide show, with a Latino friend-of-a-friend playing bright Spanish guitar in the background. But when a wedding guest came up to me at the end and said, "This was truly the best wedding I've ever been to," I believed him. It was more than just a wedding. It was something incredibly special: America at its best, a melting pot celebration of the mosaic that we are.

For that one shining morning, all the storms of past and present conflicts or intolerances faded, a rainbow appeared, and only love was present.

~Megan Pincus Kajitani

We the People

Not merely a nation but a nation of nations.
~President Lyndon B. Johnson

"I'd like to ask a special favor of you," my teacher said to us. "Madena and her mother have just moved here from Ukraine. I'd like you to make a special effort to be her friend."

Our teacher didn't need to point her out. I spotted her from clear across the lunchroom. Madena had olive skin and long, almost black hair tied into two braids that stretched all the way down her back. No one else in the whole school looked like that.

She was sitting next to her mother, and after our teacher introduced us, we sat down to eat our lunches. Madena's mother, Taira, asked us questions in heavily-accented English. We told her our names and where we lived, but the whole time Madena stared at her lunch tray, looking completely miserable. The only times she spoke were to her mother, and then it was in a language we didn't understand.

It didn't occur to me as a seventh grader how frightening it would be to move to a new country. It was a place where everything was different — the way we spoke, the things we did, even the way we dressed.

I had moved from another state just a couple of years earlier, but at that moment, I had forgotten the way my heart had pounded at school my first day and how desperate I was to make friends. I'd forgotten how scared I was to be in a new place.

Instead, I was worried about how Madena stood out. The last

thing I wanted to do was attract attention, which could invite bullying and teasing. I smiled at her, but inwardly I wished that our teacher had assigned someone else the task of being her friend.

Within days, my worries were confirmed. Kids had started calling Madena "Mother Russia," and they pulled at her braids. Madena stuck next to my friends like glue, probably because we were the only kids she'd been introduced to.

One of our friends, Valerie, talked to the rest of us. "I went to her house, you guys, and she's actually a lot of fun. We should let her be our friend."

Based on Valerie's word, I was willing to give it a try. I tried to involve her in conversations more, asking her questions directly. We invited her to get together with our group outside of school, and we told the kids who teased her to "shut up."

Madena blossomed into a girl who was extremely interesting, intelligent, and kind. She became my best friend, and when she finally let down her braids, the entire school was stunned by her beauty.

We remained friends through high school, going to football games and dances. At some point along the way, she changed from being Madena, the girl from Ukraine, to just being Madena. She was one of us — unique, yes, but 100 percent one of us.

After high school, we lost touch for a while, but reconnected about fifteen years later. We'd get together then for chats and tea, comparing stories from our love lives. I was so impressed with how fantastic she had turned out, and one of the things I most appreciated about her was how familiar she was with other cultures. While I had never left Utah, she had traveled all over the world and gained an understanding and respect for all cultures.

It was Madena who told me I needed to go to the Diwali Festival at Utah State University.

"I don't even know what that is," I said.

"It's the Hindu Festival of Lights," she explained. "A celebration. Kind of like the New Year you celebrate in America."

"I don't know," I said. "I really don't know anything about it."

"Just come," she said. "It'll be a good experience. I promise."

A Vibrant Melting Pot |

A friend of Madena's lent me a beautiful satin sari to wear to the festival. Madena came over early to help me drape it correctly. It was so elegant and lovely, but I worried I'd look out of place wearing it. Most of the attendees at the festival would be students from India who were attending school here. With my pale skin and blue eyes, I would be the one sticking out.

Madena reassured me, but just like back in middle school, I felt my anxiety rising.

At the festival, we ate delicious butter chicken and curry, and then the International Student Council put on a fantastic program with dancing and singing. Both the women in their saris and the men in their clothes looked so classy.

I learned about how Diwali spiritually signifies the victory of light over darkness and hope over despair. I pictured how beautiful it must look to see all the houses and porches lit with lanterns in celebration.

At the conclusion of the program, Madena and the students cleared the floor for dancing. I watched from the sidelines as they laughed and danced to Indian pop music. I definitely felt out of place. I didn't look like anyone else here. I didn't recognize the music. And I certainly didn't know how to dance the way they did.

A young man approached me. "Come join us," he said, gesturing to the dance floor.

"Oh, no." I shook my head. "I don't know how."

"It doesn't matter," he said. "Please, come have fun with us."

As I stepped timidly onto the dance floor, I was met with encouraging smiles and nods. After dancing for a while, the group formed a circle, and they took turns going into the center to show off their dance moves while the crowd cheered.

"Your turn," someone told me.

"Not me!" I said. "I can't dance."

But before I knew it, I was right in the middle. I sashayed my hips, hardly comparing to the skilled dancing I'd just witnessed. But still I was met with warm smiles and applause. Afterward, we joined hands and paraded around the ballroom in a circle.

I was an outsider, but they invited me, welcomed me, and greeted me with kindness. When I think about the kind of America I want to live in, I think of that night at the Diwali celebration. In my America, love and kindness are expressed to all. I don't think of us as "We the Americans;" I think of us as "We the people."

~Amanda Yardley Luzzader

Americans in Paris

I believe fundamentally in the kindness
of the American people because I
have been a beneficiary of it.
~Jose Antonio Vargas

"I always wanted to go to America," the waiter said in his thick French accent.

My friends and I gawked at him as he rounded the table and gave us our plates of food. The seven of us, having just climbed the Arc de Triomphe and trekked the entire Champs-Élysées before noon, were ravenous, and the platters of grilled chicken and crisp pita bread looked warm, inviting, and filling. We clutched our knives and forks, ready to dig in and fill our stomachs before the tour of the Musée d'Orsay later that day.

However, we ignored the meals in front of us. The waiter's sentence was brief, his words few, yet they froze us and made us glance at each other across the table before staring at him. He went about his business as if he hadn't said anything out of the ordinary.

We were in Paris, the fourth stop on our three-week tour of Europe. We were a group of college girls who had never before left the United States. Most of us had probably never ventured farther south than Virginia or farther west than Ohio.

For us, visiting Europe was an escape. Here we were in Paris, one of the most beautiful cities in the world, where the lights sparkled at night and the sun in the morning reflected on the rippling Seine. Every man and woman on the street looked like a model, and every piece of chocolate behind glass cases in candy stores looked like a work of art. We were in the city that Humphrey Bogart and Ingrid Bergman would always have, the city that artists captured on canvas, and the city where so many romantic films ended before the credits rolled.

We were in Paris, and yet this man wanted nothing more than to come to America.

"New Jersey," he said suddenly. "I would love to leave Paris and move to New Jersey."

"You don't want to move to New Jersey," the girl across from me, Marissa, said. "I'm from New Jersey. Trust me."

We all laughed, but now it was the waiter's turn to stare at us. He had dark eyes, dark skin, and shiny dark hair. Although he spoke with a French accent, he looked Middle Eastern. Like America, Paris seemed to me to be a melting pot of all different races and cultures.

"I hear that New Jersey is very nice," he said, not understanding Marissa's American sarcasm. "I have friends in New Jersey."

"But you live in Paris," another girl, Jackie, said, emphasizing the city's name as if the man didn't know. "Why would you want to move to America?"

He shrugged. "Because people are kind there. People don't care where you come from." He turned away and studied the empty drinking glasses in his hands. He was shining them. The restaurant, in an alley off the Champs-Élysées, was nearly empty. No other customers were waiting for him, so he lingered.

"It's not like that here in Paris," he continued. He glanced at us from beneath his dark lashes.

We were silent. For us, it was so hard to understand. We had grown up in America, in our own melting pot of different languages and skin colors, of different religions and sexual orientations. Perhaps that made us spoiled in a way. Perhaps that even made us blind to the struggles that so many around the world still faced, blind to the fights so many were still having for their own acceptance. We were blind to just how lucky we were to have a country to go back to that welcomed us regardless of who we worshiped or loved or what color our skin was.

"People here treat me differently because I am Muslim," he added. All at once, all the anger and frustration, the sadness and even fear, came pouring out of this young waiter. I thought of the anti-Islam riot that had filled the street outside my hotel with screams and smoking flares the day before.

He shook his head. "In America, none of that matters. People are kind," he said again.

All of us at the table had grown up learning about the "American Dream." We heard the term "Land of Opportunity." In elementary school, we dressed up like our ancestors and cooked international foods from our families' history. But for us, "American Dream" was just a phrase that politicians threw into speeches. Those days in school were days to dress up and eat food and get out of homework. None of our parents were immigrants, not even our grandparents. Our families came to America with early settlers following the Mayflower or on ships to Ellis Island. They embodied the American dream so that, many generations later, we could live it, free from fear or intolerance or hate.

And now here stood a man who embodied that same spirit our ancestors held. In only a few sentences, he showed us the kindness America harbored. He demonstrated for us the true power of the American Dream — how it transcended international boundaries and traveled across oceans. There we were in Paris, seeking to escape the seemingly mundane life back home, and here was a man working to achieve the life we had taken for granted for so long.

His head was low, and his shoulders slumped under the weight of sadness.

I have heard it said that we might never understand something until we walk in another's shoes. Our young waiter didn't merely take us for a walk in his shoes. His eyes were reflecting pools, with memories we couldn't see or even imagine, playing out before them. In only a few minutes, one man in Paris opened our eyes to the beauty of America more than any politician could.

"We hope you come to America," Marissa said. Her voice was heavy.

Without a word, he took his sparkling glasses, leaving us to our meal and our sudden silence. We all looked around the table, wishing we could help him.

When our lunch was finished, our waiter returned. He froze, his hand hovering over the table where our empty plates were left alongside a pile of euros.

"You left money," he said.

We shook our heads and smiled. "That's for you. A tip," we all tried to explain at once. Tipping isn't something that's done in most of Europe.

"But…" His eyes flickered between all of us. "Why?" His mouth was parted ever so slightly in shock.

Marissa gave him a bright smile, perhaps hoping to be the first American to show him that kindness he dreamed of, but certainly not the last. "Because you were very kind to us."

"Thank you," he breathed.

I imagined him taking the money home and hiding it away in an envelope or a box, in a jar in his kitchen or in a safe on his shelf, where he was collecting every cent he could to come to America, like so many before him did and so many will for generations to come.

-Keri Lindenmuth

Chapter 7

My Kind (of) America

Where Kindness Counts

Welcome to Tent City

If you take advantage of everything America has to
offer, there's nothing you can't accomplish.
~Geraldine Ferraro

When my family and I first set foot on American soil in 1975, we were physically exhausted, emotionally devastated, malnourished, dehydrated, homesick, and penniless, having survived the perilous journey from our war-torn homeland of Vietnam as one of the first waves of "boat people." And yet, it was still the happiest day of our lives because we had arrived in America, the land of safety, freedom, and kindness.

We had lived a life of privilege and comfort in Vietnam. My father was a successful, self-made man who had married my mother, the sheltered daughter of my industrious, widowed grandmother. We had servants, nannies, and a driver. Life was very good.

This life of privilege was abruptly ripped from underneath us when the Communists overthrew the existing government of South Vietnam on April 30, 1975. Our beloved home was no longer our home. My family and I had to flee the country during this terrifying mass exodus. We barely made it out, with just the clothes we wore and fear in our hearts. We had lost *everything*.

Beset by chaos and unrest, we boarded a small, dilapidated ship to flee the country. Our journey was plagued by physical hardship, extreme seasickness, and harsh storms. I have a blurry memory of nearly falling overboard when a severe storm rocked the ship violently, throwing my father — who was holding me in his arms — off-balance as he stood too close to the railing. I did not know how to swim, so had I fallen into the treacherous waters below, it probably would have been the end of me, and the end of my story.

Another frightening obstacle that we faced was the inadequate quantities of food and water. I remember asking my mother if we could go home because the drinking water on the ship smelled like gasoline. My mother replied simply, "We can never go home again, so please drink the water, Mai." She must have been devastated, terrified, and grief-stricken, but she did her best to remain calm.

After what seemed like an eternity of sea and air travel, we eventually landed in Camp Pendleton, California, as a result of the U.S. government program called Operation New Life. Through various collaborative efforts by the American Red Cross, the Catholic Church, and other humanitarian organizations, we received medical care and much-needed hope.

According to *The San Diego Union Tribune*, nearly 900 Marines and civilians worked for six days to erect "Tent City," a collection of 958 tents, 140 Quonset huts, a newly installed sewage system and communication lines. Tent City would eventually shelter, clothe, educate, feed, and even entertain 50,000 Vietnamese refugees. If this massive undertaking wasn't a feat that was propelled by kindness, compassion, and generosity, I don't know what is.

In retrospect, I realized that some of those same Marines may have either gallantly fought in the Vietnam War, known someone who had fought in the Vietnam War, or had lost someone who fought in the Vietnam War. And yet, there they were, working tirelessly to build a temporary home for thousands of Vietnamese refugees who were preparing for a new life in America in the aftermath of this terrible war. This realization moved me tremendously.

Even though we were living in makeshift tents, our life was finally calm for the first time in weeks. While I was too young to remember many specifics, I do have some lingering, fond memories of playing Frisbee on the warm summer days, standing in lines for delicious American foods like hot dogs and doughnuts, and seeing the smiles of the kind American Marines stationed at Camp Pendleton who helped us in innumerable ways. Considering that the Vietnamese are a race of relatively short stature, these American Marines looked like gentle giants next to my father and mother, who both stood five feet, one inch tall.

Through the Catholic Church's efforts to help Vietnamese refugees, a benevolent sponsor family took us into their home and hearts. While we lived with this sponsor family for several weeks, they were instrumental in helping us to rebuild our lives. Mom and Dad learned to drive and found employment, while my siblings and I enrolled in school. Everyone had to learn English in record time. Looking back at this time, I am certain of one undeniable truth: Had it not been for our sponsor family, there was no way that we could have successfully assimilated into our new lives. For this, I am eternally grateful to them. I am still in touch with my sponsor family, and I am so thrilled to be a part of their lives.

Forty-two years later, I am extremely proud to call myself a Vietnamese-American. When I remember those days at Camp Pendleton, I remember the kindness of the Marines, the Catholic Church, the American Red Cross and volunteers who helped to lovingly welcome us to our new home. When I think of my sponsor family, I think of the kind Americans who enriched our lives, nurtured our souls, and gave us faith in humanity, with open arms.

I am forever indebted to the compassion, hospitality, and generosity of the Americans who welcomed us in the summer of 1975. I wish that I could reach out to the countless Marines and volunteers of Camp Pendleton to express my gratitude for their kindness and to reciprocate in some way. Regretfully, I don't even know any of their names. John F. Kennedy once said: "As we express our gratitude, we must never forget that the highest appreciation is not to utter words, but to live by them." So, I will repay their charity from those many years ago by being the best American I can be. And by being kind and offering a friendly welcome to the next newcomers to our nation.

~Kristen Mai Pham

62

The Lady in Seat 26B

The secret of genius is to carry the spirit of the
child into old age, which means never
losing your enthusiasm.
~Aldous Huxley

I don't typically talk with passengers on airplanes. My flight time is reserved for falling asleep to my favorite music or turning the pages of a good book. That changed, though, on a flight from Tampa to Newark when I sat next to her — the lady in seat 26B.

After tossing my carry-on luggage into the compartment above me, I settled into my seat. I cracked open my book, anxious to discover what Harry would get into during his third year at Hogwarts.

Then she turned to me.

"And where are you traveling to? Home or on vacation?"

I closed my book. *Maybe later, Harry.*

"Heading home," I said. "You?"

"Oh, I'm heading home, too," she began. "I was visiting my sister in Florida. I come from a very large family. Nine kids! I'm the oldest still alive — eighty-nine!"

And then she laughed.

She laughed the way a schoolgirl might, full of childlike joy, innocence and whimsy in her voice. She reminded me of my own grandmother: the way she gestured with her hands, her freshly painted pink nails, her starting a conversation with a complete stranger as if we'd been friends for ages. I wouldn't have guessed she was nearly ninety, though. She held no cane or glasses, just an iPhone and ripe enthusiasm.

"Good book?" she asked, pointing to my paperback.

"Yes. Do you read?"

"Oh, I don't have time to read," she replied.

I'm sixty years younger than 26B, I thought, *yet she's the one who's too busy to read? What on earth could she be doing with her days?*

"Well," she began, "I work at Costco two days a week. I pass out the samples, you know. I just love it! I meet all sorts of folks. There are real nice people. There are also the cranky ones, but I enjoy them, too!" She laughed again, and I admired her ability to not let negative energies affect her mood. I wondered how I could manage that, too.

"My mom always said to be like a duck."

"Like a duck?" I asked.

"Yes. Have you ever seen a duck when it's wet? The water just rolls right off its back."

I've heard a lot of sayings from my grandma over the years, but this one was new to me. I liked it. *Be like a duck.*

"I'm also very active with my church," she began again, rattling off what created a schedule too busy for reading. "I meet up with my girls. I go out to dinner every Saturday night with my son and his wife. Usually Outback or Longhorn. Sometimes Chinese. Then on Sundays, I cook a big pot of sauce, and the entire family comes over to my house for dinner — my kids, grandkids, even the great-grandkids! We just sit around the kitchen table and laugh. Oh, do we laugh!"

And then she did. She laughed a great, deep belly laugh. Her face lit up. I believed each wrinkle had been created from joy, as if her body couldn't contain her happiness and so it spread out onto her face.

"Are you hungry?" she asked. Before I could answer, she was rummaging through her purse. She pulled out Ziploc bags of trail mix and a granola bar.

"Here," she said as she plopped them onto my tray table. "Eat some."

She continued to rummage.

"Oh, have you had these?" She handed me a single Werther's Original hard candy.

"Well, now I know you're as old as you claim," I said. "You just forced a hard candy on me."

We both laughed.

"What's your secret," I asked, "to sounding so happy, positive and healthy?"

"I bake a lot," she laughed. "No, really. My husband died ten years ago. I thought to myself, I'm not going to just sit around! That's when I got my Costco job. I believe in being active."

She paused for a few seconds and then turned toward me.

"Life is so good," she said. "I'm just excited every day to live it!"

I'm just excited every day to live it.

I wanted that three-hour plane ride to reroute to California so I would have more time to learn about her life, her experiences — her energy for life. I became more inspired with each mile we flew.

I told myself, *If someone who is eighty-nine years old can choose to live her life with such desire and passion, I can, too! What's the point of mindlessly dragging through life when you can be excited to live it every day? Why sleep on a plane when you can ride, eyes awake, next to someone like 26B?*

We touched down, and passengers jumped out of their seats, waiting to pull luggage from their overhead compartments and exit the plane.

26B and I remained sitting.

"Thank you for chatting with me," I said. "You are very inspiring."

"I try to be kind," she said. "When you're kind to people, they'll be kind to you."

~Katelyn Stanis

63

Chicken Soup for the Soul

Helping Hands

My values, our values, aren't about pointing fingers.
They are about offering a helping hand.
~Kathleen Blanco

At fifty-two, I was broke and homeless. When I walked into my friend's small apartment with only one suitcase and an air mattress, Barbara's warm, welcoming smile and big bear hug wrapped me in a cocoon of love and acceptance. But the packing boxes I saw scattered throughout her apartment reminded me that she was moving in two weeks, and the clock was ticking. I had to start looking for my next place to stay.

Before Barbara took me in, I'd already spent three months bouncing between various family and friends' homes. To those who knew me, it seemed my life was spinning out of control. But, more often than not, I felt at peace. Although I wasn't able to dodge the financial crash my own choices had set into motion, I had spent time every day working to quiet the fearful thoughts my difficult circumstances stirred up. I meditated. I journaled. I took long walks. And I savored all that was good in my life, which was still plentiful.

Having created this mess, I figured I probably wasn't the best judge of how to fix it. So, after giving away the bulk of my furniture, putting my most precious belongings in storage, and leaving my apartment with no idea where I was going to land, I let go of trying to figure out or control what should happen next. I surrendered completely.

Full of curiosity about what new life direction might emerge, I felt excited rather than scared, at least most of the time. When I did feel some worry or fear start to creep in through a side door, I'd close my eyes, take a few deep breaths, and reconnect with that place deep inside where I knew everything was going to be all right.

By the time I arrived at Barbara's, my new life had already begun to manifest. One day, I got a call from a friend who was inspired in a meditation to ask if I wanted to write for him. In all the years I'd worked with authors, it had never occurred to me to provide writing and book-promotion services. Without hesitation, I said, "Yes! I'd love to!" It opened up a whole new way of working with clients and earning a living.

But at that point, I was only making a few hundred dollars a month and couldn't afford to pay rent. So I placed an ad on Craigslist offering home-care services in exchange for a place to live. Since Barbara didn't have an Internet connection, I'd take my laptop and drive to a nearby Starbucks every day, where I'd order a cup of tea, connect to their Wi-Fi, and settle in for an hour or so to go online. I'd check to see if anyone had answered my ad, respond to any live-in help or house-sitting ads that looked like they could be a good fit, and remind my friends that I still needed a place to crash for a while, casting as wide a net as possible.

Several days in a row, I noticed a woman around my age who also brought her laptop with her and went online while sipping her coffee. After saying hello a few times in passing, we struck up a conversation one day and discovered we were in the same situation. Shelly, too, had to move on August first and was using Craigslist to look for a rent-exchange living situation. A woman of deep faith, Shelly trusted that God had her life well in hand. While she was taking appropriate actions to find a new place to work and live, she had a strong and steady faith that she was being guided and cared for every step of the way. We became instant friends and a source of support for each other.

The days sped by, without either of us having any success, but our spirits remained high. Even so, Shelly, who at one point had lived in her car for several months, started giving me lessons on how to live in my car safely just in case I couldn't find a place to stay. I listened intently, yet couldn't bring myself to believe it would actually come to that. So far, things had always worked out. But the fact that I was seriously considering strategies for living in my car was scary.

When I was down to the last forty-eight hours, Barbara encouraged me to work non-stop to find my next place to stay. Yet my inner guidance gave me different advice. Deciding to trust that still, small voice inside me, I spent most of Saturday curled up with my laptop, writing and living the life I wanted to create.

With the very real possibility I could be living in my car in two days, the thought I might be deluding myself certainly crossed my mind. But by the time I'd finished my daily ritual of meditation and journaling, the doubt had mostly passed.

After writing for hours, I drove to Starbucks to check my e-mail, but no one had answered my ad. On the way back, I stopped at Shelly's to drop off a book she'd loaned me.

Shelly had an unusual rent-exchange situation, in that she was paid for the work she did with a fully furnished two-bedroom vacation rental house while her employer, Miriam, lived elsewhere. She invited me to have dinner with her and spend the night in the spare bedroom, since she knew I'd been sleeping on an air mattress.

Shelly's invitation moved me deeply, not only because we'd known each other for such a short time, but because it felt like my intention to spend the day living the life I wanted to create had opened a portal through which miracles were beginning to flow.

Shelly cooked us a lovely dinner, and an idea begin to percolate as we were eating. I said to Shelly, "Since neither one of us has a place to move to on Monday, what if we bartered with Miriam for some extra time in this house? I have some diamond jewelry I'd be willing to use as payment."

At first, Shelly was against the idea. "I'm a woman of my word," she said, "and I told Miriam I'd be out of the house on Monday." But the next morning, she started to soften, and by the afternoon, we'd hatched a plan. Shelly sent an e-mail telling Miriam she needed another week in the house and would consider it payment for the extra hours she'd worked beyond their agreement. She told Miriam I was moving in, and that if we needed the house for more than a week, I had some valuable jewelry to barter with for more time.

It worked!

That evening, I went back to Barbara's, and on Monday morning, we hugged and said our goodbyes. Barbara left for her new home, and I drove over to Shelly's. Since we'd been given a week's reprieve, Shelly and I treated ourselves to a relaxing lunch before getting back to the business of finding our next living situation. When Shelly got online, she found an e-mail from a potential employer asking for an interview. Since Shelly didn't have a car and it was quite a distance away, I said I'd be happy to drive her.

When we were back at the house, I got a call from Barbara. Before she'd even made it out of town, her car had died. She needed a place to stay while shopping for a new car. I told Shelly, who said immediately, "Tell her to come on over, the more the merrier." With a daybed in the dining room, there was plenty of space for all three of us.

That night, as we were chatting about what an elegant solution life had come up with to take care of all three of us in our hour of need, my phone rang. Joyce introduced herself and said, "I'm not a big Craigslist fan. In fact, I don't really trust the people who advertise on it. But I woke up in the middle of the night inspired to check it out. I saw your ad, went to your website, and liked what I saw." Joyce was about to start another round of chemotherapy, and she wanted someone to support her through the process. I shared with her that I had taken care of my mother through her cancer journey, and we set up a time to meet.

The week sped by as I drove Shelly to her interview, she came with me to mine, and Barbara shopped for a reliable used car. Our interviews went well, so both Shelly and I had our next homes lined up, and Barbara got a great deal on a car.

There was only one problem… my job didn't start for two more weeks. As I was contemplating what to do next, Shelly said, "I'm not leaving you out in the cold. If I have to postpone my new job so we can stay in this house until you have a place to go, I will." Shelly, whom

I'd known for less than two weeks, wasn't going anywhere until she knew I was taken care of.

After calling her new employer, Shelly turned to me with a smile on her face. "Julie," she said, "go get packed. She'd rather have you come with me than have me postpone my starting date."

I stayed with Shelly in her new garage apartment for almost a week, and then spent a few nights each with other friends before moving in with Joyce. During that thirty-day period, I stayed in seven different homes — reaping the benefits of many helping hands, both seen and unseen. By the time I left Joyce's, eight months later, I was making enough money from my new author services to start paying rent again and leave homelessness behind.

What didn't get left behind — and has continued to deepen and grow since then — are my respect and appreciation for the kindness and generosity of others. When I was at my lowest point, literally broke and homeless, friends and strangers alike stepped up and offered their support in whatever way they could — whether a shoulder to lean on, a bag of groceries, or a place to stay.

~Julie Isaac

64

The Cookie Gauntlet

There is a charm about the forbidden that
makes it unspeakably desirable.
~Mark Twain

Spring blossoms burst from the earth, wafting sweet fragrances on breezes that warm both body and soul. But wait. What other scent of the season do I detect? Ah, yes — cookies.

Whether March comes in like a lion or a lamb, another rhythm of nature is as predictable as the spring equinox. Little girls, their pigtails bouncing with excitement and eyes lit with hope, will sweetly inquire, "Ma'am, would you like to buy some cookies?"

Nay! No! Nein! Nunca! My fifty-something figure reveals my abject failures from years past. No more may I indulge my taste buds with concentrated sweets. My will struggles to subdue the desires of the flesh. Unwanted saliva surges against the dam of my lips, preventing the correct words from escaping. One swallow, two — then my traitorous tongue says, "Yes, honey, I'll take two boxes of Peanut Butter Patties and two Thin Mints."

Last March, my husband Dale and I approached a big-box store. I spied the foes encamped outside the exit, their eager faces shining with hope. But this year I engaged the battle with a new tactic. I left my purse in the car so I would have no cash on hand. I entrusted the credit cards to Dale, recruited as a foot soldier to fortify my will. I gave him strict orders to ensure success. This year, I would be victorious as I ran the cookie gauntlet.

"No cookies, Dale. If I try to pause for a sniff, grab my hand and keep me moving."

"Yes, dear."

"In fact, don't even let me peek in that direction. Eye contact is deadly."

"Yes, honey."

"I'm counting on you!"

"I won't fail, my dear. No cookies."

We shopped for healthy foods — lean meats, fresh vegetables, and sugar-free condiments. I relished my success in resisting food samples, refusing each one with steely resolve. I worried slightly when my foot soldier downed a pizza bite, but congratulated myself on personal triumph despite severe temptation. Each small conquest built confidence to face the ultimate battle upon exiting the store.

In the checkout lane, I set my jaw and firmed my lips into a straight line. I turned on my internal radio and started humming "Eye of the Tiger." I envisioned my strides, confident and swift, eyes forward, gaze unswerving.

We wheeled toward the exit. The clerk eyed the items we had purchased and compared them to the receipt. She stroked it with a yellow marker and said, "Enjoy the beautiful day."

The doors were propped open, and girlish chatter echoed in the breezeway. A small stab of guilt pricked my conscience as I thought of the worthy causes supported by cookie sales. I remembered the times my own child raised funds for school and church projects and how disappointed she was when no one would buy chocolates, magazine subscriptions, or gift wrap.

"Dale, I need you to be strong." I placed both hands on the cart handle to prevent them from reaching toward the tower of temptation outside. I picked up the pace, ready to sprint if necessary.

"I'm ready, honey. No cookies." Dale's smirk did not inspire confidence. He was too relaxed, apparently underestimating our dangerous enemy.

I blazed a trail into the sunlight and feigned a search of the parking lot for our car. With my peripheral vision, I perceived a sprite approaching from the right, and I groaned. Brown, curly pigtails. Death knells began to sound when a surreptitious glance revealed she carried my favorites — Peanut Butter Patties, along with a box of Thin Mints.

Before I melted, my hero's voice intervened. "No, thank you, sweetie. No cookies for us today."

My heart swelled with pride.

"But, sir…" the child whined. My hands began to tremble, my grip loosening.

"Not today. Good luck with your sales." Dale took control of the cart with one hand and grabbed my hand with the other. He kept moving. I trailed behind.

The urchin followed us and chucked both cartons into our buggy.

The nerve! The cheek! If that little temptress thought we would stop to pay just because the cookies landed in our cart, she was sorely mistaken!

Dale stopped rolling. Tactical error! Unbidden, my eyes swept down to see tears brimming below insanely long brown lashes. A drop would escape any moment to trail down a pinkened cheek.

My hands took on a life of their own. They began swatting my pockets, searching for cash. Remembering I had emptied them, I started searching Dale's pockets, impervious to stares from passersby.

Dale gripped my questing fingers and returned them to the cart. Gazing with deliberate kindness at the child, he said, "Honey, we can't buy cookies today."

Three little words changed everything. The perpetrator's tremulous voice cried, "But they're free!"

Free? No-cost cookies? The child instantly morphed from a money-grubbing rascal to a rosy-cheeked cherub. But wait. There had to be a caveat.

"Now, honey, I know you can't give away cookies. Isn't the purpose of the sale to raise money?" Dale's voice of reason tamped down the hope that rose in my breast.

"Yes, sir," the child replied. Her eyes brightened. "A woman came out right before you and bought two boxes of cookies. But she said she couldn't eat them because she was on a diet. She wanted me to give them away."

God bless her, a kindred soul, a cookie fairy spreading love and kindness to perfect strangers! I became teary myself at the thought of enjoying Peanut Butter Patties with no guilt while also sparing a fellow dieter extra pounds. From a certain point of view, I would perform my own good deed. *One could not spurn such generosity, could one? And break a little girl's heart?*

A smile affixed itself to my face, and I tried to rescind my "no cookies" command with a hopeful glance toward Dale. He returned my grin and raised his eyebrows. Thin Mints were his favorites.

"Thank you, young lady," Dale said, "and I wish I could also thank the lady who bought them."

The girl glowed with success. "She was really nice, wasn't she?"

I basked in the joy of the moment — at least until her next revelation.

"She told me to give them to the next old couple who came out of the store."

~Rhonda Dragomir

65

A Cast of Characters

Alone we can do so little, together we can do so much.
~Helen Keller

It was the first week of September, a beautiful late summer evening that made you glad to be alive. I wanted to be outside, but I sat at the kitchen table studying for a biochemistry exam. George was relaxing, reading the newspaper. Our fourteen-year-old daughter was attending the first high school football game of the season, and our seven-year-old son was in the front yard playing soccer with a friend. Suddenly, a blood-curdling scream outside had us jumping up and racing toward the sound. My gut churned upon hearing the agonizing howl of pain coming from our child.

George and I burst through the screen door, running toward our boy who was lying on the ground screaming, "My leg, my leg!"

Rushing to his side, I cradled his head and told him to lie still and not move. Tears streamed down his face as he reached toward his contorted leg.

"Call 9-1-1," I said to my husband. I was sure his leg was broken.

At the first sound of sirens and sight of flashing lights, many neighbors flooded into the street. The ambulance and EMTs pulled into our driveway and promptly got to work. They splinted the lower half of Timmy's body and moved him onto a stretcher.

A neighbor who was a nurse approached and offered to call the surgeon she worked with to meet us in the ER. Gratefully, we said yes. Timmy was loaded into the ambulance. We followed in the car.

The ride was short, and the surgeon was waiting for us. Technicians whisked our frightened seven-year-old off to X-ray. George and I trailed alongside, holding his hand.

Minutes later, I stood next to the doctor as we looked at the films. "A spiral fracture of the femur is serious business." I could see exactly what he meant. There were a good three inches between the ends of the broken bones.

I faced the doctor. "What does this mean as far as treatment and hospitalization?"

"He'll need a pin in his leg and then two weeks in traction. When the bones are aligned, I'd put him in a hip spica cast."

"What's that?"

"It's a little smaller than a full body cast, starting just under his rib cage, extending to his toes on the fractured leg and to his knee on the uninjured one. A stabilizing bar will be attached as part of the cast to keep his legs in alignment."

I felt weak in the knees, and my mind was racing. I was in my first full year of nursing school twenty-six miles away. The only prayer I had of staying in school was to have Timmy transferred to an orthopedic specialist at the hospital in which I was doing my training. I could stay with him when I wasn't in class, do my homework in his room and spend nights in the nurse's residence. The surgeon respected my wishes and gave the order for the transfer.

That short-term plan would suffice as long as he was hospitalized, but what would we do when he was discharged in that hip spica thing? George calmly reassured me we'd take one day at a time.

As soon as our parents heard what happened, they said, "What do you need? And how soon do you need us to come?" We were relieved at their generous offer to help and set up a tentative schedule, to be firmed up as soon as we had a discharge date.

Two weeks later, we were given instructions for home care. Two people had to turn him every two hours because he was no longer a featherweight little boy, but a large, bulky plaster boy. At all costs, we could not jostle the metal skeletal pin apparatus protruding from the cast. We had to make sure he was adequately hydrated to help prevent blood clots due to his inactivity. He had cutouts in the cast to allow for bodily functions, using a bedpan and a urinal. We borrowed a mechanic's creeper so we could place him on his stomach to play. Elevated on pillows to keep the metal apparatus from touching the floor, Timmy easily pulled himself around on the ball-bearing casters while he maneuvered his little cars and Army men. We alternated him between a sofa bed downstairs during the day and his own bed at night.

Our parents lived with us and cared for Timmy for three weeks. Everyone had the tutorial on how to care for the boy in the cast. George came home for long lunches to pitch in. However, weeks loomed ahead where we had no help.

When our wonderful neighbors heard there was a possibility I'd have to leave school to take care of Timmy, one in particular became a lifesaver, setting up a schedule of volunteers to help during the work week. A nurse herself, Lynne was eager to assist. She was a godsend. Words can never express how grateful we were for her help. She brought a red stake wagon, which was padded with many pillows so she could pull Timmy around the neighborhood on nice days. She set up a chaise lounge in the shade of the front porch with, you guessed it, lots of pillows, and Tim would color or read books.

For three weeks, my neighbors covered Monday through Friday so I didn't have to take a leave of absence from school. My heart burst with thankfulness for their sacrifice and kindness.

After six weeks in the cast, Timmy was admitted to the hospital to have the contraption removed and begin physical therapy to learn to walk all over again. I stayed in the nurses' residence until he came home using a tiny walker. He was not allowed back to school until he could manage walking with crutches. When that goal was reached, George drove him to school in the morning, and Lynne picked him up in the afternoon. Both kids got home about the same time, and Margie supervised her little brother until I got home at 4:00 p.m. It was a team effort.

One afternoon in the first week of December, three months to the day after the accident, I came through the door to see my two beautiful children sitting at the table having a snack. "We have a surprise for you, Mom. Close your eyes."

"Okay, they're closed."

Several seconds passed. "Open your eyes now."

I opened my eyes to see both kids grinning from ear to ear. Timmy was standing unassisted and walked slowly toward me. I began to cry as he reached out his arms for the best hug ever.

Three years later, I graduated from nursing school, having made the dean's list six times. It humbles me to know my achievement would not have been possible without the kindness and sacrifice of family and friends to get us through a most difficult time.

~Nancy Emmick Panko

66

Two Guys

Being of service to others is what brings true happiness.
~Marie Osmond

I volunteer for a local charity, doing repairs and carpentry. One morning, Carrie from the agency phoned. There had been a break-in at our emergency housing for homeless families. Someone had kicked in the front door, overturned furniture, and smashed holes in the walls.

It didn't sound like theft. "Maybe it was the boyfriend or husband?" I suggested, since we often house women and children, and a deserted man can react with rage.

"No. The husband's there, too." Carrie told me they were a young Hispanic family—a mom, dad and two children under ten. The husband left a construction job in Puerto Rico to relocate to upstate New York for a better offer. Not long into the job, his hip was crushed in a worksite accident. Despite two surgeries, he might never walk again. Without his income, they lost their apartment. Carrie said, "Their life is falling apart. This break-in has the woman scared to death." She let that hang, so I wondered if the damage was done by someone who resented the type of people we sheltered. "We need to fix the place ASAP."

I met Carrie at the house so she could introduce me. The parents spoke almost no English, Carrie spoke almost no Spanish, and my Spanish from high school had evaporated. Another volunteer arrived to translate. The mother—Anna—seemed shell-shocked. In her twenties, she had two children, a handicapped husband, no job, and was stranded several thousand miles from family. Now someone had vandalized this last refuge. It was just lucky they had been out when the vandals arrived.

The holes in the walls screamed hate. Two were fist-sized. Another was so large that someone must have rammed a shoulder through the drywall. Anna shuddered as we inspected them. A wheelchair sat in the living room. Upstairs, I passed a bedroom in which the husband lay in bed, curled up in despair facing the wall.

I took measurements and drove off to buy materials and get my tools. When I returned, I said "Hola!" to Anna, using up a tenth of my Spanish.

She smiled politely. Then the aroma in the kitchen beckoned, a sweet, tangy flavor so potent that breathing it sent 100 calories directly to my waist. Chili bubbled on the stove. Despite the damage, her cooking made the old house feel homey.

As I repaired the drywall, the husband slid downstairs step by step on his rear end. When he reached the bottom, he used a single crutch to struggle upright on his good leg and sit in the wheelchair. He was a handsome man in his late twenties with an athletic body. Anna pointed at him and said to me, "Carlos."

"Garrett," I said. He reached up awkwardly to shake my hand, then grimaced and wheeled into the kitchen. Anna turned aside, distressed to see her man humbled. I finished screwing in the drywall so at least the dusty insides of the wall were hidden. Those angry holes insulted what America stands for. Decent people don't terrorize families down on their luck.

There wasn't much I could do about people filled with such hate, but something else was in my control. The kindness of strangers can be impersonal, even cold. That was not the case here. Carrie had rushed to help on her day off. The volunteer translator held Anna's hand while she translated. And another volunteer soon arrived to drive Anna and the children to several appointments in her own car. She brought cookies. These were good people doing their best to not remain strangers. I was proud of them. They made me feel that I should do more than just fix the damage, pat myself on the back, and drive home.

Left alone with Carlos, I wondered how that could happen. He stared from his wheelchair as I contemplated the ruined door. After stirring the chili, he had nothing else to do. I understood too well how he felt. Shortly after I retired, I suffered severe retinal detachments that threatened to blind me and left me unable to do many things I had always done. For two years, I lived in a kind of suspended animation. And I was not a thirty-year-old facing a lifetime of dependency. I wished I could have told Carlos to have patience and hope because he was young and strong, but the language barrier separated us.

The door had a keypad lock, and after I removed the outer plate and handle, I could not extract the rest of the mechanism. I began to sweat under Carlos's gaze. "Señor," he said, rolling closer. He pointed to a spot inside the lock and made a twisting motion. I started to reach for it, but then had a better impulse.

"Usted." I nodded, using another of my few Spanish words.

His hand flashed into the lock. In ten seconds, he extracted it with a grin. I unscrewed the door's top hinge, then handed Carlos the screw gun to detach the lower two. After I cut the new door to size, we worked together to mark the hinge and lock locations and rebuild the jamb. He worked eagerly, glad to be useful. I screwed in the high hinge. Carlos did the lower ones and installed the keypad. When the door did not swing smoothly, we pointed and pantomimed until we figured out what the other one meant. We soon made the adjustments.

"Bueno?" I asked.

"Si," he said, closing the heavy-duty door with a solid click. Then he reopened it and welcomed me into his kitchen. He motioned me to follow into the living room, where he pointed at the patched drywall and pantomimed covering the seams with tape and joint compound, then tapped his chest. He was not going to stay here long—a few days most likely. He had nothing invested in this house, except for his pride. He would protect his family and make the house fit for the other homeless families coming after him. Together, we would erase the holes and what they stood for.

One of the best parts of volunteering is that the stranger you offer kindness to can become a friend. That's the kind of America I am proud of. After I gathered my tools, Carlos nodded at the chili and raised an eyebrow. I understood perfectly. It was the language of hungry men.

~Garrett Bauman

67

The Streets Are Not Paved with Gold

A single act of kindness throws out roots in all directions, and the roots spring up and make new trees.
~Amelia Earhart

My mom gave away every single toy I owned except for one doll. Then that doll was accidentally decapitated by my brother riding his bike.

"You will have plenty of dolls in America," my mother assured me as she wiped away my tears. "The streets are paved with gold."

Mom, my brother and I were emigrating to America. We had to pack lightly as if we were going on a visit because no one was allowed to leave our Eastern-European country permanently. I was too young to understand why the government wouldn't allow my stepfather to go with us. "Mamko," I asked again, "why can't Daddy come with us?"

Mom answered again. "I told you, darling. It's forbidden for citizens to travel out of the country."

Imagine being told: "You can't leave the country with your family."

My brother and I were permitted to leave because Mom was a U.S. citizen.

We arrived at a New York City harbor, leaving behind an oppressive Communist regime. My first vision of the Statue of Liberty is still vivid in my mind. She stood at a distance, appearing so majestic. I'd heard about her from Mom. She symbolized liberty for all — an unequivocal contradiction of what we had left behind.

We observed the "Welcome to America" signs at the pier. The customs agent who checked our documents and passed us through echoed, "Welcome to America!" "Welcome" was the first word I learned in English.

"What does it mean?" I asked Mom.

I don't remember her exact words, but I soon learned its true meaning by the actions of Americans. They are the most welcoming people on Earth.

My grandparents met us at the pier. Before we all crammed into the waiting vehicle, I took a moment to check the sidewalk. Then this innocent eight-year-old concluded sadly, "The streets are not paved with gold."

We were moving into our grandparents' modest home in Queens, New York. It was full of relatives and tenants. When we pulled up to the house, everyone was waiting outside, cheering, "Welcome home!" A lady from next door greeted us with a bowl of spaghetti and marinara sauce. Another neighbor brought a pot of matzo ball soup.

The tiny bedroom that Mom, my brother and I shared had a sign over the bed that my cousins had colored with red, white and blue crayons. It said: "Welcome to America."

I attended school with my American cousin, Millie. Fortunately, she spoke my native language. Walking to school, we'd encounter people who greeted us warmly with a hello and a smile.

"Do you know them, Millie?" I'd ask.

"No," she replied.

"Then why are they smiling at us?" I wondered out loud.

"They're just being friendly. That's what we do," she explained.

But I was suspicious. That's not what people did in my old country. There, people walked with heads bowed, avoiding eye contact, afraid of their own shadows. The government encouraged neighbors to turn in neighbors, and family members to turn in their own relatives, out of fear. People withdrew from each other. It was safer.

I wasn't yet aware of the billions of dollars America donated each year to foreign aid or that the U.S. was always there to offer assistance to nations experiencing national disasters. As a little immigrant girl, I was only aware of how Americans treated me.

At school, the kids were so supportive.

"Let me help you with that lesson," said a child who approached me the first day. At least, that's what I thought he said. I didn't understand the English language, but I inherently understood the unspoken language of kindness.

I think I must have seemed like a hungry puppy, staring longingly at my classmates' lunches, when one little girl offered: "Want my sandwich? I'm not hungry."

Was she kidding? Peanut butter and jelly on white bread! When you're eight years old and you've never tasted peanut butter and jelly, there's nothing better! The simple snacks American kids took for granted, I considered amazing. They certainly beat my mom's day-old bread smeared with lard.

Mom went to work in a factory, sewing sleeping bags and bathing suits. She'd never sewn before, and it was the first job she ever had, but she never complained.

My clothes were hand-me-downs from Millie. Although we were the same age, I was four inches taller. The skirts were way too short, but Mom added colorful facing to the hems. When I grew some more, she added another row of facing. My long pants soon became Capri pants. Thank goodness I was as skinny as a rail, or the hand-me-downs would have been too tight and funny looking. Maybe they were funny looking, but I never knew.

No one had much in our new, lower-middle-class neighborhood in Queens. Maybe there wasn't money for fancy clothes or luxuries, but no one ever starved, and everyone shared what they had. And they helped each other in any way they could. It was more than a neighborhood; it was family.

Still, from time to time, I'd recall my mother's words, "The streets are paved with gold." And once again I would examine the concrete on the sidewalk and wonder why she had said that.

At the age of ten, I started earning my own money by walking dogs and babysitting. One day, Mom dropped by my babysitting job carrying a platter of freshly baked kolaches. I was delighted, thinking they were for me.

"Oh, no, darling. You'll have yours at home," she explained. "This is for the family here. It's time for us to give back."

"Give back? What's that?" I asked.

"It means that Americans have been so generous to us when we needed it, and now we hope to show our gratitude by returning the good deeds. You have to give back, too."

"Me? But what can I give? I have nothing." I didn't understand.

And then it occurred to me that I didn't have to give material things. Occasionally, I could walk the dogs and take care of some children pro bono. And so I did. It made me feel like a true American.

I'll always be grateful for the blessings bestowed on my family in the early years. Nowadays, when newcomers arrive in our country, our church or our neighborhood, I strive to extend to them the same warm welcome we received upon coming to America.

Decades later, the little doll without a body rests in my jewelry box, among more expensive — but not as valuable — trinkets. It's a constant reminder of how little material things mean if you don't have the kindness of friends and family, the freedom and the good fortune to live in America.

Under the jewelry box where no one can see — but I know it's there — is that simple sign of red, white and blue that our relatives placed over our bed when we arrived in this country. I don't have to see it to know it says: "Welcome to America."

No, the streets in America are not paved with gold. But they are paved with kindness and love.

~Eva Carter

68

Highway Breakdown

A fellow who does things that count, doesn't
usually need to stop to count them.
~Albert Einstein

Our PT Cruiser broke down at a dark and dismal highway rest stop somewhere between California and Arizona. With all the spectacle and force of Yellowstone's Old Faithful geyser, caustic anti-freeze steam rose from the car's engine, giving off a sour smell that turned rancid as the fumes touched our tongues.

My boyfriend Mark and I had been traveling with a fully packed car and camping trailer. We were transporting Mark's teenage son and all his belongings to Arizona so he could come live with us. Needless to say, our maiden voyage was not turning out well.

There we stood at the rest stop — sun setting, front hood open, green puddles at our feet — realizing we had a significant leak in the engine cooling system and only so much battery life left in our flashlight.

That's when I saw it… "the look."

Mark attempted to look in control of the situation while trouble-shooting, but the look dripped out and spilled all over his face. The look said, "We're screwed."

At a minimum, we needed a repair shop, a replacement hose, and more than a snow cone's chance in Hades that we could have both our car and trailer towed pronto and for less than a small fortune. Chances of that were slim to none on a Sunday night.

We were stranded. Moments after that realization, a black car appeared from out of the darkness, backing up to ours. A man of small stature stepped out of the car, wearing a neat, white shirt and light-colored shorts that hung well past his knees.

"Jou got problems with jour car?" the Spanglish-speaking man asked Mark.

"Uh, yeah, but it's no easy fix. It's leaking somewhere underneath, but I can't get under to find it."

"I mechanic. I help."

"But we can't fit..."

"Under car? No problem. I fit," the man said.

"No. You can't. It's too tight, and you'll ruin your..."

"I fit!" he said, waving an arm behind him, dismissing our concerns while going to the trunk of his car. Within seconds, he emerged with a sturdy car jack. Ours was buried under boxes, so all we could manage was to roll the front left tire onto a low curb. The little man jacked up our car even higher and gave it a good shake to make sure it was stable. Without hesitation, he slipped under the car on a blanket we laid down to protect his body and clothing.

Mark and I looked at each other quizzically.

"An angel," I uttered out loud.

"No kidding," he said, and then called down into the engine, "Hey, what's your name?"

"Rodr... g...," came the muffled reply.

"What? I can't hear you. How about I call you Rod?"

"Okay," came the reply.

Within an hour, after many radiator water refills, engine turnovers, and intense investigations in and around our car's underbelly, Rod emerged with the broken hose. Just what Mark did and didn't want to see.

Rod checked the time on his watch and then let out a sigh. "Auto parts closed." His shoulders slumped, so ours did, too. Screwed.

Then Rod perked up. "I try..." he said, animating with his hands how he would cut the damaged end off the hose and try to re-seat it.

Mark had his doubts. The hose was barely three inches long and seemed to be an exact, necessary length. "I see what you're saying, but I think we're gonna need a new hose."

"I have hose," Rod said.

"What?" Mark asked. "You have a hose?"

"Si."

"You have a hose."

"Si. But we try this first. Okay?"

Mark repeated himself one more time — one last attempt to let it sink in.

"Si," Rod said, signaling us to follow him over to his car. "I pick up today from junkyard, from old car."

In Rod's trunk were several grocery bags of parts pulled from old cars. In one of the bags were several hoses — one of which was a potential match for our broken hose. Also in the trunk were eight bags of groceries. And from inside Rod's car emerged a young mother and three small children. Immediately, I felt terrible we were imposing on not just Rod's time, but his family, as well.

Mark greeted the family and then held a lone hose up into the dim light, examining it. It wasn't perfect, but it looked like it could work. I watched his wrinkled brow relax as he turned his fascination to Rod. "Where did you come from?" Mark asked.

"Qué?... my car," Rod said.

"No, where did you come from?"

Rod tried again. "Blythe," he said, but clearly the question remained over his head.

"You're heaven sent," I said, but Rod still didn't understand.

Most of the time that Rod tended to our car, his wife and children milled around, easily keeping themselves entertained. Even when Rod's youngest son collapsed into a tear-filled meltdown after he or one of his siblings slammed a car door on his fingers, Rod checked on the crying child, but quickly returned to working on our car. Even while groceries in the back of their car were warming in the seventy-five-degree night air, Rod kept working on our car. Even though Rod's family had been out the entire day and seemed tuckered out, Rod kept working on our car.

Just about midnight, Rod and Mark fixed the car enough to make it drivable. Realizing we had a good chance of making it home, we fought back tears and squeezed Rod with heartfelt hugs. I hugged Rod's wife and thanked her profusely for her family's great kindness and patience, to which she simply said, "We had this happen to us once. We remember what it was like."

Mark and I scrounged up sixty dollars between us and gave it to Rod, apologizing for our meager offering for four hours of selfless work. We asked for his address, intending to do something more for him and his family afterwards.

"Ah… Rodrigo!" I said, as I read the name that appeared on the scratch paper.

"Si!" he said, with a big smile.

Rodrigo received our offering graciously, but seemed more concerned about us making it home safely. Without hesitation, he insisted on following us for forty miles on the highway and texted us the rest of the way until we walked in our door.

The next day, I looked up Rodrigo's name on the Internet, hoping to find out more about this exceptional man. One of the search results listed the qualities typical of people by the name of Rodrigo. It said, "You are tolerant and like to help humanity. You are generally warmhearted and give freely of your time, energy, and sympathetic understanding. Universal and humanitarian in outlook. This is a very compassionate name." We couldn't agree more.

~Susan Maddy Jones

Simple Gifts

It isn't the size of the gift that matters, but
the size of the heart that gives it.
~Eileen Elias Freeman

"Did you hear about Jane? She was taken to the hospital a few nights ago to have her appendix out. I guess it was all very sudden."

Standing on the sidewalk outside my house, my face and attention turned from my daughter and her Big Wheel to my neighbor. "No, I didn't hear anything about that. Is she okay?" My neighbor didn't know, but Jane would be coming home today.

I really liked Jane. She had two boys, a little older than my grade school-aged son and daughter. Jane and I spent many hours chatting while our young ones played games and rode bikes up and down the sidewalks. It was so surprising to hear about her surgery. I decided right then that I wanted to do something for her.

Wracking my brain, I couldn't seem to come up with a plan. Her husband had taken time off from work, so she didn't need babysitting. Her family was arriving in a few days, so they could do the shopping. What was left? Finally, I decided to volunteer to make a dinner for them.

Now I must confess that I come from a long line of bad cooks. Cooking is not our forte. My dad said his mother "boiled everything."

Volunteering for a dinner was not something I did lightly. But I figured if I called early and got my bid in, I'd have a few days to flip through some cookbooks. *You'll be fine,* I told myself. *You can do this.*

The next day, I called my friend's house, and her husband answered the phone. He was a bit flustered, and I felt so sorry for him. I'm sure the first days were tough, trying to help his wife while getting ready for family coming in, too. It was a short phone call, but I did find out that the pain pills were working and my friend was doing well. As we wound up the call, I asked him, "Would you like me to make you a dinner sometime?"

One would think I'd thrown a life preserver to a drowning man. He responded immediately and with enthusiasm, "Yes! How about tonight?"

My mind started to race. Tonight? As in the same day it is today? "Um… well… I guess… Oh, of course I will. Count on me!" I stammered as I hung up the phone. Now I was the one who was flustered. My two older children were at school, and the baby was sleeping upstairs. There was no way I was getting to the store.

Whatever this family was going to eat tonight had to be in my house right now.

I rooted through my pantry and scoured the refrigerator. The only things I could find for a meal were the ingredients for tuna casserole. I didn't even have enough lettuce for a decent salad. *Well,* I said to myself, *I promised to make dinner, so I guess this is what I'll be serving.*

I baked the casserole and a tube of ready-made biscuits. Then I quickly mixed and baked some brownies. When I was finally done preparing the meal, I wrapped everything up and walked to my friend's door to deliver my embarrassingly plain dinner. As I began the walk back to my house, mercifully under the cover of darkness, I bowed my head and hoped I'd never have to think about that meal again.

Three days later, there was a knock at the door. It was my friend's son, returning my very clean casserole dish. After thanking him, I took the dish to the kitchen, and as I placed the dish on my counter, I noticed that it had some papers in it.

The first paper I pulled out was an envelope, and inside was a thank-you note from Jane. Between friends, it's not necessary to do something like that, but that's just the kind of person she is. The second paper I pulled out was an index card with a paper attached that read, "Would you give me the recipe for your tuna casserole?"

I was stunned. *Are you kidding me?* I thought. *She wants the recipe for that?* I was really embarrassed now because here's how I make it:

Take a can of tuna. Open the can. Scrape it into a casserole dish.
Take a can of cream of mushroom soup. Open the can. Add it to the tuna.
Swirl these ingredients around for a while, and then add some cooked egg noodles.
(If you are feeling fancy, add crumbled potato chips to the top of the casserole.)
Bake at 350 degrees for a while until it's hot.

But as I stood there in the kitchen with the thank-you note in one hand and the request for my tuna casserole recipe in the other, I realized something: They really liked that meal. It wasn't fancy, and it certainly wasn't balanced, but it was enough. For that one night, my friend and her family knew there were neighbors who cared about them. I thought what I did was so inadequate, but to my friend on the receiving end, it meant the world.

That very simple dinner, delivered one night to a little house in our small town, showed me that reaching out to help someone doesn't require a big production. I saw the power in a simple gift, given with love. That meal not only fed this family, but it warmed their hearts, too.

It's easy to believe that the problems of our neighbors are so difficult or complicated that we can't possibly make a difference, but that's just not true. All across America, people are extending themselves in little acts of kindness and care to their neighbors who need a healing touch. It might look like what they do is impossibly small, but to the people they serve, those efforts mean everything.

That's a beautiful reason to continue helping those who need us. All it takes is one small act of kindness, one family to another, to make a difference. Through my small offer to provide a dinner, I joined in our nation's tradition of the simple gift, and I look forward to helping again soon. Going forward, I'm going to be more aware of the needs of my neighbors. After all, I do make one impressive tuna casserole.

~Ceil Ryan

70

Out of the Mouths of Strangers

A kind word is like a spring day.
~Russian Proverb

"I hate fat girls. I hate ugly girls." This completely unprovoked verbal assault came as my friend and I were walking into our junior high school one morning. The girl who'd spoken — an eighth-grader neither of us had ever met before — glared insolently at us as though daring us to say something back.

My friend and I just ducked our heads and hurried past, hoping our attacker wouldn't spew even more insults. I spent the rest of the day wondering if I was the ugly one, the fat one or, more likely, both.

Needless to say, my self-esteem in junior high wasn't exactly in the stratosphere.

High school was hardly an improvement. I was at band camp my freshman year when a girl I only knew a little bit from elementary school walked up to me, leaned close, and whispered, "Um, there's something coming out of your pants."

Frowning, I reached back. It felt like a tissue sticking out of the waistband. I pulled on it, and to my horror, a three-foot-long trail of toilet paper came out. It had been dangling there, like a tail, for a good half-hour, at least.

Cheeks on fire, I crumpled the toilet paper, stuffed it in my pocket, and thanked the girl for informing me. She nodded and scurried away. I could only hope no one else had seen it. Much to my dismay, I later learned that an entire group of people had noticed, and they'd actually held a *vote* over who would have to tell me!

I wish I could say things got better from there.

In my sophomore year, I ran into one of the school guidance counselors in the hallway. I didn't know her very well, but my dad, who taught biology at the school, had always spoken highly of her. I definitely wanted to make a good first impression. I greeted her warmly, and she gave me a super-friendly smile. She asked about life on the farm my family had just moved to, and I eagerly told her. We ended up in her office, having a twenty-minute discussion about horses, literature, career goals, and numerous other topics. I couldn't wait to tell my dad how well we hit it off!

Then, just as I was getting ready to leave the counselor's office, she leaned close and whispered, "Um, by the way, your fly is unzipped."

The smile wilted off my face. I looked down, and sure enough: unzipped. Plus a little bit of my white T-shirt was poking through the opening, emphasizing the gaping hole.

"I noticed it a little while ago," the counselor added, "but I didn't want to interrupt you."

"Thanks," I said faintly.

My face glowed like good old Rudolph's nose as I quickly zipped my pants and slunk out of her office, hoping I'd never see her again. Well, at least not anytime soon.

By junior year, I was a pro at checking my fly inconspicuously. I was also completely paranoid about making sure none of the T.P. that my mom insisted I drape on all public toilet seats inadvertently got stuck in my pants.

So far, there had not been a repeat of either incident.

Things were looking up… until the day I saw a girl approaching me after band class with a critical frown on her face. I quickly checked my fly, but it was properly zipped. There was no time to check for T.P.

Instead of leaning in close to whisper the bad news, the girl simply reached behind my head and pulled something out of my ponytail.

"This was in your hair," she said, holding up what appeared to be a stick.

I stared at the object for a full five seconds before realizing it was actually a thick piece of hay. It must've fallen into my hair when I was feeding the horses that morning. I explained this to the girl and thanked her for taking it out. She was polite, but I'm sure she was wondering, just like I was, how I could've missed such a thing when I was brushing my hair. It was *huge*. It might as well have been a stick. And now, I had yet another item for my daily "Try Not to Look Ridiculous" checklist: Inspect your hair for giant twigs every morning.

I wondered how many more things I would have to add to that list before my high-school years were over.

A few weeks later, I thought I was about to find out. A National Honor Society meeting had just broken up, and my friend and I were milling around, chatting with other NHS members and enjoying the post-meeting snacks. Then I saw the girl approaching. I didn't know her name, and she appeared to be headed directly for me. My stomach dipped.

When she stopped in front of me, I could feel my heart rate go up.

"I need to tell you something," the girl said. Her eyes were solemn. Her face, unreadable.

My heart was beating so hard by now that I could feel it pulsing behind my eyes. I glanced at my friend, who was standing beside me, about to have a front-row seat to my humiliation.

I looked back at the girl. "Should she leave?" I asked hesitantly, indicating my friend. "I mean is this something she shouldn't hear?"

Or that I don't want her to hear? I thought.

"She can stay," the girl said.

I swallowed loudly. Sweat was soaking through my shirt, and I tried not to draw attention to it. The girl took a deep breath and squared her shoulders. *Here it comes,* I thought, *another fat, ugly, toilet-paper-tail, fly-unzipped, stick-in-your-hair moment.*

"I just wanted you to know," she began, "that you are the prettiest girl I have ever seen in my life. You are so beautiful. And if you ever notice people staring at you, that's why."

Once I got over the sheer shock, I managed to stammer a "thank you." I was blushing so furiously, my face felt sunburned. My friend grabbed my hand and clutched it tightly, moved to tears by the display of kindness. The girl smiled and walked away.

In the years since then, I've often wondered what made her do it. Maybe she really thought I was pretty. Maybe she somehow recognized that I had self-esteem issues and she wanted to help.

Or maybe, she just woke up that morning and said to herself, "Today, I am going to walk right up to some random girl and make her feel spectacular. I am going to give her a moment that will shine so brightly in her memory, it will not only stay with her for the rest of her life, but it will also make every bad memory seem dim and insignificant by comparison. Today, I am going to make someone feel like the most beautiful, most special, most important person in the whole wide world."

And if that was her goal?

Man, she nailed it.

~Gretchen Bassier

71

Wrapped in Love

Love is always bestowed as a gift — freely,
willingly and without expectation.
~Leo Buscaglia

With the arrival of the holiday season, my heart filled with gratitude. Only months earlier, my family and I had wondered if I'd even see another Christmas after spending seventeen days in the hospital with heart problems. Still recovering from surgery, I found myself in an emotional state.

When a mammoth parcel arrived on our doorstep, I couldn't believe my eyes. The return address showed that one of my online friends had sent it — a woman from Pennsylvania whom I'd never spoken to on the phone or met in person.

Inside the cardboard box I found two gigantic, cheerfully wrapped packages along with a card. Placing them under our tree, I couldn't help the thankful tears that filled my eyes.

Of course, I sent Kate an e-mail and reprimanded her for spending her hard-earned money on me when I knew she could have used it for her family. She wrote back and informed me that two other Internet friends had gone in on the deal — Connie from Oregon and Dorann from New Jersey — both women I'd never met but who were also Chicken Soup for the Soul writers, as I was. Kate explained that it wasn't meant for Christmas, but rather a get-out-of-the-hospital surprise that had arrived late.

During the months leading up to my hospital stay, and while I was in the hospital, several of my networking friends who had known about my health troubles had shown support. They'd kept my home and online mailbox filled with messages of love, hope, prayers, and encouragement, which boosted my family's morale. And now these three special ladies had sent a gift.

Even though they weren't Christmas presents, I loved the way the red and green wrapping paper added color under our tree. It served as a blessed reminder that our family had made it through this difficult time. I told Kate and the others that if they had no objection, I'd like to save the packages for Christmas morning so I could enjoy their beauty during the coming weeks.

When Christmas arrived, our eyes glistened as I opened the card and read the inscription to my family. My voice cracked with emotion.

With all you and your hubby have been through these last couple of months, we want to make sure you stay warm and cozy this winter!
Wrapping you in our love!
Kate, Connie and Dorann xoxoxo

Their thoughtfulness touched our hearts, and they could not have picked a more perfect present — two beautiful, cozy blankets!

My friends had known that we heated with woodstoves and that, during the winter, our house can get downright chilly, especially in the morning. However, they didn't know that our many threadbare blankets had worn so thin that we'd had trouble staying warm at night in our bed. With my medical disasters, my husband had missed a lot of work, and money had been tight. New blankets were not in the picture for us.

Also, including my husband touched both of our hearts. David had suffered so many sleepless nights worrying about me, and now when he'd find himself wide awake and stressed, he had a comforting, fluffy throw to curl up in, compliments of three kind souls he'd never had contact with.

I may never meet these three women. They may never meet each other. And yet their kindness represents what I have found in my cyberspace pals who live in this great country of ours — compassionate, caring souls whom I'm honored and proud to call my dearest friends.

~Jill Burns

Chapter
8

My **Kind** (of) **America**

Making Things Happen

72

Making School Cool

Come forth into the light of things,
let Nature be your teacher.
~William Wordsworth, The Tables Turned

With no central air conditioning and no trees providing shade, the classrooms that faced south at my children's middle school got way too hot during the warmer months of the school year. I knew firsthand from my days volunteering in the school that students, staff and volunteers got overheated, and it was difficult to concentrate.

As a long-time master gardener, I knew that trees could shade those classroom windows and reduce the temperatures inside to teachable levels. If benches and shrubs were added, the front yard would be transformed into an "outdoor classroom," one that would entice teachers to bring their students outside to learn. And I imagined how wonderful it would be for our district's kids, many of whom live in apartment buildings without yards or green space, to experience the contentment of sitting on a bench under a leafy green tree during their school day.

Since I'm both a dreamer and a doer, I met with the school's PTA and described how adding trees, shrubs and benches would lower classroom temps as well as add natural beauty to the front yard. And I expressed my willingness to organize the project. The group liked the idea, but thought their fundraising efforts and volunteer time should remain focused on academics. During the meeting, I noticed that the principal, whose family has deep roots in our town and gives generously of their time and talent, listened carefully to my proposal, but he didn't comment.

Two days later, the principal called me. He said, "When people are surrounded by beauty, they are happier. When children are in a natural environment, they are calmer. When students can sit outside on a beautiful day surrounded by green trees and birds, they learn more."

He continued: "I have a school filled with energetic students. And I shared your thoughts with my staff. We all think you are very kind to offer us your skills. My staff and I want to help you transform our school's front yard. Let's meet."

At that first meeting, I promised to find a certified landscape designer who would transform our vision into a workable plan. A social studies teacher agreed to research possible grants and mock up sample lessons that would incorporate the outdoor classroom into the school's social studies curriculum. The art teacher said she would brainstorm with her colleagues and create lesson plans that would use the natural resources of a newly refurbished front yard. The science teacher said his department was enthusiastic about conducting nature-based experiments in an outdoor classroom. And the principal? He promised to talk with the district to figure out the logistics of making our vision a reality.

After a year of meetings and design revisions, the district approved a landscape plan, which was created, gratis, by a professional landscape designer who graduated from the school years earlier. I found a local company that promised to deliver topsoil at a deeply discounted price when we were ready to create the planting berms. Then I heard about a new foundation in our state that had a grant program for schools doing exactly what we were planning: planting trees to lower temperatures inside the school building as well as beautify the urban environment. I applied, and we were accepted into the program for the following year! We were promised a variety of shade trees that would thrive in our area. The trees and the labor to install them were free! And the foundation thought it was terrific that our students and staff would work alongside the professional crew to plant the trees.

Meanwhile, the social studies teacher submitted a grant application for the plan, an outdoor classroom, which we called "The Habitat for Living & Learning." And I applied for a grant from a large home improvement store. Many months later, we were notified. We won both grants!

At this point, we spoke with everyone we knew about the Habitat for Living & Learning. The hard work of digging and planting was scheduled to begin within months, so we posted the design in the front hall of the school where students, staff, parents, and locals could see it. We spoke about it at local meetings, school events and one-on-one in the community. People in our community were so very kind and we received donations and offers to help with the planting.

One sunny day, three years after my first conversation with the principal and his staff, huge trucks filled with topsoil arrived at the school. Students and staff were lined up three deep at the classroom windows, cheering and waving. It was easily one of the best days of my life.

Everyone — students, staff, and volunteers — worked to spread the topsoil over a series of days. The following week, the trees and the crew from the foundation arrived. Students and teachers worked in shifts alongside the crew for a full day. All day, I heard students ask questions: "Will trees really make our classrooms cooler?" "Why do we have to dig such a deep hole?" "Do we have to water the trees every day?" The crew and volunteers answered every question.

And today? Leafy green trees shade those formerly hot classrooms. Classes are regularly held in the Habitat for Living & Learning. Students read outside in small groups during English. They talk and laugh as they measure the ambient air temperature for an experiment during Science. Budding young photographers take photos during Art.

Word spread about what we had accomplished. Parents from other schools approached us to learn how to do something similar at their schools. I met with interested parents and the local garden club, of which I was also a member, to share resources, tips, and insights. Now most of the schools in our school district have renovated their front yards with the assistance of local volunteers, the local garden club, and eager staff and students. My heart glows every time I walk by one of our transformed schools.

~Darlene Sneden

A Little Birdie

Build a Bridge, Save a Life
~Bridge Breast Network slogan

Miss Birdie was a petite woman with an inviting smile and a loving heart, who absolutely adored children. So it was no surprise that she'd chosen a career in childcare and early education. She enjoyed interacting and caring for the children at Westflower School — where she taught sign language, shapes and colors to infants and toddlers — so much so that she would get to school early every day.

One day, while reading to the toddlers in her bright classroom adorned with Dr. Seuss sayings and characters, she felt a sharp pain in her breast that made her pause for a few moments. After catching her breath, she continued reading to the toddlers but noticed that the pain wasn't going away. Miss Birdie had been blessed with good health, and over her fifty years she had never had more than a few bad colds and a stomach virus here or there that she'd contracted from one of her "little babies." And when she did feel under the weather, over-the-counter medicines worked just fine. But this time was different. By the end of the school day, with the pain still in her breast, she was sure she needed to see a doctor.

That night, after she cooked a hearty meal of meatloaf and mashed potatoes for her family, Miss Birdie started researching breast pain on the Internet. She figured out pretty quickly that she would need a mammogram. Her salary at the school was enough to cover her

Making Things Happen | 275

household bills and allow her to take care of her family of four as a single mom, but she had very little left over at the end of every month. With no health insurance, she wondered how she'd be able to afford a mammogram. But she knew she had to get one. That's when Miss Birdie started researching options for women like her and came across the Bridge Breast Network in Dallas, Texas.

The Bridge provides free medical care to uninsured and under-insured women diagnosed with breast cancer. The Bridge's mantra is that no woman should die from breast cancer because she lacks resources. The process starts with a woman calling The Bridge looking for assistance in getting a free mammogram. The nonprofit connects that woman to free diagnostic medical services (mammograms and biopsies). Then, if she is diagnosed with breast cancer, The Bridge connects that same woman to a team of medical providers, including doctors, surgeons, oncologists, and radiologists. The medical team volunteers their time, but The Bridge is financially responsible for materials (film for the mammography machine, for example) and drug therapies (chemotherapy, for example) and can purchase these items at cost. Through its business model, The Bridge is able to leverage $1 in donations ten times so that a $100 contribution equates to $1,000 in medical care provided.

The Bridge provided Miss Birdie with a diagnostic mammogram and a needle biopsy that confirmed she did indeed have breast cancer. The Bridge then helped her navigate through the maze of medical care at no cost to her. She had a lumpectomy, eight weeks of radiation and was prescribed Tamoxifen for the next five years.

I met Miss Birdie four years later when she became my daughter McKenzie's teacher. I dropped McKenzie off one morning, rushing because I was running late for an appointment. I didn't have time for my normal morning pleasantries with Miss Birdie, and she noticed.

She asked where I was rushing off to and why I was so dressed up. (I was wearing pearls, a vibrant pink suit, and peep-toe pumps in the same shade.) I told her I had to speak at a breakfast before work and pulled my lapel pin out of my purse as she complimented me on my attire. As soon as I put on the pin, Miss Birdie recognized the double pink ribbon logo with "The Bridge" in tiny letters under it and started screaming. That's when she told me about her own experience as a client of The Bridge.

She told me how thankful she was for The Bridge — that we surely saved her life, and we did it in a way that allowed her to keep her dignity. I told her I was the Treasurer of the Board of Directors for the organization and was going to speak at our annual Bridgebuilders' breakfast where we thank our donors and ask for more contributions.

As I drove away from Westflower to battle morning traffic, I had a renewed sense of focus. I was now more determined than ever to help save the lives of hardworking women in my community who had to choose between healthcare and groceries, between mammograms and rent, or between surgery and utilities.

For the past twenty-five years, The Bridge has been saving the lives of women like Miss Birdie — 200,000 women to date. We have provided millions of dollars in free medical care. I am so proud of what we have accomplished, even as I understand there is so much more to do. Now as President of the Board of Directors for The Bridge, I have given my time, talents and resources to this organization for the past eleven years because I know what a woman faces when she is diagnosed with breast cancer. I know what she is up against emotionally *and* financially when it comes to treatment. I was diagnosed one year prior to joining The Bridge as a board member and volunteer. One year prior to my diagnosis, I lost my forty-five-year-old mother-in-law to the disease. I wanted to do something to honor her legacy so that her dying would not be in vain. I could not save her, but through our efforts at The Bridge, I am able to help save someone else's mother. Someone else's daughter. Someone else's sister. Someone else's teacher.

I am forever grateful that a "little Birdie" reminded me to never give up building bridges of hope in my community.

~Sheila Taylor-Clark

74

An Encounter with the President

The willingness of some to give their lives so that others might live never fails to evoke in us a sense of wonder and mystery.
~President Ronald Reagan

Ronald Reagan was a childhood hero of mine. In 1984, at age thirteen, I wrote to him and asked if he would honor my grandfather, a World War II veteran, in some way. He was retiring from his career as an employee of the state of Colorado and I wanted to do something special for him.

A few days prior to his retirement celebration, a large envelope arrived in the mail. Inside was a beautiful typed letter, signed by President Reagan, congratulating my grandfather on his years of service to the State of Colorado and our country.

A short time later, a smaller, handwritten note arrived from the President, simply thanking me for taking the time to write him and for being a faithful patriot. I later learned that President Reagan was famous for personally answering some of his mail, and I was lucky enough to be included in that category.

Later that year, my grandfather and I received an invitation to attend Ronald Reagan's second inauguration. Regrettably, we had to decline the invitation because we couldn't afford the plane tickets.

Years later, Washington, D.C. prepared to dedicate the World

War II Memorial on the Mall, between the Lincoln Memorial and the Washington Monument. They asked veterans to join the celebration. On May 29, 2004, my family escorted my grandfather on the most amazing trip to our nation's capital, where he, along with thousands of other veterans, was honored for his service.

By this time, I had started a military support organization that served veterans and their families, so to be around this gathering was especially humbling as veterans from every war and every branch of service descended on the District of Columbia to mark the occasion. There were more than 140,000 people there that day.

My grandfather and I shared a special moment outside the gates of the White House, reminiscing about the 1984 invitation from President Reagan that we were unable to accept.

On June 5th, President Ronald Reagan passed away, and my heart was crushed.

Two years later, President George W. Bush invited me and several other founders of military support organizations, including actor Gary Sinise, to visit him and discuss our work with military veterans and their families. It was an invitation I wasn't about to turn down again!

I remember sitting across from the President of the United States as he addressed each of us. A young boy's dream had finally come true, yet it seemed surreal.

Shortly after having our pictures taken with the President and participating in a brief press conference, we were escorted to the main section of the White House for a private tour.

I soaked up every color, every artifact, and every word I could retain. After all, very few people get an invitation to meet with a President, let alone are given a private tour of the White House.

As I entered the East Room, where I knew many grand historical receptions had taken place, I thought to myself, *Well, President Reagan, here I am! I'm twenty-two years late, but I was finally able to accept your invitation. The only thing that would have made this moment perfect is if you were here right now.*

After taking a final look, I slowly exited the East Room, my mind still processing everything I had seen and learned about the magnificent history of the People's House. And just as I turned the corner to go into a hallway, there before me was a life-size portrait of our 40th President, Ronald Wilson Reagan, seemingly looking down upon me with his ever-famous smile.

I felt like I was meeting my hero face to face! Granted, it wasn't the same as meeting the man himself, but it was the next best thing!

Not only had I met the current President of the United States and walked in the footsteps of history, but I had a divine encounter with my childhood hero, all in one day.

I had to call my grandfather and tell him about the experience. He cried on the phone as he said, "I'm glad you got to fulfill your dream. I wish I could have been with you."

And that's my kind of America, where a young boy can dream the impossible and have it come true.

~Leo Pacheco

75

A Spark

How beautiful a day can be when kindness touches it.
~George Elliston

Shortly after moving into a new Clovis, California neighborhood in 2002, I noticed my neighbors all had the same routine: drive into the driveway, use a remote control to open the garage door, and drive in with the door closing behind them. Everyone had a lawn service, which meant no one worked or puttered in their yards. Rarely did I see children playing outside. I didn't know even one of my neighbors. It seemed so impersonal and isolating to me. My neighborhood needed a spark.

The next Christmas season, it was time to be that spark. I sent invitations to each house on my street inviting the neighbors to my home for a Christmas cookie exchange. To my surprise, they all came bringing trays of freshly baked cookies.

It was a delightful evening getting to know one another. We discovered we all felt the same way — we needed to connect. Several began to talk about vandalism or other minor crimes they had experienced in our area. We agreed that the simple solution was to exchange phone numbers and alert each other to potential problems. By the end of the evening, someone offered to host the cookie exchange the following Christmas.

Two years later, in addition to what was now our annual Christmas cookie exchange, we decided to hold mid-year block parties, giving us another opportunity to connect. We received permission from the city to shut down our street for an afternoon. Neighbors brought out tables, chairs, barbecues, and lots of food. We rented a bounce house, hired a disc jockey and invited someone from the police department to speak to us. It became an annual event and included our official Community Watch meeting to discuss all issues concerning our neighborhood.

When the police department implemented the Clovis Community Watch program (CCW), I was voted to represent our neighborhood as the block captain. I met with other block captains and local police officers to help promote community safety, awareness, and connection.

In 2016, block captains were invited to work with the police on a more substantial community awareness program. We met in a local park monthly, but the cold months were coming. Someone asked, "Where can we meet during the winter?"

"My house is always open," I volunteered cheerfully.

An officer sitting behind me said jokingly, "Great! How about Thanksgiving? I am on patrol and won't get to have Thanksgiving dinner." Everyone laughed and agreed that I should open my house to everyone in attendance for Thanksgiving dinner.

"I am agreeing to host CCW meetings only," I said, dismissing that idea.

As I drove home, the words of the officer — "I am on patrol and won't get to have Thanksgiving dinner" — kept playing in my head. By the time I pulled into my garage, I made the decision that I would provide dinner for him and the other officers who kept my family safe during the holiday.

My surprised husband easily agreed when I told him, "I am preparing Thanksgiving dinner for all Clovis officers who will be on patrol Thanksgiving."

My intention was to buy, prepare, and serve the meal myself at the police station. I could not ask anyone else to give up their family time. But then my next-door neighbor asked, "What are you doing for Thanksgiving?"

"Preparing dinner for the Clovis Police who will be on patrol," I answered.

"I'll buy the turkey," he volunteered.

Another neighbor said she would cook it. Others called or came to my door to volunteer salads, side dishes, and desserts. Some offered money. So many asked to help.

Thanksgiving Day arrived. I could hardly wait to meet the other volunteers at the police station to set up for the feast that would be served later that day. Decorations in red, orange, brown and yellow gave a warm, welcoming feeling to the room. The buffet tables were over-filled with all the traditional and favorite foods associated with the holiday. By noon, everything was perfect and waiting for our special guests: Clovis police officers who could not be with their families.

The officers stepped into the break room, waiting to fill their plates from the bountiful offerings. "There are really people who would take time out from their family holiday to provide this incredible meal for us?" one asked.

"It is our honor to do this for you," I said.

The mood was light as the officers ate and shared conversation and laughs. When the last meal was served and the last officer left, it was time to clean up and go home, secure in the knowledge that these men and women were keeping our city safe. It made me happy to know that in some small way, my friends and I did something to make their holiday easier.

Just as with the cookie exchange and block parties, preparing and serving Thanksgiving dinner for police officers promises to become an annual tradition. It started with "a spark" years ago in the form of a simple idea and a simple invitation.

~Georgia A. Brackett

76

Quilting Comfort

A quilt is a treasure that follows its owner everywhere.
~Quilt Sayings

I used to work for a national Alzheimer's research program at a university. We wanted to thank the many Alzheimer's patients who volunteered to participate in our clinical research studies. But how?

As a quilter, I knew that quilts could soothe and calm anyone, from a tiny baby to a homesick college freshman. I suggested to my boss that we give lap-size quilts to the participants. I knew that the patients would appreciate them.

At first, she rejected the idea, saying we couldn't afford to buy quilts for hundreds of people.

"No, no," I told her. "Quilters will make and donate them. It won't cost us anything."

She looked at me like I was mad. "Why would a person donate a handmade quilt?"

"Because we quilters run out of people. After a while, our families and friends have all the quilts they need. We want to keep making quilts, so we make them for charity," I explained.

With that she said I could begin the project if our director agreed. He also questioned why a person would make a quilt for a stranger. "What kind of person would do that?" he asked.

"A kind one," I answered.

Ultimately, he approved the pilot project, though he had little faith it would succeed. I caught him rolling his eyes as I got out of my chair to leave his office.

I reached out to a couple of quilter friends. They agreed to send e-mails to 17,000 quilters telling them about my new project to give quilts to Alzheimer's research participants. No sooner had the e-mails gone out than offers began coming in from quilters wanting to help. I notified all of our research clinics and let them know that soon we would have quilts for them to give the study participants.

When the first box arrived, I opened it as though it were my birthday. I cooed over the sweet quilts, each handmade, each a testament of the heart.

I began shipping them to our research clinics. One of the first clinics to receive quilts was in Alabama. The study coordinator called me a few days later and told me about an elderly patient who came in to undergo a scan. She put the woman on the metal table, which was cold and hard. She began shivering before the scan started. Denise Ledlow, the study coordinator, ran back to her office and returned with a quilt that we'd sent her. She covered the woman, who stayed warm and comfortable throughout the imaging. Afterward, the woman's daughters came into the room and helped their mother sit up. All three of them fingered the colorful quilt and asked the study coordinator who it belonged to.

"It belongs to you," Denise told the elderly mother.

The woman and her daughters didn't understand. Denise turned over the quilt and showed them a label on the back that dedicated the quilt to the Alzheimer's patient who received it. The quilter thanked the patient for volunteering for research, for helping to put an end to the disease. Denise told me that the women were stunned and weepy-eyed at the unexpected generosity from someone they would never meet.

After a while, the quilts stopped coming, and I knew I had to find another source. Through a friend, we reached out to AARP, hoping for coverage in one of their publications. When an editor called, we talked about the project, and she advised me to set up a dedicated e-mail address and phone line because we would be inundated with inquiries when the story ran. The short article appeared in one of their publications that went to twenty-five million homes.

E-mails and voicemails began pouring in. We sent out instructions on where to send the quilts. It took a month for three of us to respond to all the inquiries before they began to slow down. By then, dozens of boxes of quilts began arriving at our office, where I stored them on my office shelves. It looked like a quilt shop.

As a quilter, I couldn't wait to open each box, but it wasn't just the quilts that intrigued me. In every box, we found a handwritten note or a letter thanking us for giving the quilter an opportunity to make a difference for someone with Alzheimer's. Many told stories of a loved one lost to the mind-robbing disease; others described how helpless they felt at losing a friend or family member, and how making a quilt for a research participant gave them a chance to give back. It was cathartic.

One woman wrote me a four-page letter filled with anguish and heartache. It took days to read it because of the emotion it brought out every time I opened the envelope. Another letter came from a group of seniors who made the quilt together. They asked us to hurry up and find a treatment as they felt sure they were going to develop the disease next. Reading all the heartfelt letters and cards, I thought that the least I could do was send each one a thank-you note. I began writing back to every quilter. No matter how many quilts a person sent, I sent a handwritten note each time I received a box.

I grew in awe of these quilters, these strangers who gave so generously of themselves. I knew quilters to be good people, but this level of kindness for people they would never know? It was a special sort of kindness, truly one as American as our soil. It defines us as Americans. It's what we do.

I kept a file of every note and letter I received from these astonishing people. When a new employee began working with me the following year, I handed her the bulging file and suggested she read some of the letters to get a feel for the people who were making the project possible. A short time later, she returned it. Wiping her eyes, she said she couldn't read any more letters. She dubbed it the "crying file." And it *was* a crying file, full of emotion and sorrow, but also hope for a better future.

In mid-2016, I left the university. It was tough to leave my beloved quilt project. On my last day, I checked how many quilts had come in since the project began six years earlier. The number blinked back at me on the screen. I smiled because 3,808 people suffering from a disease that could not be cured were comforted by a simple act of kindness, one stitch at a time.

~Jeffree Wyn Itrich

77

Caught Doing Good

*I think a hero is any person really intent on making
this a better place for all people.*
~Maya Angelou

The young man on the corner was waiting for the walk signal. While waiting, he jumped up like a basketball player and tossed a crumpled paper bag into the garbage pail. It bounced off the rim and landed on the ground. He could have pretended not to see where it landed, especially as the traffic light had just changed, but he slowly walked around the pail, picked up the crumpled bag from the ground and placed it gently inside. I dug around quickly in my purse, pulled out one of my green Caught Doing Good pencils and gave it to him.

"I saw you pick up the bag and throw it away for a second time, and I want you to know I appreciated that," I said.

He looked at me quizzically. "Is this a new movement I haven't heard about?" he asked. I explained it was my own thing, at least so far, and took out one of my special appreciation cards to give him. "This is great," he said. "Do you have another set so I can keep one and pass along the other?" You bet I did.

This idea began some years ago. While shopping for children's gifts at a teachers' store, I bought a bunch of pencils imprinted with the phrase: Caught Doing Good. These pencils would be used by elementary school teachers to acknowledge their students' good work.

What I envisioned, however, was another use for these pencils. After all, grown-ups deserve recognition, too. We all want to be appreciated. Since it "takes a village" to raise an adult, I thought these pencils would start a conversation in the "village."

I designed a vertical business card on which was printed:

Caught Doing Good
I saw you.
You did a nice thing.
It was appreciated.
Your decision
to share a kindness
will inspire others
to do the same.
THANK YOU

Whenever I observed ordinary people doing what was, to me, the right thing, I'd give them a pencil and a card, and then tell them what I'd seen them do.

One bone-chilling, rainy evening before Christmas, on a bus that seemed filled to capacity with people rushing home from work, the driver spotted a woman across the street running to catch the bus. She was pushing a child in a wheelchair. The driver waited, put down the ramp, and had everyone squeeze even more tightly together to make room for this mother and child. When I got off the bus, I gave the young driver one of my Caught Doing Good pencils and let him know I recognized and appreciated what he had done. The driver replied, "It's really nothing. It's how I was raised." Even if it was part of who he was, the deed was so thoughtful and kind, it just had to be acknowledged.

Another day, as I was walking home, I passed two boys, about twelve years old, playing catch. When one threw the ball, it came too near my face, and I moved quickly out of the way. Suddenly, the other boy rushed over. He said, "So sorry, miss. I hope we didn't hit you. Are you okay?" He was very worried. I reassured him I was all right and gave him a Caught Doing Good pencil for his concern. In addition, I said he must have wonderful parents who'd taught him to be so kind and polite. He beamed.

It takes so little to make people feel noticed, appreciated and valued. Last year, I gave a bunch of those pencils to the entire pharmacy department of a local drugstore. In my experience, everyone who works there is respectful, kind, and helpful. It was time to let them know how grateful I was.

Another time, I observed a little girl sitting across from her mom between a young man and me on the bus. She was diligently reading advertisements out loud for her mother. At one point, she glanced up at the young man's hat. "Brooklyn" was printed on the cap in sparkly rhinestones. "I like your hat," she said.

Without missing a beat, the young man nodded and said, "And I like that you are reading." Before I got off that bus, I gave the young man one of my Caught Doing Good cards. I told him I'd heard what he'd said to the little girl, and that it was so important for adults to encourage children to read. He was taken aback for a second, but then he said, "Thank you," and read the card. "This is great," he said. "I'll pass it along."

I've shared these card-and-pencil sets with friends and family, and at meetings. Everyone reports how much fun it is to give them out. My granddaughter gave one to a customer where she was working. The man had helped an older woman with a wobbly shopping cart by giving her his more stable one. My granddaughter asked for more cards and pencils because "this is so much fun!" My sister gave one to a ladies' room attendant at a rest stop who, after mopping the floor, remained there to warn patrons to be careful on the wet floor. The overworked woman was so grateful for the kindness and recognition that she began to cry. My sister told her she deserved this because she was doing her best to protect people.

Whenever we are together and see someone being kind or thoughtful, my friends and family say to me, "Give that person a pencil." As a result, I now carry my green pencils and blue cards wherever I go. What a wonderful way to make my way through the day, always looking for the good in every situation and the good people in every crowd!

~Judith M. Lukin

78

The Kindness Rocks Project

Please know that I think this is a beautiful gift
that you are sharing with this world.
It has helped in healing souls today.
~From a Kindness Rocks recipient, October 2015

I am fortunate to live on Cape Cod, a peninsula located on the eastern edge of Massachusetts. It is a place where visitors from around the world come to experience the beauty and serenity found in its magnificent land and seascape. The beach is where I go to exercise both physically and spiritually.

Oftentimes, while on my morning walk, I'll whisper, "Send me a piece of sea glass or a heart-shaped rock as a sign." I'm speaking to my mom and dad. It may seem a bit crazy to some, but I do feel that connection on my walks. On the days when the perfect heart rock does manifest itself or the rare piece of sea glass washes up on the shore, I believe my decisions are being guided from above.

Losing my parents in my twenties was extremely difficult. One year after my wedding, my mother succumbed to breast cancer. She was my most influential role model because of her selflessness, her kindness towards others, and the creative gifts she shared with the world. My father remains the most caring and charismatic person I have ever met. He was my hero and instilled in me that caring for others was simply what we do, without hesitation, recognition, or attachment to any outcome.

When I found myself in a perfect storm two years ago, I missed the guidance and support of my parents. I was raising three teenage daughters, with all that entails, plus I had just gone through a complicated business partnership that ended in the sale of my company. I needed to find an outlet that would give me purpose and meaning, so I volunteered for various nonprofit organizations, including one that involved taking a humanitarian trip to India with Cross-Cultural Solutions. There, I was assigned to a small school in the Himalayas where I taught English to schoolchildren. The surroundings were simple — a classroom hut made of stucco and straw.

I witnessed how simple acts of kindness had so much impact on those who have so little. Even the smallest gesture, such as a smile or a hug, was a gift. It created a connection.

A month after my return from India, I was on my morning walk when I had an epiphany. I realized that many of the people I came across while walking on the beach were probably searching for inspiration as well. The beach is where many go to be introspective. I started focusing my awareness on others by observing their behavior. It was all too familiar.

The next morning, I packed a Sharpie pen in my pocket and headed out on my morning walk. I began writing kind words of encouragement on smooth, flat stones and randomly dropping them along the beach. I tried to put a lot of thought into the words I chose, taking into consideration how they would make me feel if I discovered one on my walk. Would I truly see it as a sign or a message that was meant for me?

A friend of mine found one of the rocks and texted me a photo of it. What were the chances of that? This is a large beach with literally *millions* of rocks. No exaggeration. She mentioned how much the rock had affected her, and that she recognized my handwriting. It was no secret to her that I walked that beach daily.

I denied responsibility. Insecurity and fear of judgment prevented me from being honest with her. She sensed otherwise and said, "Well, if it was you who dropped it, you really made my day."

Her words lingered in my thoughts. I considered confessing, but

Making Things Happen |

decided that remaining anonymous made the act more impactful. The focus would remain on the message for the person who discovered it. The Kindness Rocks Project was born.

Soon, I began painting and dropping rocks on a daily basis — outside the grocery store, along the beach, at the post office, wherever my travels took me. My daughter suggested that I add a hashtag to the back of each rock. This would enable me to remain anonymous while connecting with rock recipients. Not only were people now sharing photos on social media, but also an emotional narration of how the rock made them feel.

On the way home from her last chemotherapy appointment, one woman commented that "finding a rock was an unexpected blessing in her day," and she saw the rock as a simple reminder of her strength and courage. This made me very emotional. The Kindness Rocks Project is a true example of the saying "It's better to give than to receive."

One day, while searching the Internet, I uncovered a video posted by a high school girl on YouTube expressing her gratitude for a kindness rock she had found earlier in the day. She was in her bedroom speaking to the camera as if she was having a conversation with a friend. She talked courageously about her ongoing battle with depression. Tears filled her eyes when she described a rock that she had found. It read: *Don't ever give up or give in*. This moment had a profound effect on her. She described that rock as a symbol that someone cared, and she believed the message was specifically meant for her.

In just two years, I am humbled and full of gratitude for the 23,000 people who have joined the project and turned it into a movement. Kindness truly is contagious! Please join us in The Kindness Rocks Project.

~Megan Murphy

Editor's note: To learn more, visit http://thekindnessrocksproject.com

79

Recipe for an Open Heart

Food is a central activity of mankind and one of the
single most significant trademarks of a culture.
~Mark Kurlansky

"Y ou had a restaurant?" new friends will ask.

I nod. "An international store and café."

"Wow. Where?" I can see the wheels turning. Had they known it?

"In New England, before we moved cross-country."

Roots and Wings is no more.

"I've dreamed of opening a restaurant," some say with a faraway look.

We had, too. Sometimes, I'm in awe that we actually did it. A lifetime of experiences led to our decision, but it started with a barn.

It was a venerable old barn with weathered wood siding and an antique weathervane. Long ago, it served as the carriage house for the inn down the road. The first floor featured horse stalls and "rentable" space; the second floor, a hayloft that could double as a ballroom. It stood strong and solid, right next to the little river that ran through our Massachusetts hill town. It almost dwarfed the 1850s brick colonial that came with it. What stories these buildings could tell!

And it was for sale. Could we afford it — not just the financial investment, but also the time and energy? Between work, volunteering and raising our two daughters, life was full.

The barn conjured up visions of a day spa, community center and local artists' studio. The house offered more practical and immediate possibilities. The previous owners raised three boys downstairs. Upstairs were two apartments: one a writer's work studio, the other home to two women and their big dog, who, on command, carried a full bag of potatoes up the stairs.

A friend wanted to rent the downstairs for her gourmet popcorn and molded chocolates business. Licensed in songbird rehabilitation, she also hoped to start a bird sanctuary in our back yard. We made an offer. Shortly after we signed the title papers, she chose to move to a bigger town up the road. We wandered around the first floor, getting over our shock, and realized we were falling in love with the space ourselves: the welcoming country kitchen, the broad front porch. An idea began to take shape.

Ever since we met in graduate school in Maine (I, a Midwestern farm girl, my husband just arrived from India), we had shared a keen interest in other cultures. Together, we explored cuisines, languages and music with our international friends in Maine and later in the Midwest. When we returned to New England, we started serving my husband's popular home-style Indian food at our town's annual fall festival and at fundraising dinners for our daughters' school. Sometimes, I taught international vegetarian cooking and nutrition classes, too.

"Let's open our own place!"

"We'll sell kits of our favorite recipes with pre-measured spices and staples," he said.

"And offer fair-trade handicrafts, music and books from around the world," I said.

"We'll have a weekend café, and maybe cooking classes."

"Our guests can explore the world through all their senses," I added.

Roots and Wings, International Store and Café, was born.

Weekdays, I ran the store and occasionally served lunches while my husband worked his "day job" as an electrical engineer. Weekends, he managed the café — and the stove. I'd come early to start the dal or other time-consuming dishes and open the store. He'd prepare the rest. Our daughters helped us serve when they could. We also catered meditation conferences, yoga retreats, a wedding, and a kosher meal after an adoption-naming ceremony.

The kitchen had a large "island" that opened into the dining area so we could talk to our guests, share cooking techniques, or tell a few jokes as we cooked or plated their food. Picture windows front and back made the room bright and cheery. Guests often invited us to sit with them after their meal, where conversations wove from food and travel to technology like earth-monitoring satellites or science topics like health and climate change.

Even twenty years later, Roots and Wings still conjures up powerful memories. We developed the division of labor we still employ for special events: I manage the baking, breads and lentil soups; my husband handles the specialty dishes and entertainment. We fine-tuned techniques for teaching cooking and catering to people with special needs.

I don't miss the anxieties: *Is there enough food? Will it be ready on time?* Or the endless deliberations on what to sell in the store. But I can still smell the cardamom and curry wafting through the air. I see the colorful patterns of Guatemalan fabric, the intricately woven baskets of local artists. I hear the animated conversations, the crunch of crispy potato-stuffed dosas being enjoyed, the exotic instruments and voices lifted in song.

The best memories are of the people. A Peruvian immigrant who designed murals throughout South America created our beautiful Roots and Wings sign, which we still have. Neighbors came with their daughter whom they adopted from India to share our Indian meals. A friend with Filipino heritage frequented the café for food and conversation, sometimes bringing his mother, an expert in Esperanto, the international language. He introduced friends who became regulars as well: she a yoga teacher who studied yoga in India, he a music promoter with a multicultural background. We invited her to teach our yoga classes and often sat late into the night chatting over tea and dessert.

World travelers and those who weren't came to buy unique gifts or cooking ingredients. One couple claimed "asbestos tongues" and craved the hottest sauces we could find. Others tried their hand at cooking exotic dishes. A family who lived far out in the woods became our only takeout customers. What a surprise to discover we would be moving to the California town where she grew up.

We served mostly Indian vegetarian cuisine with a smattering of Middle Eastern and other Asian foods. Occasionally, we added traditional New England fare like baked beans and Indian pudding with local maple syrup.

A family visiting from Scotland read about us in the local paper. They spent a whole day with us, enjoying a meal, perusing our handicrafts, sharing stories. Neighbors around the corner often came for lunch with their small children. Their jazz band played for our daughter's high-school graduation party on the café porch. Even the rain didn't dampen our spirits that day.

One year, we offered a Festivals of Lights dinner celebrating Diwali, Christmas, Hanukah, Kwanzaa and New Year's. We served traditional foods from all the celebrations, accompanied by holiday music. It was so popular we had to schedule a second evening, which was ushered in by a winter storm. A falling snow-laden tree barely missed one of the cars, but everyone arrived safely, and we were all cozy and warm in our little café.

Roots and Wings earned us little profit, but what we gained in those two-and-a-half years was priceless. It was a bittersweet time when we closed our doors. The long hours and sore feet are distant memories, but the stories will always be treasured. We never had time to do more with the barn. I'm okay with that. It started with a barn, but it became a community.

~Susan Rothrock Deo

Seeing a Need

Act as if what you do makes a difference. It does.
~William James

few years ago, my husband and I traveled to Ethiopia for a conference on Africa and the Bible. Because the Ethiopian Orthodox Church evolved in Africa instead of Europe, it has a cadre of scriptures and saints that Westerners know little about.

After the conference, we flew north to trek the underground churches of Lalibela. There, eleven churches were sculpted, each from a monolithic rock, back in the 1200s. During that era, craftsmen used ancient tools to hollow out giant boulders, transforming them into sanctuaries.

Most intriguing were the hundreds of priests garbed in white flowing robes, swaying from side to side, chanting. When the service drew to a close, we meandered through the labyrinth of churches.

At one point, while taking a shortcut around a tukul hut village to our van, I came across a boy dragging his torso across the dirt. His legs were completely non-functional. He pulled his body across the stones with two wooden blocks to avoid cutting his hands. Never had I seen such a forlorn child.

I wanted to take his photograph but didn't want to embarrass him. Then I remembered our guide's admonition: If we wanted to take a photo of someone, we should give him or her a bit of money in exchange for the favor… so I handed him a few Ethiopian birr, and he posed for me.

A week later, back in the United States, I eagerly downloaded my photos. There was the boy on my computer, his harrowing eyes still glaring at me. He had shriveled legs and two wooden blocks clutched tightly in his hands.

I felt his desperation and wondered what kind of wheelchair might help someone living in a straw hut in the rugged Lasta Mountains. The boy became my angel, but unlike other angels, he haunted me.

I placed his photo on my screensaver, and over the next two years, I breathed a prayer for him every time I opened my computer. I also began my search for a specialty wheelchair that a person living in a developing country with a shriveled arm and no functional legs could maneuver.

Finally, I discovered the Festival of Sharing, a relief auction sponsored by Methodists in Missouri. As I clicked through their charities, without a word of warning, the wheelchair found me!

Meandering from link to link, I discovered the Personal Energy Transportation (PET) hand-cranked wheelchair, built of forged steel and wood, and virtually unbreakable. These chairs navigate rugged terrain and are designed to take a beating.

To my surprise, one of the few stores in the country that sold PETs was located in Moundridge, Kansas, just sixteen miles from my home. I called the store and they said they'd be happy to ship a PET wheelchair to the boy in Ethiopia, assuming I could provide a name and address for him.

Unfortunately, he lived in a tukul hut village with no mailbox and no address. Nor did I know his name. All I had was his photograph.

Fortunately, Jane Kurtz, a Caldecott-winning children's author who grew up in Ethiopia, lived forty miles down the interstate. I dialed Jane, and she connected me with a young man named Habtu. She and her husband sponsored Habtu through a school in Ethiopia. Conveniently, Habtu hailed from Lalibela.

Perfect! I thought. *Habtu can go to the village and find the boy.*

I e-mailed Habtu the photo. Then I waited… and prayed.

Days later, a message from Habtu flashed across my screen.

"I found the boy!" he shouted. "His name is Sinku. He lives with his mother in a tukul hut on the edge of the village."

My heart leaped for joy.

A few days later, we hauled a PET to the airport and sent it to Addis Ababa, Ethiopia. Soon afterward, Habtu e-mailed and said he received the PET. We bought him a ticket to fly over the Simien Mountains and deliver it to Sinku.

Today, Sinku's photo smiles at me on my desk. Because of him, our students travel to Ethiopia to deliver PETs to the poor and we have provided mobility to sixteen people so far. The tragedy is that thousands more still need them.

~Jeanne Jacoby Smith

The Good Fairy Returns

True charity is the desire to be useful to
others without thought of recompense.
~Emanuel Swedenborg

When I was a small child, my mother suffered a difficult pregnancy that required her to nap every afternoon. Lonely and bored one afternoon, I decided to straighten up the house while she slept. Carefully, I tiptoed around, emptying ashtrays into the trashcan (my father was a two-pack-a-day man) and wiping out ashy residue. Then I began collecting and rinsing dirty dishes, plumping sofa cushions just as I'd seen her do, straightening magazines and newspapers on the coffee table, returning stray playthings to the toy chest, and re-shelving books. When I was done, I settled on the couch and quietly read, waiting for Mother to wake up.

"Honey," she exclaimed, walking into the living room. "Everything looks so nice. Did you do this?"

"No, not me. Must have been a good fairy."

She started to correct me but instead joined in the pretense. "Aren't we lucky to have such a helpful visitor? Maybe she'll come every day while I nap." And so she did until Mother safely delivered my little sister.

On May Day, we made little paper cornucopias with painted paper and doilies. Filling these cones with flowers from our garden, we walked around our neighborhood and hung their ribbon handles on the doorknobs of those who had delivered tuna noodle casseroles, fruit salad, and plates of cookies after Mom returned from the hospital.

Ringing doorbells, we then hid around the corner, smiling as we imagined the pleasure our little baskets would give the recipients. Our anonymity deepened the joy for both of us. This joy in anonymous giving is something I've continued to practice, with my own family, whether it's a few bills in the donation box of a church, a twenty-dollar bill along with a "God Bless" to a panhandler, "adopting" families financially, or my husband collecting spare change all year in a German stein to drop in the kettle of the first bell-ringing Salvation Army volunteer he spies during the Christmas season.

Eighteen months or so ago, he and I were pleasantly surprised when our financial advisor suggested it would be wiser to give the windfall from an IRA to nonprofits. If gifted to our children and grandchildren, it would be taxed at a high rate; if given to nonprofits, they would get the full amount. Since we fulfill our family commitments in other ways, we had no problem with her suggestion. Neither did we have difficulty selecting two charities, as we had both devoted many volunteer hours to organizations whose programs, goals and staffs we fully support. We also had no hesitation in deciding to make our gifts anonymous.

Some would say that gifts should be made public in hopes of influencing others to follow our example. But we don't believe either of us is that influential, nor is the point of our giving to encourage potential donors. If a program or cause is worthy of support, people will make up their own minds, whether they know of other donors or not. And giving anonymously keeps the focus not on the gift or the givers, but the cause itself.

Just like when I was a child tiptoeing around the living room or neighborhood pretending to be a good fairy, it's a secret delight to do something without recognition. These days, when we attend meetings, and hear staff and volunteers making plans to enrich their programs or add facilities that otherwise wouldn't have been possible, it just feels good to be anonymous donors.

~SuzAnne C. Cole

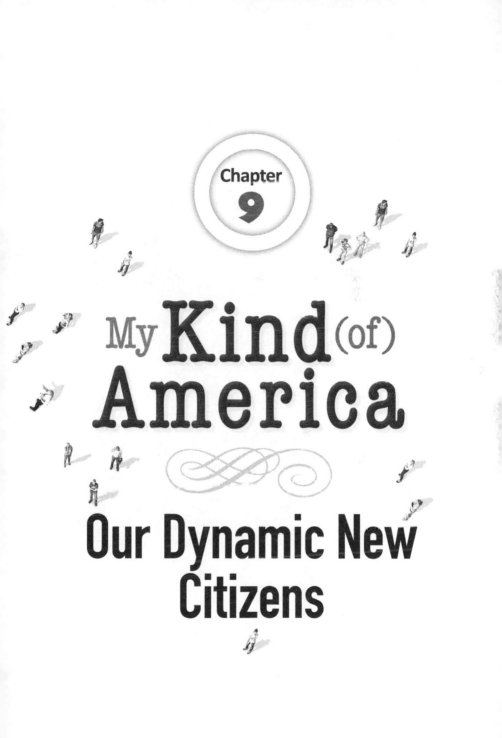

Chapter

9

My Kind (of) America

Our Dynamic New Citizens

Mission Accomplished

*My mission in life is not merely to survive, but
to thrive; and to do so with some passion, some
compassion, some humor, and some style.*
~Maya Angelou

To say I was excited is an understatement. It was my
eighteenth birthday, and I was about to realize my dream.

Most kids can't wait to grow up, but for different reasons
from mine. They want the right to stay out late, be independent
of their parents and, maybe, have a drink legally. All I ever wanted
since I came to the U.S. ten years earlier was to become a citizen of
this country I loved. It was my mission. As soon as I turned eighteen,
I applied for naturalization.

My brother's friend Val also applied. He was in his mid-twenties
and had been in the U.S. for five years. Both our families had fled
Czechoslovakia to escape Communist oppression.

To become naturalized, one is required to take an English speaking and written test. U.S. Citizenship and Immigration Services gives
applicants a hundred questions, with answers, on U.S. civics. Up to
ten random questions could be asked. Of those, six had to be answered
correctly.

I wasn't worried about myself because I had been a good student.
I was concerned about Val, who had never attended school in the U.S.
and spoke broken English.

When I asked him how his studies were going, he answered

boldly: "No sweat. Piece of cake." Although he had a limited English vocabulary and a heavy accent, he had easily picked up American clichés and slang.

Several days before our naturalization hearings, an urgent knock sounded on the door of my family's apartment. My brother opened the door to a panic-stricken Val.

"What's wrong, Val?" I asked, concerned. "Come in. Come in."

Poor Val began, his English worse than ever. "I remember nothing. I don't know what I going to do. I never pass test. I try study but is so confusing."

"Relax, Val. Relax." I tried to calm him down. "We'll get you ready."

I could see why he'd be anxious. While I studied earnestly, Val was more interested in hanging out at the local bar and grill with his buddies, meeting girls.

That evening and several other agonizing evenings later, I tutored Val. I quizzed him, coached him and did everything I possibly could to get the correct answers into his head.

"What are the first three words of the Constitution?"

"We, the peoples."

"Name one branch of the government."

Val hesitated but finally guessed correctly, "Congress."

Then the day came for our interviews. At a government building in New York City, a USCIS officer would determine if we would be naturalized. Even as we rode in Val's beat-up, old Pontiac, I quizzed him.

"Name one of the two longest rivers in the U.S."

"The Missipi."

Close enough, I thought.

I started to relax, thinking Val might pass this test after all.

When we reached the USCIS offices, we parked the car and entered the lobby.

There we were ushered into a crowded waiting room with people of all nationalities. To my surprise, it was packed. *Did I think a couple of Czechoslovakians like Val and I were the only ones applying for citizenship in this incredible country?* There were Europeans, Africans, Asians,

Middle Easterners, Mexicans, Australians and others. Val and I took our seats among other hopeful applicants.

The girl next to me was with her parents. She must have been about my age. She and her family had come from Hungary. They had fled their country during the Hungarian Revolution, taking refuge in Western Europe until they were able to enter the U.S. She was as thrilled as I was. Her mom was overwhelmed with joy, wiping her tears discreetly. We shared our excitement, and I felt as if we were sisters. I still remember her name: Anika.

Val sat next to an elderly couple who were holding hands, obviously overwhelmed with emotion. They were from Ukraine. Val had no problem conversing with them, partly in broken Russian and partly in English.

We exchanged stories of our lives and expressed our hopes for our futures as U.S. citizens. Immigrants from all over revealed how grateful they were to be in the best country in the world. Some spoke with joy. Others held back tears. We had something in common. It was as if we were family, and I guess we were.

One by one, we were called for our interviews. Val went before me. The desk of his interviewing immigration officer was in the front of the room, still in my view. I watched as Val raised his right hand, as if taking an oath. Later, I learned it was an oath to tell the truth and nothing but the truth.

A few minutes later, my name was called. I eagerly approached the officer's desk. His demeanor was friendly and encouraging. I breezed through my speaking and written exams. The civics test was next. I had studied the sample questions so well that I had no problem giving the correct answers.

My CIS officer congratulated me and informed me that I had passed. I would be notified when to appear for the Oath of Allegiance ceremony where I would receive my naturalization documents. I was elated, to say the least. I was one step closer to realizing my dream and becoming a U.S. citizen.

Back in the waiting room, I found a seat in the front row where

I could observe Val still being questioned. *Why was he taking so long?* I was beginning to worry.

Suddenly, I heard raucous laughter coming from Val's interviewing officer. But Val was not laughing. This made me nervous.

At last, Val stood up. I watched as his CIS officer shook his hand and, still laughing as if he had heard the best joke ever, bid him goodbye with a pat on his back.

Finally, Val was walking toward me. He looked baffled, but not necessarily troubled.

"How'd it go, Val?" I couldn't wait to hear. "What was so funny? What did you do?"

"Nothing," answered Val. "He just ask me final question."

"Which was…?" I prompted.

"Who was first president of United States?"

"Well, what was your answer?"

"George Washington Bridge," answered Val, as if it were obvious.

A month later, Val and I returned to the USCIS building to take our Oath of Allegiance. We left the building proudly, our precious citizenship papers in our hands.

Returning home over the George Washington Bridge, our voices rang out joyfully, singing "God Bless America." Nothing could stop us now. We were young and free, and anything was possible in these United States of America. It was a blessed day.

Mission accomplished.

~Eva Carter

83

A Special Kind of Support

*There is no exercise better for the heart than
reaching down and lifting people up.*
~John Holmes

As my English Language Development (ELD) students filed in the first day of school, I couldn't help but remember my own beginnings in this country as a seventeen-year-old immigrant who arrived in New York twenty-nine years ago. I spoke no English, had never been to high school, and had been in various foster homes since I was nine years old.

My story is the typical one of a young immigrant coming to America looking for better opportunities. In reality, my intention was not to stay. I was here to learn English and then go back to find a better job and thus have a better life.

The women in my family never had the opportunity to attend school, and they made their living cleaning houses and washing clothes. It was an honest living, but I knew I wanted to do something more. As soon as I arrived here, I started fighting for my right to a better life. I found work at a factory that paid me three dollars an hour and then enrolled in English as a Second Language (ESL) classes at night. Later, I became a live-in housekeeper because it made it easy for me to work and go to school to obtain my General Educational Development (GED) diploma. The people I worked for were the first of a number of people who were kind to me and helped me to pursue a higher education.

After being in America for a year and obtaining my GED, my employers lent me a thousand dollars so I could take some college classes at a nearby private institution. I did this for a semester, but found it too expensive to attend school. Penniless and undocumented, I thought about going back, but then I received a letter from my aunt telling me that my mother, whom I had never met, lived in California. I called her and took a Greyhound across the country for three days to meet her for the first time.

My legalization took eight years, during which I found different types of work: housekeeper, babysitter, cashier, and dog sitter. After improving my English, I worked as a receptionist and legal secretary. I did all this while attending five different community colleges and getting ready to transfer as soon as I received my documents.

It was hard at times, but a few people supported me along the way and lent me a kind hand. While waiting in line at a lunch function, I struck up a conversation with a nice lady and her husband who would later become two of my biggest supporters and mentors. My friends had left without me, and the couple offered me a ride home. They also invited me over for Thanksgiving dinner, picking me up and dropping me off because I did not have a car or know how to drive. Meeting Mr. and Mrs. P was probably one of the best things that ever happened to me. They were and still are very supportive, extremely loving, and just the most kind and generous people I have ever met. Ever since that day, they have included me for every holiday. They also steered me toward a teaching career, gave me advice, offered money for rent when I was about to be evicted, and were generous with their understanding, patience, and love. For the first time, I felt like someone honestly cared for me and loved me for who I was.

I am now an English teacher, hold a master's degree, obtained a National Board credential, and was named a California State Teacher of the Year. One of the reasons I have been successful is because I always had the support and guidance of Mr. and Mrs. P.

Looking into the future, I would also like to become a mentor to people like me. I believe that we should give back to the people who have been there for us. I am a passionate teacher because I know that with love, support, hard work, patience, and acceptance, all students can be successful and thrive — just as I have. As my students take a seat to begin a new academic year, I see myself in them. I want to be the Mr. and Mrs. P in their lives.

~Isela Jacome Lieber

84

Rescue

*The most beautiful people I've known are those who
have known trials, have known struggles, have known
loss, and have found their way out of the depths.*
~Elisabeth Kübler-Ross

In 2010, Jacques and his sister Marie survived the earthquake that destroyed Port au Prince, Haiti. Their mother and father didn't survive. They were rescued by an uncle they barely knew. At the time of the disaster Jacques was six and his sister was only four. They had no food or water, no place to sleep, and no place to keep dry. They were just two kids on the verge of death along with thousands of others. Their uncle and his friend managed to smuggle them on board an old freighter that was headed to the Bahamas to bring back food and supplies.

They were both very hungry, and Marie cried most of the time. She was seasick and hurt from the quake. They huddled together to keep warm all day while the old ship chugged north to Nassau. The captain of the ship told his passengers that if they were discovered in Nassau, they would be sent back to Haiti, so he dropped them off at a small island where the authorities were more lenient. They found many Haitian families living and working on the island, and for the first time in a month they had food, water, and a dry, warm place to sleep.

Their uncle and his friend wanted to cross the Gulf Stream and wind up in Florida. Jacques told me later that he can remember his uncle telling anyone who would listen that America was the "Land of the Free," and that their lives would be better there. Several large fishing boats passed by the island on their way to the fishing grounds on the edge of the Bahamas bank. They hitched a ride and landed at another small island close to Bimini, just forty miles from Florida. They had already travelled more than a thousand miles, so another forty didn't seem like much of a problem.

It took a month for their uncle to repair the old wooden boat he had salvaged from a junk pile. He added a mast and made a sail from some tattered bed sheets. He patched the holes in the hull with tarpaper and resin, and built a small covered deck at the front so Marie and Jacques could keep dry. He calculated that the forty-mile journey would take about twenty hours if the wind stayed steady from the east. Jacques scrounged a loaf of bread and a dozen stale buns, and together with a plastic jug of water they set sail for America.

For three days and nights, they searched the horizon for land, but saw nothing but waves. They had eaten all the food and were out of water. Marie was constantly sick. She shivered with fright and winced in pain whenever Jacques hugged her. As Jacques told me later, "We knew we were lost, and we prayed silently for a miracle. On the fifth day, our prayers were answered."

The Coast Guard cutter *Bluefin* found them drifting northward in the Gulf Stream. They learned later that they thought they were all dead. Petty Officer Jeanne Dumas was assigned to care for the two children. They were both carried to the sick bay, where they were cleaned up and given some water and liquid food. Marie was not conscious. The Petty Officer stayed with them throughout the night and refused to be replaced until she knew they were going to survive.

At the Coast Guard base in Miami, Marie and Jacques were granted a thirty-day stay due to their physical condition. Their uncle and his friend were due to be sent back to Haiti, and the two kids would also be sent back at the end of their stay.

Petty Officer Jeanne Dumas visited them almost every day. She spoke French and told them that her mother had been born in Haiti and had married an American sailor. From the X-rays it was discovered that Marie had been crushed in the earthquake and would have to undergo an operation to repair some internal damage. The doctor was amazed that she had not complained of the pain she must have been in. Her operation secured them both an additional ninety-day reprieve from rehabilitation to Haiti.

During the next three months, they became very close to Jeanne and me. We treated them like our own kids, and were generous with our love for them both. As the days ticked by, they knew that the day of departure back to an orphanage in Haiti was approaching. Jacques knew that the prospect of a life of poverty would be impossible for Marie to understand after having endured the journey to America. Her sad future sat heavily on Jacques' mind every night when he went to bed.

Marie was finally released from the hospital and declared fit and healthy. Jeanne decided to have a small party to celebrate the occasion, but Jacques knew that Marie's bill of good health meant the end of their stay with Jeanne and me in America. He didn't feel like celebrating, and his mood put a damper on the party. Jeanne knew why they were so sad and told them she had some news to share with them. We had secretly applied to adopt them, and the adoption had been granted. They could both stay!

Jacques is thirteen now. His little sister Marie is eleven and a typical American kid sister. As Jacques confided to me one day, "Don't let her know, but she's the bravest kid I've ever known, and I'm proud to be her big brother. Not a day goes by that we both don't thank God and the U.S. Coast Guard for bringing us safely to America."

~Derek Hawkins

85

Safe Harbor

*Every house where love abides and friendship is a
guest, is surely home, and home, sweet home
for there the heart can rest.*
~Henry van Dyke

Last fall, I was invited to a monthly meeting with a local
agency that resettles refugees in our community. This gathering brings volunteers together to figure out what the refugee families need and how we can support them. My church
missions group sent me as an ambassador to gather information and
see how we could get involved.

At the first meeting, I discovered that local residents had already
provided support to ten families from the Congo and Syria. Local
businessmen and civic leaders were providing needed services pro bono.
Volunteers were buzzing with enthusiasm as their efforts had already
met many of the refugees' basic needs. A few refugee families shared
their stories of tragedy and loss. In broken English, they expressed how
thankful they were for help in finding jobs and getting their children
enrolled in school.

I left that meeting invigorated by what was happening in this little
pocket of my community. Like most Americans, I was aware of the
millions of refugee families displaced globally, but hadn't thought long
and hard about the troubles they face on a daily basis. It wasn't until
I was staring into the faces of several beautiful families that I realized
how tough this crisis is for so many millions of human beings.

I decided to mention to my boss that one of the Syrian fathers would be a good fit at work. In no time, my employer hired him. In a conversation with my sister, I mentioned a family that needed to be "adopted" and her church got involved.

Then, I decided to organize a dinner and invite these Syrian families over for a meal.

In preparation for the dinner, I found a small market in town that sold Halal meats. One of the employees there, a woman who had emigrated from Syria as a girl twenty years ago, helped me find some of the items I needed. I promised to come back so we could talk again. I was fascinated to learn that we already had a Syrian population in our city.

Driving home to prepare the meal, I realized this would be the first time our guests would be in an American home.

That night, the adults looked tired but happy as they came inside. The children stayed close to their parents at first, possibly fearing the unknown but visibly curious. Communication was minimal. My brother-in-law had downloaded an app to help with translation before they arrived. When the family was there, we quickly realized that technology isn't always as intuitive as the human touch. We finished our conversations with hand signals, and then gathered in the kitchen and living room for drinks and snacks.

The children followed my nephews outside to play. My nephews picked up the soccer ball to toss around, and in no time the children were laughing and playing together. One of the Syrian dads jumped in and tossed the ball around for a while. Soon my brother-in-law joined in. The smaller children were having a good time riding the scooters and bikes in circles around the deck. The adults seemed to relax, breaking into comfortable smiles, as they enjoyed watching the children play together.

That night, you could hear several rich and lively conversations going on in Arabic, English and a mixed version of both.

Over dinner, my husband and I had a chance to learn more about my Syrian co-worker Ajar and his wife and son. Ajar had been hired by my employer a few months earlier and had already earned a reputation as a hard worker. Now, it was paying off. With smiles, he showed us two free movie tickets he had earned by going above and beyond what was required. He had also saved enough money to buy a car. We learned that his family is Kurdish, one of the largest ethnic minorities in Syria. Because of ISIS, their family was in constant, serious danger. They had seen death firsthand and came close themselves. Ajar expressed how thankful he was to be safe. "America is a very good country."

After dinner, the kids ran around the house. I couldn't help but notice the huge grins on their faces every time they ran by.

As I watched these two beautiful families with their young children find comfort in friendship, I realized the relief they felt being here in America, despite all the hardships. They had been forced to live in refugee camps in Turkey and Jordan before arriving here.

That night, I sensed they were beginning to breathe freely as we broke bread together in their new country. The families left with smiles and seemed visibly refreshed by the visit. They shared just how thankful they were for new friends in a foreign land. We decided to host another dinner and continue to share life with them.

Watching my family, friends, co-workers and community get involved has opened my eyes to see that it doesn't take much to be kind. My employer donated winter jackets to every refugee to get through our cold winters. Co-workers donated unused goods lying around their houses to help some of the families. My sister-in-law has talked of organizing a get-together for the moms. My sister is helping a family with practical needs, like transportation to dentist and doctor appointments. A church in our community donated a storage unit where household items and clothes for the families can be stored until they are needed. I volunteer occasionally to help organize the unit so that it's easy to find everything.

These are the stories that get passed down to the next generation. One kindness continues to build on the next. America's beauty lies in the thread of these experiences. When ordinary people choose to strengthen the weary by extending themselves in kindness, a beautiful human encounter happens. When tired, storm-tossed souls can find a safe harbor here, my America is an extraordinary place to live.

~Jen P. Simmons

86

The Citizens' Daughter

Volunteering is the ultimate exercise in democracy. You vote in elections once a year, but when you volunteer, you vote every day about the kind of community you want to live in.

~Author Unknown

Squinting to see my path in the Honolulu sun, I finally found the entrance to the building. Instructions told me to take the elevator to the fourth floor and to check in with security. I was to present a government-issued ID and have my bags scanned on the belt. This process done, I proceeded to the Ceremony Room decorated with the seal of the U.S. Department of Homeland Security and the words "U.S. Citizenship and Immigration Services" underneath. I had a flashback to the last time I had been in a ceremony room like this one more than thirty years ago.

***

"For goodness sake, Gwen. Sit down, please!" It was the last period of the last day of school in June 1983, and my teacher was clearly exasperated trying to keep a class of twenty third-graders quiet. Even I was unusually jumpy for "such a quiet and model student."

"I'm sorry, Miss. I'm too excited to sit still."

"And why's that? Surely you can last for just thirty more minutes."

I practically burst out of my chair. "My mommy's going to become a U.S. citizen today!" I declared proudly.

My classmates looked on with mild interest as my teacher attempted to turn my story into the final teaching moment for the year. We had spent the last few weeks of school learning about immigration, and my classmates were used to the stories I passed on from my parents about growing up in another country called the Philippines. I was excited not only because my brother and I were going to do something special after school, but that for once my mother was home all day instead of working.

That afternoon, I stood with a gallery of other families as I watched Mom wave a little American flag in her left hand and raise her right hand to take the Oath of Allegiance. What I didn't understand was why my mother had the biggest smile on her face, like she had won the lottery. I had never seen her so happy. The image of my mother standing there in a blue suit and red blouse made an impression on me that has lasted my entire life. Indeed, the older I got and the more I heard of my parents' story in relation to the world around me, the more I understood why this day was one of the most important days of not only Mom's life, but my own.

***

My mother and father moved to this country in the 1960s, part of the last wave of immigrants from the Philippines who came to the U.S. to study and fill professional jobs. They grew up in a country heavily damaged from World War II, but with strong American ties. Their first language was English. The Philippine school system was based on an American educational curriculum. The movies, clothes, pop culture, music, and everything they were exposed to was American. It was no wonder, then, that they had always wanted to live and raise a family in this country.

It wasn't easy. Times were different back then for working women, especially those of color, and when my mother became pregnant with me after starting a new job, she panicked. She was certain that she was going to be fired. Fortunately, her boss was a very kind man who saw the potential in this young woman he had decided to mentor, and he let my mother work from home for a while after giving birth. Three weeks after I was born, my mother could be seen sneaking me into the office and hiding me under her desk so she could continue working. That man, Mr. Grossman, has been a family friend ever since.

My life would have been so different if I had not been born and raised in this country. And I ponder how much I owe the blessings in my life to not only my parents, but to the people who showed our immigrant family numerous acts of kindness throughout my childhood. From Mr. Grossman, who let my mother keep her job, to the neighbor who called for an ambulance when my grandfather had a heart attack, to the numerous women who helped my grandmother grocery shop — there was never a shortage of people who wanted to help and make us part of the community.

The kindness that I received growing up has inspired me to give back to my own community through volunteerism. I've been blessed to work with everyone from the homeless, to people with disabilities, to public-health advocates. But until that day in Honolulu a few months ago, I had never worked with immigrants.

I've never forgotten the sight of my mother dressed in red and blue — the one whose every decision in life was made for us. I've never forgotten the huge gift my parents gave to me in the form of an American birthright, and I've looked for a way to honor that gift in just the right way. So, when I saw a notification that the U.S. Citizenship and Immigration Services office was going to offer U.S. citizenship teacher training in Honolulu, I jumped at the opportunity to attend.

And that's why, when introductions were made, I swallowed tears before I introduced myself as Gwen, the American-born daughter of naturalized U.S. citizens. In a few short months, I will be the one helping prospective citizens prepare for the interview and exam. It's a decision I made with Mom and Dad in mind. And a decision I made to honor those Americans who showered us with such kindness and love. To this citizens' daughter, the words "thank you" will never be enough.

~Gwen Navarrete Klapperich

87

The Price of Peace

Peace cannot be achieved through violence; it can
only be attained through understanding.
~Ralph Waldo Emerson

He came to the United States, as refugees do, fleeing persecution and danger in his native country. Marko was born in Bosnia to Serbian Orthodox parents, although he practiced no religion. He had the equivalent of a master's degree and enjoyed a high level, managerial job. In Serbia, he would have been easily accepted, but in Bosnia — where Serbs, Croatians and Muslims were all fighting each other — he was not accepted. He had the further complication of having married a Croatian woman.

He tried to keep a low profile, but eventually lost his good job. When he and his wife started receiving threats, they applied for refugee status so they could begin a new life without fear of religious persecution and violence.

They passed the lengthy scrutiny of the U.S. refugee-vetting process and were finally cleared to go to the United States. Our international refugee center in Ohio sponsored them and helped settle them in a modest apartment. Although they were both well educated in their native language — she was a lawyer — they attended my English as a Second Language classes at the center.

My classes functioned as a sort of mini-United Nations. In addition to the former Yugoslavian factions, we also had refugees from

Burma, Iraq, Laos, Somalia, Sudan and other war-torn countries. All of the refugees had a story, and the stories were far beyond our normal American experience to understand — from having their houses burned down around them, to being used as human shields, to being left for dead in a pile of people of the "wrong" religion or politics who had just been shot.

In English class, it was easy to tell who had been enemies in their native countries. They sat on opposite sides of the classroom and avoided each other before and after class. Whatever their backgrounds, my most important rule was You May Not Bring Your Enmity into This Classroom. Everyone had to get along or at least tolerate one another while we were learning English. Part of our unspoken curriculum was also for these displaced and emotionally battered people to learn that the U.S. is a friendly, welcoming place for all, no matter your religion or ethnicity.

I got to know Marko better than some of my other students — partly because his English was better than most — but also because he had an insatiable desire to learn everything he could about his new country.

After class, he peppered me with questions about many aspects of American life. "What is a Whopper? Do I need to pay to go to the national park? How can I get a driver's license? What does 'No way, Jose' mean?"

Some questions were easy; some were not — such as when he asked me why there were so many different churches and religions here and how people of different faiths could coexist peacefully. We talked about the concept of freedom of religion and the wisdom of our founding fathers in separating church and state, and the fact that every person is free to choose which church to attend — or none at all — as he or she pleases. It was hard for him to understand because it was so different in his country, where religious arguments had been going on for centuries, causing bloodshed and forcing many people, like him, to abandon their native land. How did Americans with such different backgrounds live together in peace?

Although Marko was not religious himself, his intellectual curiosity about it led him to ask if he could visit my church to see what an American house of worship was all about. So we took him to church with us one Sunday.

He took in everything in respectful silence. At one point in our Protestant service, the minister said, "The peace of the Lord be always with you." The congregation responded, "And also with you," and then we turned to the people around us, smiled, shook hands, and wished them peace.

Marko shook the first offered hand in stunned silence. Then as he realized what people were saying, his eyes shone. Complete strangers were smiling at him, an outsider, a refugee, and wishing him *peace*! It was what he had been forced to leave his homeland to find, and find it he did.

~Becky S. Tompkins

88

From the Mideast to the Midwest

*We on this continent should never forget that men first
crossed the Atlantic not to find soil for their ploughs
but to secure liberty for their souls.*
~Robert J. McCracken

My wife and I were both born in the Midwest, and that's where we live now. But my wife spent her childhood years in the Middle East, where her parents took her to be raised. Shortly after we married, her cousin Zaid came to our town from Baghdad to attend grad school at the University of Missouri. It was halfway into the Iraq War, a time when the situation in his country was growing more desperate by the day. Zaid was eager to settle in and start the process of moving his wife and two young daughters out of Baghdad.

It took several months, but he was finally able to arrange for his family to join him in Missouri. Before coming to the United States, Zaid had experienced a taste of the Western world, and he admired many aspects of life in the West. It's fair to say that he was extremely grateful for the opportunity to live in the U.S. and study at an American university. His wife Shah'laa, at least in the beginning, didn't share his enthusiasm for the West. It was apparent from the first time I met her that she came from Iraq harboring some strong negative feelings about America.

Shah'laa's attitude was something I'd not experienced in any of the Iraqis I'd met before. When I visited the Middle East, everyone treated me warmly. Shah'laa, in contrast, was initially very cold. As I would later come to understand, she had been deeply affected by the events in her country. She arrived in Missouri in a state of shock. She'd been forced to live in conditions no one ever should.

Even before I met Shah'laa and her daughters, I became aware of an incident they'd witnessed en route to the Baghdad airport, their last drive through the city before departing Iraq. At a checkpoint not far from the airport, the car in front of them was stopped. After a brief pause, one of the Iraqi guards at the checkpoint aimed his gun into the car and fired at pointblank range, killing one of the passengers.

I can't even begin to imagine what it was like for Shah'laa and her girls in those tense moments, sitting behind the one that had just been fired upon, knowing that they'd soon be forced to pass through the same checkpoint. Fortunately, Shah'laa and her daughters easily cleared the security check. But the cold-blooded murder they'd witnessed was the last image of their country they carried with them onto the plane as they ventured off to America... the very nation that, in the minds of some, was responsible for ushering in this chaos.

Knowing what she'd been through, I was especially cautious with Shah'laa at our first meeting. I felt a certain kind of responsibility since I was the first American she and her daughters would officially meet on U.S. soil. I felt that I was representing my country, and I wanted to show this Iraqi woman a different side of America than she'd seen up to that point. Just as Arabs in the Arab world pride themselves on their hospitality, I wanted to show Shah'laa and her girls what Midwestern hospitality and generosity looked like.

As if the trauma at the checkpoint wasn't enough, it turned out that the suitcases Shah'laa checked at the Baghdad airport were lost in transit, meaning she and her girls arrived with nothing more than a few carry-on items. Zaid had accumulated a few possessions during his months in America, but he lacked most of the things necessary to sustain a household. Luckily for him and his family, I happened to know someone who was skilled at acquiring things quickly and very cheaply.

The day after Zaid's family arrived in Missouri, a large truck pulled into the driveway of the apartment he'd rented for them. Driven by my brother-in-law, the truck was loaded from stem to stern with furniture, clothing, bedding, towels, pots, pans, plates, utensils, small appliances, decorations, food, toys, and other miscellaneous items. I'd always known that my mom had a knack for finding bargains at yard sales, but on this occasion she outdid herself. When she heard that Zaid's wife and daughters were coming to the area and that they had next to nothing in terms of possessions, Mom got to work. She became a woman on a mission. Within a very short time, with help from her sisters and a few co-workers, she managed to procure everything a family of four would need to get a household up and running.

I was stunned by the sheer quantity of goods my family delivered to the door that day. Shah'laa stood and watched while my brother-in-law and I began unloading the truck. Glancing over at her from time to time, I could tell that she was confused, perhaps even a bit troubled by what she saw. We'd already assured her and Zaid that these things we were carrying into the apartment were gifts; there was no expectation of repayment. Even though Mom and her helpers had acquired most of the items at deeply discounted prices, the truckload was still worth several hundred dollars altogether, a sum greater than this newly transplanted Iraqi family could afford to spend at the moment. The value of the merchandise may have been weighing on Shah'laa's mind, but it seemed there was something else, something more, behind her unease.

At one point, I noticed her place her hand on her husband's shoulder, stopping him mid-step. Leaning toward him, she proceeded to say something to him in Arabic: an emphatic question, it seemed from her tone. Later, I would find out what her question to him had been.

"Why are they doing this, Zaid? Why are they being so nice? They are Americans!"

It's been several years since Shah'laa and her daughters moved to the U.S. from war-torn Iraq. Over time, I've seen her attitude toward America — and especially toward Americans — change considerably. She's become close to many of her neighbors, along with others in the community. I believe she's come to truly appreciate that she landed on U.S. soil, and that she now has so many people here who care about her. It took her uprooting her whole life and moving several thousand miles to come to know the real America, but I believe she finally does. She now understands the true spirit of this country. And I will forever feel proud of my Missouri-born and -bred family for the way they welcomed an Iraqi family to our home in America's heartland.

~Anthony Clark

89

American Sharon

Life is a celebration of awakenings, of new beginnings,
and wonderful surprises that enlighten the soul.
~Cielo

T he night before Sharon's U.S. citizenship test, I heard a knock on my back door. My friend, who had emigrated from India, stood in the moonlight with her well-worn study booklet in hand.

"Quiz me," Sharon deadpanned.

Shaking my head, I couldn't help but laugh. "I knew you'd be popping over here tonight!"

Sharon's back yard and my back yard face each other. Even though we are in different phases of family life, we quickly became friends by sharing a yard. While Sharon is busy running her two young children to swim practice, play dates, and birthday parties, I'm busy daydreaming about the day my adult children make me a grandmother. Yet years together have made us more like family.

I skimmed the booklet as I snuggled into my living room couch, and Sharon settled in on the overstuffed leather recliner. The questions took me back to my high school civics class where we studied public law, U.S. government and the role we play as citizens.

The longer I quizzed Sharon, the more I couldn't help but wonder: *How well would I do if I took a residency exam in Bangalore, India?* Hmmm... my intuition tells me, not so well. Even though Sharon's pronunciation of Ws sound like Vs, she was acing this practice exam.

"How many U.S. Senators are there?"

"100."

"Who led America through World War I?"

"Wilson Woodrow."

"Well, it's Woodrow Wilson, but close enough."

To pass the naturalization process, an applicant must get six out of ten randomly selected questions right. The next day, Sharon answered the first six questions in a row correctly and was given a date to come back and take the official Oath of Allegiance.

The day she exuberantly took her oath marked the completion of her extensive process to become an American citizen. Sharon, her husband, and youngest child traveled to Hartford for the ceremony, but little did she know the festivities were only beginning.

A few weeks later, in celebration of her accomplishment, my family threw her a traditional backyard American barbecue, complete with Nan's potato salad and Fran's homemade apple pie. The invitation asked all guests to bring Sharon a fun red, white, and blue present. Sharon's pile of mementos grew to look like a bride's dowry. Stars and stripes flip-flops, a stars and stripes pillow, Fourth of July–motif placemats, and a coffee mug that read YOU DID IT were among the treasures.

As she unwrapped each gift, neighbors and friends told their own tales of naturalization. Fatima, a native of Portugal, shared her journey to become an American citizen. As a French-Canadian teenager, Steve crossed the border with his parents to begin a family business. Deepak, who was lucky enough to have family in this country to sponsor him, enrolled in the college of his choice and, in due course, became a U.S. citizen.

By evening's end, the red, white, and blue tree streamers and silver-foil stars that so perfectly decorated the trees were tangled and dangling from the branches they'd so cleverly adorned. No one cared. The last of the partygoers were lined up, barefoot, on the damp grass. American Sharon — a nickname she chose for herself and befitting our country's giddiest citizen — became our impromptu Bollywood dance instructor.

On that spring day, through kindness, generosity and heartfelt stories, our Connecticut neighborhood became its own little United Nations. That's my kind of America.

~Beth A. Molinaro

90

They Call Me "Friend"

A smile is the universal welcome.
~Max Eastman

I parked my car at the address I'd been given. *Here goes,* I thought. I walked to the door and knocked. Had I been visiting a friend, I might not have felt this churn in my stomach, the fear that I was in the wrong place.

The door swung open, and two young women and their children greeted me with smiles.

"I am Lisa," I said. "I am here to pick up your mother."

The women smiled. No one in the house spoke English, and since I spoke not a word of Arabic, our conversation was all smiles and gestures. They ushered their mother to the door, and I helped her down the steps. I pointed to my van, and she circled to the passenger side. I unlocked the doors and sat in the driver's seat. My passenger was still in the street, looking at the door of the van.

"Oh!" I exclaimed. I scurried out of my seat and around the van to open the door for her. As we settled in our seats, I helped with her seat belt, silently chiding myself for not being more aware of the cultural differences. This woman had lived most of her sixty years in Iraq. She was new to our country and community. A weight of responsibility settled on me. For the next couple of hours, she was in my care.

I typed the address of the doctor's office into my phone and let the GPS guide us to another part of the city that was new to me. I'd been volunteering with a refugee resettlement agency for a couple of months, and this was my first stint as a driver. I parked on the street in front of the office and helped my passenger out of the car. I wanted to get her inside quickly, so I left the meter empty.

At check-in, I started to fill out her paperwork with the information that was in my e-mail and on her medical card and immigration paperwork. Then I told the receptionist I needed to go outside and put money in the meter.

"Oh, we have a parking lot around back," she said. I glanced at my charge. "She'll be fine," the receptionist said.

I hurried out to the van and drove it around the block, all the time worrying about the woman. *Was I the only familiar face to her?* I didn't want to be gone long. In a matter of minutes, I was back in the office, sitting next to her, working on the paperwork. Her son, who spoke both English and Arabic, would be joining us when he finished work.

So, we waited. We couldn't make small talk. Sometimes, I looked her way and offered a reassuring smile. She seemed used to waiting. I watched the other people in the office, wondering what they might be thinking about this wide-eyed American girl sitting next to a Middle Eastern woman in traditional clothing. I was instantly protective.

When her son passed by the window, the woman's entire face displayed joy. She said some words in Arabic and pointed toward the street. I didn't have to speak her language to know she was happy to see her son. He entered the office, and I slid over a seat so he could sit next to his mother. He thanked me for bringing her, and soon they were engaged in conversation. About what, I did not know.

At one point, the son leaned over and told me his mother wanted to make a meal for me. She was inviting me to dinner, and if I could not come for dinner, she wanted him to get my number so that I could come pick it up. I thought about my schedule for the rest of the day. I had to pick up my husband from work. I knew enough about Middle Eastern culture to know that staying for dinner would not be a quick affair. I smiled and said, "Okay," thinking that I could exchange numbers with the son before I dropped them off at home.

They finished the appointment, and the son asked if I could walk with them to another place nearby so his mother could fill a prescription. I agreed, and we stayed together. The son told me how hard it was to be the only person in his family who spoke English. He had to work and go to all of the medical appointments for his family: his wife, children, mother, and sister-in-law. He had been in the United States for a few months longer than the rest of his family, so he had a head start acclimating to American culture.

When that appointment was finished, we walked back to the van. The son informed me that he would not be riding back with us because he needed to pick up some things for his family. He would walk home when he was done. He bid his mother goodbye, and I helped her back into the van.

A few minutes later, we had returned to her house. I parked the car and walked her to the door. Her family stood in the doorway, beckoning me to come in. I had no way to tell them that I wanted to join them but had to go. I said the words and hoped my face expressed my desire to be with them but the need to leave. I pointed to the van. I smiled. I waved goodbye.

They smiled in return and seemed to understand that I could not stay.

I drove away. And I haven't seen them again.

But I will never forget this act of kindness. It was not what I did for them, but what they wanted to do for me.

This pattern of kindness would be repeated in future encounters with newly arrived refugees. More than once, a Congolese family of ten has fed us a meal from their homeland when we only offered friendship in return. The oldest son even gave my husband a bottle of African hot sauce from his personal stash. I have been invited to homes of people I've known for an hour. They call me "friend" after one meeting.

I have not committed any great acts of kindness. I've simply tried to put myself in their place. What kindness would I want to be shown if I was new in a community? New in a country?

My refugee friends have showed me that kindness is not limited to language or culture. The country that welcomes them is a place where they, too, can show welcome.

~Lisa M. Bartelt

Back to Basics

Many persons have a wrong idea of what constitutes
true happiness. It is not attained through
self-gratification but through fidelity
to a worthy purpose.
~Helen Keller

"You know what's cool? Our names start with the same letter!" With my green marker I drew two thick parallel lines and connected them with a neat horizontal line.

"H." She let the letter linger on her tongue. Her face wrinkled into a child-like smile. She had learned her first English letter at the age of thirty-five.

I volunteered at my local library two days a week. It was only because I had nothing else to do. I was fresh off the boat waiting for the immigration gods to approve my work visa. I missed working, but I was free from the shackles of the alarm clock. So I cooked elaborate meals, went on long, unhurried walks or read at the park until my husband got home.

For me, being a volunteer literacy tutor was like a justification for being a *hausfrau*. I only did it so that I could respond with something interesting to all those people who constantly asked, "What do you do all day?" The freedom to do whatever I wanted was amazing, but there were days when I felt like I was vanishing. Telling people that

I helped adults learn to read and write made me hurt less. It was all for a selfish reason.

Helena and her daughters had fled Sierra Leone, which was ravaged by a decade-long civil war. We were both new to this country. But unlike me, she didn't have the luxury of time, and she couldn't read English.

The program matched Helena and me as learner and tutor. I made an ambitious lesson plan. I was confident that I would be able to teach her to read within a few months. We started with phonics. "A says aah, B says buh." We practiced five letters each day. I sang to her and showed her videos. She did wonderfully, repeating what I taught her, but she would forget everything by our next meeting. One step forward, two steps backward. I could tell she wasn't enjoying it.

One particularly frustrating day, she was a full hour late. I was about to leave when I saw her walking in, her pink quilted jacket bright against her clear dark skin and her glistening black hair in a tight topknot. I was annoyed, I was putting in all this effort to teach her, and she didn't even care to tell me she would be late.

"Helena, you're late! Why didn't you call me?" My annoyance was very clear.

"Sorry, but I lost my job today, and I didn't have no money to buy a calling card." Her voice was calm.

"I'm sorry, Helena. I had no idea." I felt like an idiot.

"It's okay. I look for another job tomorrow." She was smiling. Her optimism amazed me.

"Let's go for a walk and get some coffee. No studying today." She smiled at that, too.

There was a sharp nip in the air that fall evening. We walked down the tree-lined avenue that housed the library and waited on the sidewalk to cross the street. I pressed the push-to-walk button. From the opposite side, the "Don't Walk" sign shone bright and clear. But she didn't wait. She stepped onto the street, ready to dodge an approaching car.

"Helena, wait! You've got to wait for the 'Walk' sign to come on." I held her back.

"Where?" she looked at me, completely clueless.

It struck me then. She wasn't looking at the signal at all. She couldn't read it! I realized that I was taking the pedagogical approach to teach an adult to read.

"How do you get to work and the library?" I asked.

"I take a bus."

"And how do you know where to get off?"

"I know I have to get off when the bus turns at the brown brick building."

I was amazed. She couldn't do the things we take for granted, like reading road signs, but her hardiness and optimism were incredible. Her life was tough, but she was happy to be here with her little girls, away from the war.

I now understood that she didn't need phonics first. She needed to be able to read road signs and bus route maps to make her life a tad easier. And just like that, volunteering became much more than something I did to pass time. I was responsible for making a difference in someone's life. My sense of purpose was back.

"Let's print a map of your bus route tomorrow and learn to read that." I finally knew what to do next.

~Hema Nataraju

My Kind (of) America

Role Models

92

Letters from America

*The one good thing about not seeing you
is that I can write you letters.*
~Svetlana Alliluyeva

"I want to sponsor a child, Mama," my seven-year-old said, looking up at me while I stared at photos of African orphans strung across our church lobby.

We had just finished watching a video of children rescued from war-torn Sudan after their parents were killed and their homes destroyed.

"I do, too, Desirée, but I can't afford it."

"I'll pay for it," she pleaded. "I'll pay for it."

I looked down at her adoringly. "How, Baby?"

"With my allowance," she exclaimed.

Her allowance was five dollars a week, not quite enough to cover the thirty-dollar monthly fee. I was a single mom in my last year of college. We lived off of student financial aid, my part-time job on campus, and public assistance. I could barely provide for my own child, let alone someone else's. I couldn't take on another financial commitment.

But if I stopped eating in the college cafeteria, I thought to myself, *I could cover the rest of the sponsorship.*

"You'd be giving up your entire allowance, Desirée."

"I know," she said. "It's okay."

"That's very generous of you, sweetie," I said. "You have a kind heart."

Even though it meant a longer commitment, I wanted my daughter to be pen pals with a child her age. We picked a girl named Teddy. Desirée liked the name. We received a photo and biography of Teddy. Her hair was so short we thought she was a boy. But she was a little girl with eyes as wide as her smile. Teddy liked playing kickball and going to school, and she wanted to be an accountant when she grew up. She was a triplet, an occurrence so rare in her country that they didn't have a word for it. Teddy's father was killed in front of her, leaving her mother unable to care for their six children in a Ugandan refugee camp. Teddy's only hope was to find an American sponsor family whose support would give her shelter in an orphanage, along with an education, food, clothing, and medical care.

Desirée couldn't wait to write to Teddy and get a letter from her. Since Uganda is part of the Commonwealth of Nations, language wasn't a barrier, but there was a cultural and economic learning curve. Desirée had to learn how to put herself in Teddy's shoes when she wrote. Complaining about school, having to eat vegetables, or not getting a puppy for Christmas were all things African children couldn't understand. Desirée loved going to the mailbox and was so excited when she got Teddy's letters. We watched Teddy grow up over the years through school photos that we framed or put up on our refrigerator. We sent her photos as well, along with bookmarks and stickers of teddy bears.

For years, Desirée went without an allowance and said nothing about it. After I graduated from college and got my first full-time job, I was able to give her a bigger allowance so that she would have some spending money left over, but nothing close to what her friends got.

Through times of unemployment and economic hardships, we still managed to honor our monthly commitment to Teddy. Through the distractions of adolescence and the terrible teens, Desirée wrote faithfully to her pen pal across the globe.

We sponsored Teddy until she was grown up, out of school, and no longer needed our financial support. The experience inspired me to travel to Uganda as a volunteer and write profiles on orphans to help them find sponsors. While I was there, I got to meet Teddy in person. Guides took me to where she was staying for her last year in school. When we pulled up to the property, I couldn't believe that the seven-year-old girl we first saw in a photo was now the grown woman standing in front of me. It was surreal. As we embraced each other like long-lost relatives, I thought about what might have been if I had walked away from those photos hanging in the church that day.

"Mum," Teddy said, "I want to show you something."

She grabbed me by the hand and pulled me to a concrete room full of bunk beds from floor to ceiling. Because of space issues, each child was only allowed to have one small trunk and whatever they could fit in it. Teddy grabbed hers, opened it up and pulled out a bundle of letters tied with a ripped piece of cloth. She had kept all the correspondence and photos we sent her going back eleven years. I was overcome with emotion. I had no idea what getting those letters from America meant to her.

My girls, who grew up together through airmail, are now twenty-eight years old. Desirée works with children and is pursuing a master's degree in social work. Teddy is an accountant and works in a big city. They don't send letters to each other anymore. They Skype.

~Adrienne A. Aguirre

93

I'll Rise and Fight Again

*Most of the important things in the world have been
accomplished by people who have kept on trying when
there seemed to be no hope at all.*
~Dale Carnegie

George Cress was fourteen in 1771 when he worked on a ship to earn his passage from Ireland to America. Six years later, when he was twenty, he was fighting beside General George Washington in the American Revolution. George Cress was the first of my ancestors to leave Ireland and immigrate to the American colonies. He was my great-great-great-great-grandfather.

George Cress was wounded at the Battle of Whitehorse Tavern (also known as the Battle of the Clouds) in 1777. He was left for dead in a field, and Washington's troops moved on. George lay there bleeding and waiting to die. When the bleeding stopped on the third day, he got to his knees, and then to his feet, and marched after Washington, catching up with him a few days later. George continued to fight under Washington until the war ended and he was given some acreage and a two-dollar-a-month pension for his service. He said he was an American before there was an America.

"I am hurt, but I am not slain. I'll lay me down and bleed awhile. Then I'll rise and fight again" is a quote from an early 17th-century ballad about a man named Andrew Barton. He was a Scottish privateer, but it could have been written about George.

Over fifty members of my family have served in the Army, Navy and Marines since the 1700s. They have fought in six wars, and many were seriously wounded, but none died from their wounds.

Whenever I have faced overwhelming trials, heartbreak, illness or crushing disappointments, I have thought of my ancestor George Cress and what he would do.

Our family has faced some hard times — illness, death, and all the usual things that everyone faces in life. My husband died in a car accident, and our house burned to the ground six months later. I was a widow with four teenage children, and then I was homeless and had to file for bankruptcy.

A neighbor took in our family temporarily until I could come up with a plan, but I didn't have a plan. One bitterly cold winter night, while my children were in sleeping bags on my neighbor's living room floor, I decided to slip outside to get some fresh air and listen to the silence of the winter night, hoping for peace and comfort.

"I need help," I whispered. Before I could finish my prayer, I slipped on the ice and fell flat on my back in the snow.

Before I could cry or feel sorry for myself — and even before I knew whether or not I had hurt myself — I thought about George Cress. He'd fought for something he'd believed in. He'd been wounded and left behind for dead. He'd lain in the snow, alone and cold and bleeding for three days. He could have given up and died. He could have been bitter and angry that his fellow soldiers had left him for dead and moved on, but he'd gotten up, marched on, fought more battles and lived a good, long life.

I'd been wounded, and I'd mourned, and now it was time to get up and fight again.

The next week, I applied for twenty-one jobs, and was given one full-time job and two part-time jobs. I found an apartment for my children and myself, and I worked three jobs for the next year until I was financially stable and able to live on the income from one job. My daughter graduated from high school and enrolled at the university. One of my sons joined the Navy, and my other two sons got steady work. We made it. We survived.

A fourteen-year-old boy came to a strange land, completely alone, with nothing but the clothes on his back. Six years later, he fought against impossible odds to create a new country. If George Cress had given up and died, I wouldn't be here, my children wouldn't be here, and hundreds of his descendants wouldn't be here. He did more than survive — 240 years later, he is still an inspiration to our family.

In fact, his story has been repeated so many times in our family that we don't even need to tell it anymore. When we are facing overwhelming odds, we just say "George," and that is enough to remind us we don't quit or give up.

~April Knight

And Then
There Were Eight

Wherever there is a human in need, there is
an opportunity for kindness and to
make a difference.
~Kevin Heath

Sometimes, kindness just happens — without much fore-thought or fanfare. An opportunity presents itself and there you are in a position to make someone smile. A compassionate word, a sympathetic touch, or a simple gesture can happen in the most unexpected places. Even the Costco Food Court.

After a full day of babysitting our three-year-old granddaughter, my husband and I made a last-minute decision to head to Costco for gas. But we didn't go to our neighborhood store where we normally fill up. The gas app on our iPad advised us that the best fuel price could be found at another Costco a little farther away. We weren't in a hurry, and my always-sensible husband thought it was worth the extra time to get the better deal. Once there, however, neither of us felt like cooking, so we made another last-minute decision — to eat a quick dinner at the food court.

After consuming a hot dog (for him) and a piece of pizza (for me), we sat there sharing an ice cream and unwinding from the rigors of chasing a toddler. A couple of kids sat next to us. Then came two more and another two and another two until there were eight. The oldest girl, who looked to be in her early teens, was tasked with getting drinks for her younger siblings. However, she was preoccupied with her purse, not sure whether she should set it down on the bench or take it with her to the soda fountain.

"Daddy! Daddy!" she called to a gentleman who was placing an order at the counter. "Is it okay if I leave my purse here?"

"Daddy" nodded, and after carefully laying down her purse, she went to get the drinks. We watched with a smile as "Daddy" approached the table and then doled out pizza to an enthusiastic group of hungry boys and girls. They ranged from early teens down to a toddler that "Daddy" had to feed. It was evident that many of these youngsters were disabled in one way or another. Then we heard one little girl's quiet prayer before digging into her dinner: "Thank you, God, for my family. Thank you, God, for this food; and thank you, God, for the adoption." She couldn't have been more than seven or eight, and her simple sincerity moved us.

My husband and I exchanged looks. We were on the same page. After forty-plus years of marriage, we don't always have to talk. He got up and quietly asked "Daddy" if he could buy the kids some ice cream. The man was very touched and said it would be all right.

"This fine gentleman," he announced to his brood, "would like to buy each of you an ice cream — after you eat your pizza." The children cheered! It was the most noise they'd made since they sat down.

As my husband went up to the food counter, the man smiled. "We've been out since early this morning," he sighed. "Our day started at 8:30 with the baby's physical-therapy appointment. We are in the process of adopting him, and we had lots of errands to run."

He further told me that their last stop for the day was Costco, where the Tire Center was working on their truck. He thought he'd treat the kids to pizza while they waited.

"You have a wonderful family," I told him. "Your kids are well behaved, and they all seem so happy." Just watching them made me happy.

"This is my life," he grinned. "But I know I am blessed, and I love it."

My husband returned and told "Daddy" that the ice creams were paid for, and he could pick them up whenever he was ready. A boisterous chorus of thank-yous followed.

Buying eight ice creams at the Costco Food Court seemed like a trivial thing compared to the selfless choices made by this good man. God knows what those children may have witnessed or lived through until he gave them a loving home. Two things I know for sure: Eight little people enjoyed their dessert that night, and we went home feeling happy to have shared a moment with such a beautiful family.

Like I said before, sometimes kindness just happens. It can even come wrapped in ice cream at the Costco Food Court.

~Debra Ann Pawlak

The Whistling Postman

The clearest sign of wisdom is continued cheerfulness.
~Michel Montaigne

"**C**ome on, Spencer! We have to pick up your brother and sisters," I told my son enthusiastically, hoping he would get excited and get into our van. At nineteen months, he was at the age when he had just learned the word "No" and the art of selective hearing. I had spent part of the afternoon playing with him in the back yard and discovering our new neighborhood. We had moved into our new home two days prior, and it was nice to take a break from unpacking. With much prompting, I finally got Spencer buckled into his car seat, and we were on our way.

I was new to south New Jersey, and I didn't have the time yet to explore our new town. I had made a test drive to my children's school the day before, and this was the first time I would officially be picking them up. I was running a few minutes late due to my son's antics. To make matters worse, I must have made a wrong turn because nothing looked familiar to me. As each turn led me to more unfamiliar surroundings, I was getting nervous. I was lost, and I was going to be late for my kids' first day in a new school.

I need to stop and ask someone where the school is, I thought, but there was nobody walking the streets of the small rural town. As I eased to a stop sign, I did a double take. Walking down the street was a tall man dressed in a patriotic outfit of red, white and blue, and carrying a mail bag. I rolled down the window and asked the mail carrier where the school was. He was friendly and gave me easy directions. After I thanked him, he continued on his way as he whistled a cheerful tune.

When I got to the school office to sign out my children, I apologized for being late. I smiled at the secretary and said, "I got lost, but I was lucky enough to get directions from a patriotic mail carrier." She looked up at me, grinning from ear to ear, and replied, "Ahhh, you met David Bohn, Pemberton Borough's whistling mailman!" She told me he dressed up each month for different holidays. This month, he was dressed for Columbus Day. She told me the next month he would be walking his mail route as a pilgrim for Thanksgiving. Come December, he would be Santa Claus!

I started to work as a freelance photographer and wrote articles for the township newspaper a few months later. I was encouraged to be on the lookout for human-interest stories. Dave came to mind immediately. Luckily, the next time I saw him, he agreed to be interviewed and photographed.

On the day of the interview, I went to the post office to meet Dave on his lunch break. I went there for the sole purpose of getting a story and a few photos. Never did I dream I would walk out of there amazed. Dave told me he knew every child's name and birthday on his mail route. For their birthdays, he gifted the children with an origami ring he made from a dollar bill. Residents knew he was approaching by his delightful whistling tunes. Dave started to grow a beard in early fall, so by the time Christmas came, he would have a nice white beard to go with his Santa outfit. I asked why he was referred to as the whistling mailman.

"I originally started whistling so the neighborhood dogs would get used to me. Now all the dogs know me, but I love whistling as I walk," he said with a laugh.

"Is there anything else you'd like to add?" I asked.

Dave got serious. "I'm a United States Army veteran and served in Vietnam. I served with the 87th Engineer Battalion in Cam Rahn Bay from August 1967 through August 1968," he said proudly, and his smile returned. After the interview, I took some photos of Dave wearing another red, white, and blue outfit to celebrate the birthday of Dr. Martin Luther King, Jr.

After the story ran, Dave was such an inspiration to others that he was nominated by a local resident for Citizen of the Year in 2004. He was presented with a plaque by the Pemberton Rotary Club. When accepting his award, Dave remained humble. "I just like to make others smile," he told family and friends who had gathered on his behalf.

Over the next nine years, I occasionally took photos of Dave dressed up on his mail route for several different newspapers. One morning, I got a call from Dave. "I'll be retiring next month. How would you like to take some photos of my last walk on my route?" I had to admit, it was bittersweet. Dave had been a mail carrier in the same town for forty-three years. Twenty of those years, he dressed up for holidays, gave out birthday rings and, of course, whistled. Now that chapter would be ending.

In December 2012, I caught up with him to take photos as he delivered his last batch of mail. I thought it would be a sad day for Dave but, instead, there he was in his Santa outfit, smiling and happy. "I'm really looking forward to retirement. I have a lot planned," he said with a grin.

Nowadays, Dave is very active and still making a difference. He built a twenty-foot scoreboard on the side of his barn for the Summer Olympics. "A lot of folks may not have time to keep up with the Olympics. I want to make it easier for them to follow along," he explained when asked why he did it. Next to the scoreboard were more than 200 small flags representing each country that participated in the Olympics. For Veteran's Day, Dave painted a map of Vietnam on another side of the barn with the names of relatives and local residents who served. Seventy flags fluttered in the breeze, representing all fifty states, Vietnam territories and military services. Other flags represented POW/MIAs, Vietnam veterans, and the post office, accompanied by a large, nine-and-a-half by five-foot American flag. A hand-painted sign read: *Honoring all those who served.*

Dave continues to make the community smile. He is such an inspiration to everyone he meets, including my family. We've all received one of his dollar-bill origami rings on our birthdays, but the biggest gift of all has been his kindness and friendship.

~Dorann Weber

96

Touch a Life
with a Cup of Coffee

*It doesn't matter where you're from — or how you
feel... There's always peace in a strong cup of coffee.*
~Gabriel Bá, Daytripper

Instead of waiting in the hospital parking lot for my husband
to pick me up, I walked to the adjoining strip mall to see what
I might find. Lo and behold, there was a café. Glancing at the
sign above the door, I couldn't believe it: "Drink Coffee. Do
Good." I had recently finished a book by Jonathan David Golden, the
founder of Land of a Thousand Hills Coffee Company, which owns
this café. His company partners with coffee farmers in Rwanda and
provides them with money and training to grow better coffee and
benefit their villages.

Rwanda is all about forgiveness, hope and healing. In 1994, Rwanda
experienced a genocide that left approximately 800,000 people dead,
with millions of people widowed or orphaned. Since this tragedy, the
Rwandan government has made a commitment to restoring this nation.
These communities had to learn to forgive and continue living together
knowing the horrors their families had suffered. Some families only
have one surviving member. So, along with the memories and painful
nightmares of the loss of their loved ones, they must also carry on alone.

In Jonathan's book, he talks about a man and a woman who grew
up together as childhood friends. Once the genocide began, the man

joined the death squads, came back to his neighborhood and killed all the woman's family members. Then he uprooted all the coffee trees in their neighborhood. The man went to prison after the war. While in prison, he listened to an Anglican bishop who spoke of reconciliation and forgiveness. The woman, who was all alone, began speaking with her pastor. Her pastor explained to her that this man would be returning to his village, and that she needed to learn to forgive him.

These two people are working hard at reconciling their lives and the painful past. The government gave each of them a parcel of land to grow coffee. They eventually combined their parcels and worked together to rebuild their lives. This type of story is multiplied many times over in Rwanda. This is how a coffee garden can create a cup of forgiveness.

After finishing Jonathan's book and discovering this café, I knew I wanted to learn more about this story. Upon entering the café, there was a certain feeling of warmth and a "come in and leave the world behind" attitude similar to sitting next to a blazing fireplace on a cold winter night.

The décor had an African flair to it. The large photographs on the wall were of farmers and children in Rwanda. The furniture was a mix of high-tops and cozier two-person tables along the wall. In one corner was a conversation area (known as the "bus stop") with chairs and tables arranged to promote conversation. On the other side of the room was a world map with a little paper arrow pointing to the location in Rwanda.

I ordered a latte and lunch and spent about an hour enjoying my new coffee home. The time I spent there felt like a virtual trip to Rwanda. I was hooked. The Rwandan people had made their way into my heart in just one visit.

I had the opportunity to sit down with Belinda Ewers, president of Come To The Well Foundation, the 501(c)(3) ministry that operates the cafe, along with manager Julie Taylor to talk about the unique coffee shop. It is a place of refuge, renewal, and relaxation—a quiet place to decompress. People will come in and spend hours there. There's a sense of community.

The goal of the café is to serve people the best they can. In regard to their employees, it's all about their heart, not about their experience or what they've done before. They look for employees who are people-oriented. It's the young and the old working together — sharing knowledge, experience and hope. This is a place to come and leave the world outside. There are no magazines, brochures or newspapers on the tables. The focus of the café is to support the people of Rwanda as well as the local community.

The baristas don't keep their tips. Everything that goes into the tip basket goes out to someone in the community, but not in the form of cash. They have given back to the community in over twenty-five ways, such as buying hearing aids for a man who couldn't afford them, helping a single mother pay the electric bill, providing for a great-grandmother who was raising her grandkids, and purchasing food for people who were down and out.

Jonathan not only does fair trade, but also collaborative trade to build up the community through the Do Good Initiative. Through donations to special projects, people in the farming communities are able to address poverty and meet economic needs. One current project is a water catchment system for a Bwenda community. This project came about after Jonathan realized that the women and children spent about three hours a day retrieving water. Another project involves the farmers raising a herd of sheep for widows, who shear the wool, and then sell it to a designer in New York to put into her sweaters. They also started a forgiveness school for the victims of the genocide.

Land of a Thousand Hills has cafés in many towns in Georgia, as well as in Virginia, Texas, Massachusetts, and Florida. No matter where you find them, you'll get an excellent cup of coffee and you'll be helping out a farmer in Rwanda.

~JP Waggoner

97

Going Bald for a Cause

*Sacrifice has great value in that it not only achieves
personal success but builds successful
communities, nations and humanity.*
~Vishwas Chavan

The gymnasium smelled of cafeteria food, athletic gear, and excited children. Energy buzzed as each class of kindergarten through fifth graders filed in and sat in giggling, chattering rows. This was the big day — the kickoff to the St. Baldrick's event — and they knew what was coming. A fourth grade teacher was about to have his head shaved.

The St. Baldrick's Foundation funds children's cancer research. Their monies come from participants offering to publicly shave their heads in exchange for donations to the fund. Thanks to my friend Judy's efforts, the program was brought to our elementary school, and the idea took off. When fourth-grade teacher Mr. Leckron offered to shave his blond locks for the good of the cause, students scrambled to collect pledges. Then, over thirty kids — both boys and girls — signed up to be shaved as well. Community members and parents stepped forward. Local hair stylists and barbers offered their services. Kids, parents, and supporters of all ages signed up to organize coin drives, assemble raffles, pledge their monies, or volunteer their time. I served as treasurer, and early estimates indicated the event would surpass its $5,000 goal.

That May afternoon, the school assembled to recognize the program and kick off the afterschool community shaving event. Students shushed one another as the principal stepped to the microphone and introduced the guests. Our town's mayor—in his heartfelt, gentle style—congratulated the students on their enthusiasm and compassion. He emphasized how seemingly small acts of service can create large, positive change in the world.

Next, a mother and son shared their story of his childhood leukemia, and how St. Baldrick's funded research that was crucial to his treatment and recovery. I could see the kids connecting their fundraising efforts with his struggle. His story illustrated how the program was making a difference for real people. Witnessing the students—my kids among them—reminded me to never underestimate the power and energy of our young people.

When the barber stepped forward and beckoned Mr. Leckron with her shears, the giggles and excitement swelled. They played it up well, with the barber gesturing him to the stage while he shook his head and pretended to be afraid. Everyone cheered as Mr. Leckron walked forward and took his seat. Then the barber's razor buzzed, the kids leaned forward, and everyone held their breath. When she shaved a path right down the center of his head, everyone roared with laughter. My heart pounded, and my eyes welled at the joy filling that gymnasium. What a great teacher! What a great event! What remarkable lessons of generosity and good humor taught in a half-hour assembly.

In that moment, I realized how much I love my little village. I felt such pride for my daughters' school and the community that supports it. My heart was full. A day later, when I tallied the final proceeds, I wept at the total. Our little school raised over $10,000.

There is a phrase, "It takes a village to raise a child." Some think it is trite and politicized, but I believe it's alive and well across our country. We are a nation of communities—whether they are towns, suburbs, neighborhoods, or villages. Within them, people demonstrate heart and kindness every day, especially toward the youngest and neediest among us.

I know my community isn't the only place where this happens. I simply got to see it clearly in my village one May afternoon. Yet I'm certain when you look around your hometown, you'll find teachers who go the extra mile, officials who serve and encourage others to participate, and children who shave their heads or share their allowance to help sick kids they'll never meet.

Each day, through efforts large and small, our communities make our nation strong.

~Katie O'Connell

98

Love Wins

*If one member suffers, all suffer together; if one
member is honored, all rejoice together.*
~1 Corinthians 12:26

In May 2010, a tragedy took place in the small town of New Berlin, Pennsylvania. My friend, Mike Hobbins, was turkey hunting and was accidently shot by another hunter. This terrible event ultimately brought my family and the Hobbins family together in an unforeseen but beautiful way.

The shooting resulted in multiple brain aneurysms and the loss of vision in both of Mike's eyes. He endured months of medical treatment and schooling for the blind, but perhaps the most profound loss was the loss of something that most of us take for granted… an ordinary life. Mike never imagined when he woke up that spring morning that it was the last time he would see his lovely wife or his children, or see the woods where he loved spending his free time.

The community where Mike and his wife raised their family immediately rallied around them. They sold T-shirts, held bake sales and car washes, and eventually organized a Bingo game in Mike's honor to raise money for his medical treatments and living expenses. The Hobbins family had suffered a horrific blow, but through the compassion of others they learned what it means when people come together in love.

I was among many who wanted to help Mike and his family, and I felt good about participating in the fundraisers. At the time of the accident, Mike was just a casual acquaintance. I knew him only as one of the high school football coaches who at one time had coached my son, Taylor.

Mike's situation resonated with me because a few years prior, my stepbrother had been shot and killed in a random drive-by shooting. I knew firsthand how suddenly life could change. But what I did not know was the realistic, day-to-day impact of a tragedy of this magnitude. In the weeks and months following Mike's accident, I remember talking with friends, wishing that I had something more tangible to offer. My wish was that in the midst of such sadness, the Hobbins family could find peace and hope.

Mike ultimately lost his job of several years, and his wife assumed the role of full-time caregiver, while they both transitioned to their new normal. And while it appeared the dust had settled, a lot of the challenges were just beginning. Survivors of something like this often have a way of hiding the reality of the situations they are facing from the rest of the world. As neighbors and friends, we only get to see what those suffering are able to reveal to us. The Hobbins family would prove to be stronger than the challenges they faced, and I would learn firsthand just how much strength they possessed.

Two and a half years after Mike's accident, my son Taylor fell down the stairs in our home. He was twenty-one years old at the time, and the fall created a devastating blow to his entire being. My son was in a coma for weeks, and when he did emerge, he would be forever changed. While falling, Taylor sustained countless blows to his frontal lobe, and severely damaged the right and left sides of his brain. He spent weeks in the intensive- and special-care units and months in an acute rehabilitation hospital. Taylor's fall occurred on Thanksgiving Eve in 2012, and our lives would become defined by traumatic brain injury from that day forward.

Our family lived in the town adjacent to the Hobbins family, and many of our friends were connected. Since Taylor and our youngest son Tanner had both played football, Mike was familiar with them both. Some of the first people to come and sit with us in the long, quiet corridors of the hospital would be the football coaches. To these men, football was not just a game, it was a family. And although Mike was no longer coaching, he was still very much a part of the team.

Similar to the days following Mike's accident, a team gathered around us, and "Team Taylor" was formed. These teams were a practical way for others to show their support, and gave people the chance to participate and help when they weren't sure what else to do.

The rehab hospital we chose for Taylor was about three hours from our home. I lived on the campus with him, and the rest of our family made the trip on weekends. Taylor slowly began to emerge from his coma, and he started the process of relearning the little things. Much like Mike, he would have to work tirelessly to become a shadow of who he had been before the fall, and the challenges were great.

I took a leave of absence that resulted in many unmet financial needs. To be honest, our finances were not something that I could allow myself to think about, so I made a choice to trust that somehow, some way, things would work out. My energy had to be focused on supporting Taylor and our family in this initial stage of his recovery. But our reality was that bills were piling up and would continue to do so.

In March 2013, a few months after Taylor's fall and almost two years after Mike's accident, the leaders of "Team Mike" approached one of Taylor's best friends. The annual Mike Hobbins Recovery Bingo was once again taking place, and Mike and his wife Terry found themselves wanting to pay forward the kindness they had received. What was so interesting about this is that the Hobbinses were not that far into their own journey and still had tremendous needs of their own. However, they saw a chance to help a neighbor the same way they had been helped.

The Bingo turned into quite an event. Countless area businesses donated items to be raffled. The football team and numerous other individuals donated their time to bake things, flip burgers, and work the Bingo game and concession stand that would feed the crowd.

The Bingo was the first time that I had really been with a crowd since Taylor's accident occurred, and I trembled with grief as I experienced the uncharted territory of brokenness and fear. Mike and Terry stood by me that first year, and as I looked out into the crowd, many people were wearing their "Team Taylor" shirts... including Mike's entire family. In essence, they were saying, "When one suffers, we all suffer." They reminded me beautifully that we were not alone in this.

I stood in awe as a man and his wife, who would become our treasured friends, gave our family half of the funds that were raised that day. They knew the road we walked, and they knew they had to do something. This unsolicited and beautiful act of kindness has continued since 2013, and has eased our financial burdens over the last three years.

In 2016, we made a decision that we would embrace another family, one whose son was battling brain cancer, and the kindness continued. What the Hobbins family did for us was one of the sweetest things I have ever witnessed, and we are using them as role models now and paying it forward.

~Nicole V. Bingaman

99

American Courage

When you look at a person, any person, everyone has
a story. Everyone has gone through something
that has changed their life.
~Deepika Padukone

I was a reporter with the *Harmony Journal* newspaper and we were getting out the Labor Day edition. I was trying to come up with a story about the average, everyday worker, but I was blocked. Finally, I grabbed a cup of coffee, walked down to the pocket park in the town square and sat on the bench watching life go by.

A few minutes after I sat down, an elderly gentleman shuffled up with the help of a cane and sat next to me. We said our hellos, and I went back to scribbling thoughts on my notepad. After a bit, he asked what I was writing about. I told him I was working on an article about working men and women on Labor Day. He nodded his head and sat quietly for a while. Stumped about what to write, I turned to him and asked if he had worked any out-of-the-ordinary jobs. He smiled and said, "No more than millions of other men and women in my day."

I asked, "And what was that?"

He smiled and said, "World War II."

I inspected him closer, thinking, *What harder labor can there be than war?* Finally, I asked the age-old question, "What did you do during the war?"

Looking down at his shoes, he seemed to be dredging up old

memories. I sat waiting, giving him time, not wishing to intrude on his thoughts. A minute or two went by, and he seemed to be struggling to make a decision.

"I didn't do any more than anyone else in that war."

"Don't you realize that you are a part of the Greatest Generation?" I asked.

He chuckled. "No more than any generation would have done facing what we did. Remember, we didn't ask for the title; it was forced on us."

"Yes, but coming off the Great Depression right into a world war was a double whammy for your generation."

He went back to looking at his shoes. "We might have been a little more self-reliant than the young ones today, but when you're thrown into a situation like that, you just have to adapt."

I grabbed my pen and notepad. I had my Labor Day article sitting right next to me. I introduced myself and asked his name.

"John Leonard," he answered.

"Would you mind if I interviewed you for my Labor Day article for the paper?"

"I suppose that would be alright, but I don't know if it would be that interesting for your newspaper."

"Oh, I think it would be perfect. Why don't you tell me something about your wartime experience?"

John Leonard leaned over his cane and gazed out at the town square. "I was nineteen years old when I joined the Merchant Marine. I had lived around boats all my life on the Sound and Outer Banks of North Carolina, so it was an easy choice."

"When did you join the Merchant Marine?"

"I enlisted in the summer of 1941. I trained as a radio operator, and that fall I was aboard the *Mary Buchanan* loaded with lend/lease war materials. We dropped the cargo off in Great Britain, and we were about a hundred miles out of Norfolk when I received a radio transmission that Pearl Harbor was bombed."

"What changed for you after that?"

"Well, we knew the Atlantic was full of German subs, and the trip back was going to be a lot more dangerous. The Navy came in and placed cannons fore and aft, and machine guns starboard and port on the bridge. They also armed us with rifles, Tommy guns and side arms. We had to make room for a small contingent of sailors to man the cannons."

"How did you feel about going back again?"

"I knew we would be going back in convoy with Navy destroyers escorting us, so we felt a little more secure than going it alone. I was worried about the subs, but I was more concerned at that time with going across the Atlantic in the middle of winter. As far as I knew, at that time, a winter storm was just as dangerous. Little did I know that was not to be the case."

"Why do you say that?"

John Leonard thought for a moment. "On my second trip, we were only a couple hundred miles west of Ireland when we started to have engine trouble. We had to slow down to work on it. We started to lag behind the convoy, but a destroyer stayed with us for a while. During the night, a bad storm came upon us, and we were separated and alone. By midnight, we were dead in the water. We broke radio silence and tried to call for help, but communications were sporadic due to the storm. A few of us were in the galley having coffee. I glanced at the clock, and it was 01:30. In an instant, there was a blinding flash. After the blast, it was all a blur; I don't even remember how I got into the water." John Leonard quieted for a moment. Reliving the scene was affecting him.

"Were you injured?"

"At that time, I was too dazed to feel anything. I was pulled onto a raft with five others. We clung for dear life with waves two stories high rolling above us. It was pitch black except for the burning ship listing badly. We paddled frantically to get away from the burning oil. We were shrouded in darkness when we spotted a searchlight. We were set to holler out for help when we saw a German sub lit up by the burning ship. They were machine-gunning people in the water. The searchlight swept the area, and we heard sporadic gunfire when they would spot someone. Finally, they got tired of slaughtering my mates, and they fired their cannon and sunk the *Mary B.*

John Leonard was in a zone, focused on another life. I didn't want to intrude.

"On our third day, the sun came out, and the sea calmed. Sometime before noon, a fishing boat spotted us. We stood up waving and screaming and almost swamped the raft. Three Irish fishermen hauled us up onto their boat. We hugged and kissed them. I'm ashamed to say that over the years I've forgotten their names, but their faces are etched in my mind.

"They brought us into their village of Kilbaha at the mouth of the River Shannon. We were all taken to a nearby hospital. I didn't know before, but I had burns on my hands and arms and a broken leg. I was in the hospital for two months because my leg wasn't healing well."

"How long did you stay in Kilbaha?" I asked.

"Well, after the hospital stay, they released me to a sailors' rest home that had been converted into a physical-therapy clinic. I spent another six months there building up strength in my shattered leg. I still have to walk with this cane today."

I looked closer at his cane. It was gnarled wood with a rounded top for his hand. "That's a distinctive-looking cane. Where did you get it?"

"My physical-therapy nurse gave it to me after they got as far as they could go trying to rehabilitate my bum leg. She told me it had two purposes: I could use it to help me walk, and it could be used as a shillelagh to protect me from any uncouth ne'er-do-wells about."

"Was she your nurse for the whole time you were in therapy?" I asked.

John Leonard's eyes lit up. "Ah, yes, and I was lucky to have her."

"What was she like?"

John Leonard smiled, turned and looked at me. "She was the most beautiful woman I had ever met. She had flaming red hair. It was ragamuffin curly and cut short. Her milk-white skin had a spray of freckles across her nose and cheeks. The first time we met, I could feel myself being pulled into her intense green eyes. Her Irish lilt sounded like poetry to my ears. We were inseparable for my whole stay in Kilbaha."

"Did you love her?"

John Leonard chuckled. "How could I not?"

"What did you do after you got out of rehab?"

"Oh, I had a few more crossings and ended up teaching radiomen in the U.S."

I was scribbling furiously in my notebook when I felt that someone was standing in front of our bench.

"So, here is where you got off to, Johnny, bending this poor lad's ear." She smiled at me. "He escaped from the beauty parlor — couldn't stand all us old ladies cackling away. Did you, m'dear? Shall we go to lunch now, Johnny darlin'?"

John Leonard's eyes twinkled as he looked up into her intense green eyes. The flaming red hair had given way to gray, but the spray of freckles across her nose and cheeks still lingered. Her beauty may have faded a bit over the years, but it was still there. He leaned over to me and whispered, "I told you she was beautiful."

With some effort, he put his weight on the cane and stood. John Leonard then took his Irish beauty's hand, and they slowly walked down the street arm in arm. I watched as young people hurried past them, oblivious to the invisible old couple that was in their way.

~Thomas R. Hurd

100

The Generosity of a Stranger

*You cannot do a kindness too soon because you
never know how soon it will be too late.*
~Ralph Waldo Emerson

I was a seasonal employee in Glacier National Park when I met Kelly Tufo. Kelly was a tourist who'd come seeking peace for his broken heart and was staying there indefinitely. I needed to leave to heal my own wounds, but I had neither the will nor the money. I'd quit my job, but the property manager was a friend, so she allowed me to stay on in my cabin.

Kelly and I were both in limbo.

For three years after college, I'd relied on the same group of friends. We worked summers in Montana and winters in Colorado. In spring and fall, we traveled to Mexico, Europe, and Alaska. We'd spend every penny, and then return to employee housing and service-industry jobs.

I wanted to go to graduate school. I wanted to stop obsessing over my ex-boyfriend, whose bed I could see from my own. But my bank account was empty, and I didn't know how to say goodbye.

Kelly was open hearted and gregarious. He listened as much as he spoke. When tourists asked for hiking suggestions, we directed them to Iceberg Lake or Ptarmigan Tunnel, trails that were beautiful but sure to be packed with others who'd gotten the same advice. When Kelly asked, we took him with us, rock scrambling on ancient goat trails with no other humans in sight. We shared our best secrets with Kelly.

One afternoon, we sat in a patch of wildflowers, feet dangling in a waterfall pool. My friend Andrea and I fantasized about having $2,000 — a grand sum at the time. "I could live like a queen for a year in Mexico," Andrea said. That night, Kelly took me aside. He thanked me for reminding him how lucky he was. "I have $2,000 in the bank and then some. I have a business that allows me to earn more and to retreat into the wilderness when I need it. I have everything," he said.

The following day, park rangers noticed that Kelly had overstayed his fourteen-day limit in the campground. He rented a room in the motel and left me a note with an extra key. "I got two beds," it read. "Make yourself at home."

The motel cushioned my imminent departure. It allowed me to say goodbye on my own terms, not just to the people I loved but to the community we'd built over the years, to a lifestyle, to the wilderness that had become home. At first, I was apprehensive. I worried briefly that Kelly might expect something, might crawl into bed with me after nursing his sorrows at the bar. But I rarely saw him in those days, save a passing hello or a note of encouragement and a granola bar left on my nightstand. Kelly was out saying his own goodbyes.

One morning, he handed me an envelope. "It's time for us both to go," he said. He made me promise not to open it until I'd crossed state lines. Then he scrawled his address on a scrap of paper and tucked it into my pocket. Kelly had given me the gift of time, and now he was giving me another gift — a push out the door. The last time I saw him, he was standing at a bank of pay phones at the edge of the road, a receiver in one hand and the other waving goodbye.

That night, I read Kelly's letter. He'd given me another gift: $300 to get home. "Pay me back when you're a famous writer — or pay it forward. It's up to you," he'd written. When I reached into my pocket for his address, it was gone.

For years, I searched. I scoured California telephone books. I asked people if they knew him. Eventually, I Googled and Facebooked. Finally, in 2007, I found him. Kelly Tufo died in a rock-climbing accident in the San Jacinto Mountains at forty-one years old.

Although I'd known him only briefly, I mourned. Kelly had given selflessly to a stranger. Now I'd never be able to tell him that I got over my ex, went to graduate school, and published my writing. I'd never be able to pay him back. So I took Kelly up on his alternative.

When I adjusted for inflation, the debt grew to $500. I wanted to give someone the full amount, but I was paralyzed by choice. Besides, I couldn't afford to give that much at once. Instead, I bought groceries when the mom in front of me in line fell short, and I paid for the elderly man behind me at the coffee shop. When the gas station cashier complimented me on my necklace, I gave it to her. Each time I paid it forward, I deducted from my debt and said a silent thank-you to Kelly.

Kelly used to say that he always found what he needed in the wilderness. When I do have larger sums of money, I'll sponsor wilderness trips for urban youth in Kelly's name. I've stopped keeping track of my debt, but I still pay it forward. And I still thank Kelly Tufo, who didn't just help me up when I was down, but made me a more observant, more generous person in the process.

~Sayzie Koldys

It's a Wonderful World

When strangers start acting like neighbors...
communities are reinvigorated.
~Ralph Nader

I was in line at the grocery store waiting to pay for a couple of items I needed for dinner. I was in a good mood, thinking about the nice lunch I had just had with a good friend.

A woman near my own age was behind me in line. She had one can of cake frosting and was counting a handful of change to pay for it. When she saw me looking at her, she said, "Have you ever been unemployed? I'm counting this ahead of time so I won't be embarrassed."

I said, "Yes, I've been there."

She asked what I did for a living now. I told her I was self-employed, and money was still a bit tight, but I assured her that it *does* get better. I looked more closely at her then. She was clean, but her clothes were old and ragged. Her eyes were red as if she'd been crying. Her face was wrinkled from worry, and her hands were weathered and old looking.

It had been a couple of scary years financially for my husband and me. Things were getting better, but I remembered in the past counting the items in my cart and mentally calculating the total so I wouldn't be embarrassed at the checkout by not having enough money. I often had to put some items back on the shelf.

All that this woman wanted was a can of frosting, and I could do that for her. But I wondered how to do it so as to not embarrass her. I quietly picked up the can and put it on my side of the separator on the belt. When she objected, I told her, "Someone just bought me lunch, and now it's my turn to do something nice." She was stunned, and tears welled up in her eyes. I guessed it wasn't the first time that day that she had cried, but at least this time maybe they were tears of relief.

The cashier was a kind woman and saw what was happening. She was very subtle about the transaction and slid the frosting into a separate bag for my new friend. The woman smiled at me as she walked away with her sweet treasure. I could tell it had made her day that someone cared enough to help. It didn't matter to me if she was frosting cupcakes for her grandkids or eating it all with a spoon; it did me good to do it!

That experience made me imagine what a wonderful world it would be if everyone paid attention to what others might need and, if we could, helped them without expecting anything in return.

I remember what my neighbor did for us during our tough times. We have three critters that depend on us — two beautiful dogs and a parakeet. We love them all very much, but I was afraid we were going to have to find new homes for them because we didn't know how we were going to feed them. One day, we opened the front door to find a huge bag of dog food and a big canister of parakeet food on the front porch, courtesy of our neighbor Becky. She knew we were struggling and wanted to help. After I dried my tears of gratitude, I went to thank her. She reminded me of a time when she lost her job, and we bought her groceries. I had forgotten about that, but she hadn't.

Tough financial times can form a bond of support throughout the community... neighbor helping neighbor and stranger helping stranger. Maybe instead of wishing and hoping for a better world, we can create it one act of kindness at a time.

~Stephanie Pifer-Stone

Meet Our Contributors

Kristi Adams served as a weapons officer in the U.S. Air Force. She now lives in Germany with her husband, serving on active duty, and the world's neediest rescue cat. Kristi is a travel writer for Europe's *Stars and Stripes*. This is her third story published in the *Chicken Soup for the Soul* series. Reach her on Twitter @KAdamsBooks.

Adrienne A. Aguirre is a graduate of CSU San Marcos, and has a Master of Arts in Theology Studies from Bethel Seminary San Diego. Adrienne is a hospice chaplain and bereavement counselor. She's also a prison volunteer. Adrienne enjoys playing roller hockey and inspirational writing. E-mail her at 2240521@gmail.com.

Mary Anglin-Coulter is a writer, graphic designer, and paralegal from the bourbon capital of the world. This story is her sixth contribution to the *Chicken Soup for the Soul* series of inspirational stories. She has a wife and three daughters, all of whom enjoy art, concerts, theater, and movies.

Bernice Angoh is a prolific writer and poet who has been dubbed "the Maya Angelou of our time." She enjoys traveling, experiencing different cultures, and connecting with people. She plans to publish her first novel and children's book series sometime this year. Bernice has two children, Nina, thirteen, and Ricky, six.

Kelly Bakshi, M.S. Ed., taught seventh grade American History for eleven years. She has authored four nonfiction school library books in the Social Studies genre. Kelly is a believer in the American dream and feels that all things are possible in this great country of ours.

Lisa M. Bartelt has been asking questions and writing stories for most of her life. She was a journalist and editor for newspapers in Illinois before moving to Pennsylvania, where she lives with her husband and two kids. Her days are spent blogging, writing fiction, drinking coffee, and helping refugees adjust to the U.S.

Gretchen Bassier works as a home healthcare aide. She is the proud aunt of Julia, Tommy, Landon, and Brady. Gretchen writes short stories and novels, and hopes to start a nonprofit to benefit feral cats. Visit her blog for writing resources, reviews, story links and more at astheheroflies.wordpress.com.

Garrett Bauman retired a few years ago as a professor of English at Monroe Community College in Rochester, NY. He and his wife divide their time between their rural home in the Finger Lakes region of New York and Hilton Head Island in South Carolina. His work has been in a dozen *Chicken Soup for the Soul* books.

Nicole V. Bingaman lives with her husband and two of their children in the small town of Mifflinburg, PA. Since 2014, Nicole has been a strong voice in the traumatic brain injury and caregiving communities. Nicole's first book, *Falling Away from You*, was released in 2015.

Georgia A. Brackett and her husband are retired. They owned and operated an HVAC/R company and general construction company for thirty years. She has a passion for helping her community through the local police department Community Watch Program. Penny Childers suggested she write and submit her story.

Jill Burns lives in the mountains of West Virginia with her wonderful family. She's a retired piano teacher and performer. She enjoys writing, music, gardening, nature, and spending time with her grandchildren.

This is **Lorraine Cannistra's** ninth story in a *Chicken Soup for the Soul* book. Her first book, *More the Same than Different*, will be out in the fall. She loves cooking, writing, wheelchair ballroom dancing, laughing out loud and her service dog, Leah. Connect with her at lorrainecannistra.com.

Eva Carter is a freelance writer and photographer. She lives in Dallas, TX with her Canadian husband, Larry. They have three grown children and five grandchildren. E-mail her at evacarter@sbcglobal.net.

Anthony Clark is a teacher and professional storyteller who has published several books and dozens of stories and articles. He's written books about science, history, mythology, and business for adults and children. He offers writing and storytelling workshops. Anthony lives near St. Louis. Learn more at writeforyoursupper.com.

SuzAnne C. Cole is a former college English instructor, a mother, and grandmother of eight. She enjoys traveling, hiking, volunteering and fundraising for the local library. Her essays have been published in *Newsweek*, the *Houston Chronicle*, *San Antonio Express-News*, and many anthologies including two previous *Chicken Soup for the Soul* books.

Karen Cooper is a pantologist and short story author. Her stories have appeared in *True Romance*, *True Love*, and recently in *Chicken Soup for the Soul: My Very Good, Very Bad Dog*. She enjoys crochet, foraging, and learning new things. You can follow her blog, *Illuminate Your Path*, at illuminateyourpath.blogspot.com.

Susan Rothrock Deo enjoys sharing the wonders of nature and the diversity of the human spirit as a teacher and a writer living in Southern California. She continues to learn about people and their cultures through literature, conversation, food and music, and focuses on adult essays and children's literature in her writing.

Rhonda Dragomir is a graduate of Asbury University and lives in Wilmore, KY. She is a pastor's wife and mother of one daughter, whom she adopted from Romania in 1990. Rhonda finds humor in most situations, especially the quirky things that happen in everyday life. E-mail her at rhonda@dragomirgroup.com.

Melissa Edmondson is proud to have her sixth story featured in the *Chicken Soup for the Soul* series. She is the author of a book of essays entitled *Lessons Abound* and a book of poetry entitled *Searching for Home: The Poetic Musings of a Wanderer*. Visit her blog at missyspublicjunk. wordpress.com.

Victoria Fedden received her MFA in Creative Writing in 2009. She lives in South Florida with her husband and daughter, and teaches college writing. Her memoir, *This Is Not My Beautiful Life*, was published in 2016. She enjoys yoga, poetry, gardening, and the beach.

Linda Feist, a Buffalo, NY native, resides in North Florida pursuing her first love — writing. Published in *The Buffalo News*, *Chicken Soup for the Soul* series, and a 2016 Royal Palm Literary Award finalist, Linda's short fiction, "Einstein," will appear in The Florida Writers Association Collections 2017. To write — is to share life!

Sabrina Forest received her Bachelor of Arts from the University of Minnesota in 1998. She is a freelance writer who alternates living between her home in Minnesota and her second home in Canada with her husband. Sabrina is an avid baker and a keen lover of all things outdoors. She plans to write young adult novels.

Marianne Fosnow resides in South Carolina. She enjoys reading, writing, photography, and spending time with her family. She is delighted and proud to have a story included in this book.

Cynthia M. Gary is a Physician Assistant in rural North Carolina, where she is blessed to help people achieve physical and mental wellness. She balances her challenging profession with dance, writing, scrapbooking, and outdoor activities. She is forever grateful to her parents, Mary and John Gary. E-mail her at CynCynCreates@gmail.com.

Heidi Gaul lives in Oregon's Willamette Valley with her husband and furry family. Her stories appear in nine *Chicken Soup for the Soul* anthologies, and her devotions are featured in several *Upper Room* devotionals. Heidi's passion is travel, be it around the block or the world.

Shirley P. Gumert has had good responses from readers of her previous stories in the *Chicken Soup for the Soul* series. She has also been published in newspapers (*Santa Fe Reporter*, *Houston Chronicle's Texas Magazine*), anthologies, and blasts e-mails to her grandchildren from her Texas Hill Country home, where she lives with her husband John.

Elizabeth Harsany, an Oklahoma native, is a high school English teacher at Canton Preparatory High School in Canton, MI. She has been teaching for nine years and has often been inspired and motivated by her students. She is lovingly supported by her husband Joshua and their one-year-old son Zachary.

Derek Hawkins is the author of several books on a wide variety of fiction subjects. He was educated in England and Canada and now resides in Florida. Learn more at writerofnote.com.

David Hull retired from teaching after twenty-six years in the field and he now spends his days reading, writing, gardening, and watching way too much cable news on television. E-mail him at Davidhull59@aol.com.

After his Vietnam military service, **Thomas R. Hurd** moved to Florida and spent a thirty-year career in the dental technology field. In 1993 he sold his business and retired to the mountains of North Carolina. Not content with retirement, he became a reporter and columnist for two newspapers. He now lives and writes in Florida.

Zehra Hussain is currently a senior at the University of North Texas in Denton, TX. She is pursuing a Bachelor of Arts in Political Science with a minor in Medical Anthropology. Zehra is an aspiring physician and hopes to combine both her passion for medicine and politics in order to shape global health.

Robbie Iobst has written three books: a devotional called *Joy Dance*; a novel, *Cecilia Jackson's Last Chance*; and *Caught* written by Robbie and her husband John. John and she have a marriage ministry called Caught In His Arms. Learn more at www.caughtinhisarms.com.

Julie Isaac is an award-winning author and book coach. As the founder of WritingSpirit, Julie's provided writing solutions, tools, and support to thousands of writers since 2003. She received a BA in English from San Francisco State University, has been published in several anthologies, and is a life-long journaler.

Jeffree Wyn Itrich has been writing since childhood. Trained as a journalist, she has four books in print, numerous articles and a blog, thegoodnessprinciple.com. Jeffree works in health communications and lives in San Diego, CA with her husband. When not writing, she quilts by hand. E-mail her at jeffreewyn@gmail.com.

Susan Maddy Jones is a former computer-science nerd rewired for creativity and spending time in nature, not cubicles. She blogs about navigating life's ups and downs at SwimmingInTheMud.wordpress.

com and about her awesome camping, hiking, and DIY adventures at TeardropAdventures.com. E-mail her at susan.jones326@gmail.com.

Megan Pincus Kajitani is a writer, editor, and educator. Her writing has appeared in publications such as *The Chronicle of Higher Education*, *Mothering* magazine, and *Huffington Post*, and books including *Mama, PhD* and *Chicken Soup for the Soul: Inspiration for Teachers*. As Meeg Pincus, she also writes nonfiction for children.

Kathryn Kingsbury writes, weeds, and takes blurry photos of birds in Madison, WI. She blogs about these things and more at seasonofplenty.com.

Gwen Navarrete Klapperich is the proud and grateful daughter of U.S. citizens Eli Navarrete and Ginny Gutierrez. She thanks her mother for passing on her gift of writing and love of words, and for inspiring her to tell this story. Gwen has also contributed stories to two other *Chicken Soup for the Soul* books.

April Knight is a freelance author. Her most recent published romance novel is *Stars in the Desert*. She's the mother of two sons and a daughter who "make life sparkle."

Sayzie Koldys is a Maine-based writer, sailor, and chef, who sometimes manages to combine all three skills under one paycheck. She's passionate about the ocean, tropical island cuisine, and maintaining friendships far and wide. You can read more of her work at opercula.net and SayzieJane.com.

Isela Jacome Lieber, an immigrant from Ecuador, came to the U.S. at seventeen. She learned English, went to college, and is now an English teacher to many immigrant students like herself. Isela recently was awarded the recognition of LAUSD, Los Angeles and California Teacher of the Year. She lives in Southern California.

Keri Lindenmuth earned her BA in English and Writing Arts Certification from Moravian College. She currently works as a web content writer for a tech company. "Americans in Paris" is her second essay published in the *Chicken Soup for the Soul* series. She resides in eastern Pennsylvania with her family.

Ilana Long is the author of *Ziggy's Big Idea* (Kar-Ben Publishing). She is a columnist for *The Tico Times,* Costa Rica's English language newspaper. Besides writing, Ilana travels and lives abroad, hikes, teaches, and parents her twin teens. She is seeking representation for her comic fantasy novel. E-mail her at ilanalong@hotmail.com.

Judith M. Lukin received a Master's in Social Work, a Master's in Adult Education, and a Certificate in Nonprofit Management, all from Columbia University. She worked with community organizations, wrote grants, and was Executive Director of the Caring Community in New York City. She continues writing about listening and questioning.

Amanda Yardley Luzzader is an award-winning writer and poet. She is currently employed as a grant writer for a Utah nonprofit organization. She is a devout cat person and mom to two incredibly bright boys. Follow her Facebook page for information on where to find her stories at facebook.com/authoramandaluzzader.

Marsha Warren Mittman's had numerous poems/prose selections published in various journals, magazines and anthologies (U.S./England), including previous *Chicken Soup for the Soul* books. A chapbook was accepted by Finishing Line and a memoir is under consideration. She's received eight U.S. poetry awards and four prose distinctions.

Beth A. (Waterkotte) Molinaro is a member of the Candlewood Writers Workshop in Danbury, CT. Like her writing, Beth is warmhearted and quick-witted. Her work can also been found in *Chicken Soup for the Soul: Shaping the New You*. E-mail her at bethannmolinaro@gmail.com.

Linda Morel publishes personal essays and is a food columnist at the *Jewish Exponent*. She received an MFA in creative writing from The New School. Linda teaches writing through Teachers & Writers Collaborative. She is writing a family memoir. She lives in Manhattan with her husband. E-mail her at lindamorel2@gmail.

Ann Morrow is a writer, humorist and frequent contributor to Chicken Soup for the Soul. She and her husband live in the beautiful Black Hills of South Dakota, where she is currently working on a middle-grade novel. Visit Ann online at www.annmorrow.net.

Courtney Lynn Mroch is the Ambassador of Dark and Paranormal Tourism for Haunt Jaunts, a travel site and radio show for restless spirits. When she's not exploring haunted places or writing, it's a safe bet you'll find her on a tennis court or yoga mat somewhere. She lives in Nashville, TN with her husband.

Megan Murphy is a Women's Empowerment Coach, Kindness Activist and Inspirational Speaker. She is Founder of The Kindness Rocks Project, a business mentor for SCORE, freelance writer, and Vice President of Flower Angels USA. She resides on Cape Cod, MA with her husband, three daughters and two giant dogs.

Nell Musolf is a freelance writer in the Midwest. Her writing has appeared in a number of publications. She enjoys writing about family, friends, pets and life. She blogs at nellmusolf.com.

Hema Nataraju is an emerging writer with a particular interest in personal essays and historical fiction. Her work has been featured on *Huffington Post*, *The Sunlight Press*, *The Aerogram*, and WordPress's *Discover*. Hema lives in the San Francisco Bay Area with her husband and her four-year-old daughter.

Katie O'Connell is a former teacher turned writer who loves when her stories help others on their journeys. In addition to several *Chicken Soup for the Soul* anthologies, her work has appeared in *Reader's Digest*, *Sasee*, and online sites such as *Scary Mommy* and *Patheos*. Follow her work at blog.heartwiredwriting.com.

Linda O'Connell is an accomplished writer and teacher from St. Louis, MO. A positive thinker, she writes from the heart, bares her soul, and finds humor in everyday situations. Linda enjoys a hearty laugh, the beach, and will write for dark chocolate. Read more at lindaoconnell. blogspot.com.

Tiffany O'Connor, Ph.D., holds a Doctorate in Philosophy and a Master of Business Administration degree in Marketing. She is an accomplished freelance writer. Tiffany is married to her high school sweetheart and is the mother of two amazing boys. She chronicles her experiences raising boys at hashtaglifewithboys.com.

Vincent Olson served four years in the U.S. Air Force and later received his bachelor's in English Education from Southern Illinois University. He and his wife have one son. He teaches high school English in Illinois. In addition to short stories, Vincent also writes screenplays, poetry and novels, and is a freelance animator.

Leo Pacheco is a best-selling author, speaker, minister, and entrepreneur. He founded three faith-based nonprofit organizations and is the CEO of Lion's Crest Group, LLC. He and his family live near Orlando, FL, where he enjoys working and relaxing at the beach.

Nancy Panko is an eight-time contributor to the *Chicken Soup for the Soul* series. She is a member of the Cary Writing Circle, The Light of Carolina Christian Writers Group, The Military Writers Society of America, and the author of *Guiding Missal*.

Debra Ann Pawlak recently co-wrote a Civil War novel, *Soldier, Spy, Heroine*, based on the real life of Sarah Emma Edmonds. Her work has also appeared in *Michigan History* magazine and *Pennsylvania Heritage*. In addition, she has written a nonfiction book called *Bringing Up Oscar: The Men and Women Who Founded the Academy*.

Chaplain Sunday Pearson is in ministry and will tell you that what she does is an outward manifestation of God's extravagant love for her. She has two daughters, three grandsons and has been married to her "swede-heart" for over forty years. She is working on her first book. E-mail her at sundayp@sbcglobal.net.

Alf Pettersen is a professor at a small college in Montana. He has been published widely in many fields and also does fine letterpress printing. He lives with his wife and daughter in Helena, MT.

Julia Pfeiffer lives in beautiful rural Vermont with her wife and son. She is a construction Project Manager by day, and enjoys playing ice hockey, roller derby, and wielding power tools in her spare time.

At age forty-four, **Kristen Mai Pham** finally pursued her dream of becoming a writer. She lives in California with her best friend and writing partner, Paul. Together, they write inspirational screenplays. Kristen will eat anything that has chocolate on it and she has probably watched *Star Wars* a thousand times. But who's counting.

Stephanie Pifer-Stone is an Interfaith Minister who has a degree in Holistic Theology and studied Religious Literacy at Harvard Divinity School. *Becoming Egg-straordinary* is her first book about releasing your inner butterfly. In addition to her husband and their furry kids, her passions include yoga, writing, and cooking.

Lou Zywicki Prudhomme is a teacher, writer, grief counselor, and volunteer chaplain with a Bachelor of Arts and a master's degree from the University of Minnesota Duluth. She is the mother of four and grandmother to fifteen, with homes in Minnesota and Florida. No day is ever long enough for everything she loves to do.

Natalie June Reilly is a proud American, an author, and the founder of Nothing but Love Notes, a mission to thank our nation's heroes with handwritten love for their service to our country and our communities. Those heroes include our military, veterans, and first responders. Send Natalie a note at girlwriter68@hotmail.com.

Mark Rickerby has written over a dozen stories for the *Chicken Soup for the Soul* series. He also co-authored his father's memoir, *The Other Belfast*; released a CD of songs (*Great Big World*) for his daughters, Marli and Emma; and is Head Writer for an upcoming Western TV show, *Big Sky*. Visit him at markrickerby.com.

Sioux Roslawski retired from public school and is now a middle school teacher at St. James the Greater. She is a teacher consultant for the Gateway Writing Project, has a son and daughter along with a granddaughter. Currently, Sioux's working on a historical fiction manuscript and blogs at siouxspage.blogspot.com.

Lauren B. H. Rossato knits, gardens, and cooks in Silver Spring, MD. She recently realized she has over fifty books in her library that she has not read; if you need to find her, she will be lost in a book.

Natalie M. Rotunda helps small/mid-sized businesses by writing copy that attracts and keeps customers. She edits nonfiction books, and she served as editor for a regional women's magazine. She's written hundreds of articles for publication. She loves family time, old classic movies, hiking, and herb gardening.

Stephen Rusiniak is from Wayne, NJ and was a police detective specializing in juvenile/family matters. Today he shares his thoughts through his writing, including stories in several books in the *Chicken Soup for the Soul* series. Contact him via Facebook, on Twitter @StephenRusiniak or by visiting stephenrusiniak.com.

Tracy Rusiniak showed her father, Stephen, a frequent *Chicken Soup for the Soul* contributor, her college entrance essay about a church mission trip to Appalachia. Together they crafted her submission into the story found in this book. Now a college graduate, Tracy, originally from New Jersey, is currently living in Hawaii.

Ceil Ryan is a wife, mom, and nana living in the Midwest. After working more than twenty years, she hung up her nurse's cap to start writing, speaking, and blogging full-time. Her passion is sharing personal stories with an emphasis on faith and encouragement.

Jane Self is a freelance writer and editor living in Durham, NC. She retired as Features Editor from a New York Times affiliate in Alabama after twenty years in the newspaper business. She has published two nonfiction books and hundreds of personal columns and feature articles. E-mail her at jane@janeself.com.

Jen P. Simmons currently lives with her husband and extended family in the beautiful Sierra Nevada mountain range. Jen is an outdoor and travel enthusiast, loves the local coffee shop and fully enjoys inspiring men and women to live well mentally, spiritually and physically. Her life motto: "Live Well, Laugh Often, Love Much."

Carol Nash Smith is a retired English and journalism teacher who loves to travel. She and her husband are both writers. They are interested in many facets of our world including wildlife, petroglyphs, and the culture of our country as well as others. She has an MFA in Journalism from the University of Arkansas at Little Rock.

Jeanne Jacoby Smith is Professor Emerita of English and Teacher Education at McPherson College in Kansas. She has a BA, MA, and Ed.D. She is the author of *Refugees: A Family's Search for Freedom and a Church That Helped Them Find It*. Jeanne and her husband, Herb, travel with their college students to Ethiopia each year.

Darlene Sneden, writer and editor, currently divides her time between New Jersey and South Carolina. She knows a great adventure is around every corner. It's all in the attitude! To follow along, check out her blog at adventuresofamiddleagemom.com.

Katelyn Stanis is a Journalism major who grew up in Michigan. She currently lives in Jersey City and enjoys running, barre classes, and yoga. She writes personal essays and is currently working on her first novel. For inquiries, contact Katelyn at katelyn.stanis@gmail.com or visit her site at katelynstanis.com.

Rabbi and college professor, now retired, **Dr. Stern** devotes himself to interfaith causes. He is the Founder and Past-President of the Orange County Interfaith Network and the Chair of the Orange County Council of Religious Leaders. He writes mostly about life in first-century Palestine and lectures throughout California.

Noelle Sterne has a Ph.D. from Columbia University and has published over 400 essays, writing craft and spiritual articles, fiction, poems, and guest blogs. Her book, *Challenges in Writing Your Dissertation*, evolved from her academic editing and coaching practice. Her book, *Trust Your Life*, helps readers/writers reach lifelong yearnings.

L.A. Strucke is a frequent contributor to the *Chicken Soup for the Soul* series as well as *Guideposts* magazine. She graduated from Rowan University with a degree in Communication. Her hobbies are painting, piano, and songwriting. Strucke is the mother of four fabulous children. Follow her at lastrucke.com.

Sheila Taylor-Clark is a CPA in Lewisville, TX. Her passions are writing, public speaking, and performing community service. A two-time breast cancer survivor, Sheila is married to Nate Clark and has a daughter, McKenzie. She hopes to publish her first novel soon and can be e-mailed at shaycpa@msn.com.

Becky S. Tompkins enjoys working with words, both profession-ally — as a former teacher of English to refugees, freelance writer, and copy editor — and in her spare time. Besides reading and writing, she enjoys learning, cooking, gardening, and spending time with her family.

Award-winning author **Susan Traugh's** work has appeared in several *Chicken Soup for the Soul* books plus local and national magazines. Her young adult novel, *The Edge of Brilliance,* and her special education teen series, *Daily Living Skills,* can be found on her website at susantraugh. com. Susan lives in San Diego with her family.

Miriam Van Scott is an author and photographer whose credits include children's books, magazine articles, television productions, website content and reference works. Her latest titles include *Song of Old: An Advent Calendar for the Spirit* and the *Shakespeare Goes Pop* series. For more information, visit miriamvanscott.com.

JP Waggoner is a freelance photographer/travel writer based in Florida during winter and the Blue Ridge Mountains of Georgia in summer. Her adventures are mostly around beaches and back country roads. She's been published at PinkPangea.com, MilesGeek.com and TravelPostMonthly. com. Adventure and travel are her first loves.

Kelly Sullivan Walden is on a mission to awaken the world to the power of dreams. She is the author of ten books, including *Chicken Soup for the Soul: Dreams & Premonitions, I Had the Strangest Dream, It's All in Your Dreams,* and the *Dream Oracle Cards.* It is whispered she is the love child of Lucille Ball and Carl Jung.

K. Michael Ware is a retired Fighter Pilot and Airline Pilot. He is a graduate of West Virginia University and Troy State University. He and his wife, Suzanne, reside in Collierville, TN and are the proud parents of three children. He is a "professional volunteer" and enjoys golf and playing with his six grandkids.

Benny Wasserman began a second career as an Einstein impersonator. He revised his book, *Presidents Were Teenagers Too*, in 2017. His stories have been published in the *Los Angeles Times*, *Reminisce*, *Good Old Days* and the *Chicken Soup for the Soul* series. He is an avid reader and ping-pong player. E-mail him at wassben@aol.com.

Dorann Weber is a freelance photographer for a New Jersey newspaper and a Getty Images contributor. She has a love for writing, especially if it inspires and makes people laugh. She has four adult children, one teenager, and three grandchildren who call her Mimi. Dorann lives with husband and family in the Pinelands of South New Jersey.

From a young age, **Carla Erin Wiggins** has had a love of reading. Wanting to share this passion with others, Erin became a freelance writer in 2010 after completing multiple writing courses through Mississippi State University. Since that time, she has written and published three children's books with plans to release a fourth book in the coming year.

Known as the Silver Nightingale, **Laura Sue Wilansky** is a flautist whose music delights, inspires, and comforts. This arts journalist, composer, poet and artist received President Obama's Volunteer Service Award for her over twenty years of hospice music work. Peruse her music, poetry, activism and more at SilverNightingale.com.

Following a career in Nuclear Medicine, **Melissa Wootan** is joyfully exploring her creative side. She enjoys writing and is a regular guest on *San Antonio Living*, an hour-long lifestyle show on San Antonio's NBC affiliate, where she shares all of her best DIY/decorating tips. Contact her through Facebook at facebook.com/chicvintique.

Allison Yates is a freelance writer and lover of great conversations, human connection and travel. Since graduating from Indiana University in International Studies with a focus on human rights, she's lived and worked in Spain and Australia. She enjoys hiking, goofy dancing and exploring a city by foot.

Lynn Yates is a writer, editor, and public speaker in the southeastern United States. She has been proudly married to her husband, Dan, for thirty-three years. Honoring his wishes, she is using a pseudonym for "The Least We Can Do."

Meet Amy Newmark

Amy Newmark is the bestselling author, editor-in-chief, and publisher of the *Chicken Soup for the Soul* book series. Since 2008, she has published 140 new books, most of them national bestsellers in the U.S. and Canada, more than doubling the number of Chicken Soup for the Soul titles in print today. She is also the author of *Simply Happy*, a crash course in Chicken Soup for the Soul advice and wisdom that is filled with easy-to-implement, practical tips for having a better life.

Amy is credited with revitalizing the Chicken Soup for the Soul brand, which has been a publishing industry phenomenon since the first book came out in 1993. By compiling inspirational and aspirational true stories curated from ordinary people who have had extraordinary experiences, Amy has kept the twenty-four-year-old Chicken Soup for the Soul brand fresh and relevant.

Amy graduated *magna cum laude* from Harvard University where she majored in Portuguese and minored in French. She then embarked on a three-decade career as a Wall Street analyst, a hedge fund manager, and a corporate executive in the technology field. She is a Chartered Financial Analyst.

Her return to literary pursuits was inevitable, as her honors thesis in college involved traveling throughout Brazil's impoverished northeast region, collecting stories from regular people. She is delighted to have come full circle in her writing career — from collecting stories "from the people" in Brazil as a twenty-year-old to, three decades later, collecting stories "from the people" for Chicken Soup for the Soul.

When Amy and her husband Bill, the CEO of Chicken Soup for the Soul, are not working, they are visiting their four grown children.

Follow Amy on Twitter @amynewmark. Listen to her free daily podcast, The Chicken Soup for the Soul Podcast, at www.chickensoup. podbean.com, or find it on iTunes, the Podcasts app on iPhone, or on your favorite podcast app on other devices.

Thank You

We owe huge thanks to all of our contributors and fans. This book was a last-minute addition to our schedule, based on our belief that America needed stories on this topic, and we were overwhelmed by the response. As always, we were overwhelmed with submissions and all of them were wonderful. We could only publish a small percentage of the stories that were submitted, but we read every single one and even the ones that do not appear in the book had an influence on what went into the final manuscript.

We owe special thanks to Ronelle Frankel, who read all the stories, and to Susan Heim, who did the first round of editing.

Associate Publisher D'ette Corona continued to be Amy's right-hand woman in creating the final manuscript and working with all our wonderful writers. Barbara LoMonaco and Kristiana Pastir, along with Elaine Kimbler, jumped in at the end to proof, proof, proof. And yes, there will always be typos anyway, so feel free to let us know about them at webmaster@chickensoupforthesoul.com and we will correct them in future printings.

The whole publishing team deserves a hand, including Maureen Peltier, Victor Cataldo, Mary Fisher, and Daniel Zaccari, who turned our manuscript into this beautiful book.

Sharing Happiness,
Inspiration, and Hope

Real people sharing real stories, every day, all over the world. In 2007, *USA Today* named *Chicken Soup for the Soul* one of the five most memorable books in the last quarter-century. With over 100 million books sold to date in the U.S. and Canada alone, more than 250 titles in print, and translations into nearly fifty languages, "chicken soup for the soul®" is one of the world's best-known phrases.

Today, twenty-four years after we first began sharing happiness, inspiration and hope through our books, we continue to delight our readers with new titles, but have also evolved beyond the bookstore with super premium pet food, television shows, podcasts, positive journalism from aplus.com, and licensed products, all revolving around true stories, as we continue "changing the world one story at a time®." Thanks for reading!

Share with Us

We all have had Chicken Soup for the Soul moments in our lives. If you would like to share your story or poem with millions of people around the world, go to chickensoup.com and click on "Submit Your Story." You may be able to help another reader and become a published author at the same time. Some of our past contributors have launched writing and speaking careers from the publication of their stories in our books!

We only accept story submissions via our website. They are no longer accepted via mail or fax.

To contact us regarding other matters, please send us an e-mail through webmaster@chickensoupforthesoul.com, or fax or write us at:

Chicken Soup for the Soul
P.O. Box 700
Cos Cob, CT 06807-0700
Fax: 203-861-7194

One more note from your friends at Chicken Soup for the Soul: Occasionally, we receive an unsolicited book manuscript from one of our readers, and we would like to respectfully inform you that we do not accept unsolicited manuscripts and we must discard the ones that appear.

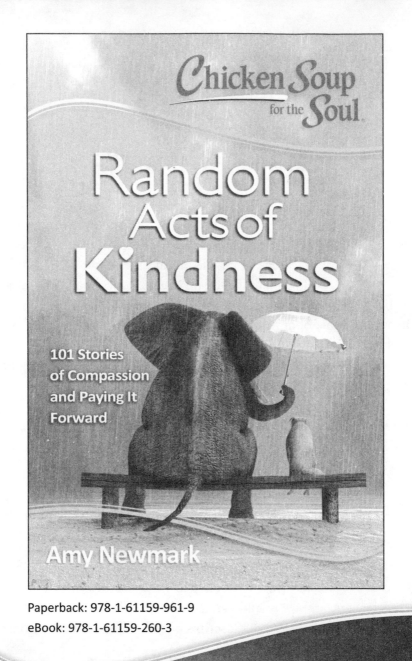

Paperback: 978-1-61159-961-9
eBook: 978-1-61159-260-3

More great stories about

Chicken Soup for the Soul®

The Spirit of America

101 Stories about What Makes Our Country Great

Amy Newmark
Foreword by Lee Woodruff

STAND UP FOR HEROES

Royalties from this book benefit the Bob Woodruff Foundation's Stand Up for Heroes program for veterans

Paperback: 978-1-61159-960-2
eBook: 978-1-61159-259-7

our kind America

Chicken Soup
for the Soul

Changing your life one story at a time®
www.chickensoup.com